PROFESSIONAL DEVELOPMENT SERIES

LEADERSHIP
Nine Keys to Success

GEORGE MANNING

Professor of Psychology
Northern Kentucky University

KENT CURTIS

Professor of Industrial Technology and Education
Northern Kentucky University

U256
PUBLISHED BY
SOUTH-WESTERN PUBLISHING CO.
CINCINNATI, OH   WEST CHICAGO, IL   DALLAS, TX   LIVERMORE, CA

ISBN: 0-538-21256-X
Library of Congress Catalog Card Number: 86-62748

8 9 10 11 E 8 7 6 5

Printed in the United States of America

About The Authors

Dr. George Manning

Dr. Kent Curtis

George Manning is a professor of psychology and business at Northern Kentucky University. He is a consultant to business, industry, and government; his clients include AT&T, Sun Oil, IBM, Marriott Corporation, United Auto Workers, the Internal Revenue Service, and the National Institutes of Health. He lectures on economic and social issues including quality of work life, work force values, and business ethics. He serves as advisor to such diverse industries and professions as energy, transportation, justice, health, finance, labor, commerce, and the military.

He received graduation honors from George Williams College, the University of Cincinnati, and the University of Vienna. He was selected Professor of the Year at Northern Kentucky University, where his teaching areas include management and organization, organizational psychology, and personal adjustment. He maintains an active program of research and study in organizational psychology. His current studies and interests include the changing meaning of work, leadership development, and coping skills for personal and social change.

Kent Curtis has served as an administrator and faculty member at Northern Kentucky University since its inception in 1970. He is a professor in the departments of industrial technology and education. His teaching areas include supervisory development, human relations in business and industry, techniques of research design, counseling, and group dynamics.

He received a baccalaureate degree in biology from Centre College, a master's in counseling from Xavier University, and a doctorate in adult technical education from the University of Cincinnati. He has designed numerous employee and management training and development programs, which are presented to Fortune 500 companies, small businesses, and federal, state, and local government agencies.

Kent also presents open seminars and on-site programs in the areas of time and stress management, communication skills, and team building. His current studies and interests include developing effective "executive pairs" (secretary/manager teams); the manager as an effective teacher; and improving the quality of work life in organizations using employee involvement groups.

PREFACE

Each book in *The Human Side of Work* is special in its own way. *Leadership* is unique in that it helps not only the leader but everyone affected by the leader. If you have ever been the victim of a bad boss, or the beneficiary of a good one, you know how important leadership can be. The "nine keys" format teaches concepts, principles, and techniques of effective leadership in a creative way that is appropriate for both new and experienced managers.

Our goal is for you to use this book to become the type of manager you would want to have. Subjects include the importance of leadership, why people assume leadership positions, the personal qualities of effective leaders, the relationship between leadership style and types of employees, principles of effective supervision, how to give orders, delegation skills, the importance of training, the role of discipline, and the role of formal authority.

Specific topics, questions, and activities include:

- What are your *social motives*? Why would you want to be a leader? Are you an eagle, a beaver, or a bunny? See pages 14–21.

- Learn key *leadership skills* — how to give orders, delegate effectively, and develop subordinates. See pages 27–29, 85–91, 98–115.

- Do you possess the *critical qualities* all leaders should have? See pages 41–45.

- What is your *leadership style?* See pages 51–57.

- Do you use or abuse the *power of position?* See pages 58–68.

- How do you rate on the *Leadership Report Card?* Do you employ the universal principles of effective leadership? See pages 76–85.

HOW TO USE THIS BOOK

This is a desk book for ready reference, a handbook for teaching others, and a workbook for personal development in the area of leadership. The material is arranged in a logical sequence for learning.

The best approach is to *interact* with the material. Read the narrative, take the tests and exercises, examine the interpretations, and review the

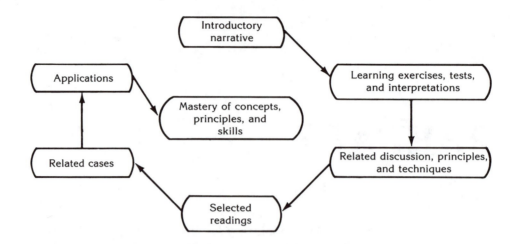

principles and techniques—then ask: "How does this apply to me? How can I use this concept or information to improve myself or my organization?" Then take action. Also, use the related readings, cases, and applications to improve your knowledge and skills.

To increase interest and improve overall learning, try the following:

1. Use the learning objectives, discussion questions, and study quizzes included in each part of the book. This will focus your reading, improve comprehension, and increase retention of the material.

2. Share your tests and exercises with family, friends, and co-workers, especially those who are interested in leadership development. In this way, you can make tangible use of what you learn and may even help others.

3. Write in the book. Use the margins; underline; write your own ideas and personalize the material.

Good luck in your learning!

HOW TO TEACH FROM THIS BOOK

Personalize *Leadership*—for yourself and for the learner. Use the information, exercises, questions, activities, and tests to complement your own teaching style and resources; use any or all of the materials provided to suit the needs and goals of the group.

Steps

First, scan the material for topics and exercises. Second, outline a curriculum and lesson plan based on time frames and learning goals. Third, arrange learning aids, media, and other resources for smooth instruction. For assistance in this area, refer to the suggested readings, cases, applications, and films that accompany each part of the text. Also, see Appendix A for suggestions on teaching, testing, and grading as well as for information about other books in *The Human Side of Work* series.

Instruction

Multimedia, multimethod instruction usually works best. Each class period ideally would include a lecture to set the stage, a learning exercise to personalize the subject, a discussion to interpret results, and related activities such as cases and readings to increase knowledge and skills. A film, followed by group discussion and panel debate, is an ideal learning enhancer. See Appendix C for an annotated list of excellent films.

Final Note

Because this book is easy to read and covers the factual information needed by the learner, class periods should be used primarily for group involvement. Learning activities and group discussion will personalize the subject and promote maximum enjoyment and learning.

Leadership: Nine Keys to Success is a popular and useful book. Readers relate to such topics as leadership motives, qualities, styles, principles, and techniques. But they won't learn the material unless they get personally involved with it. As the instructor, the more practical you can make it for them, the better; the more personalized, the better. In this spirit, we conclude with a favorite proverb:

> I listen and I hear;
> I see and I remember;
> I do and I understand.
>
> *Confucius* (551–479 B.C.)

Good luck in your teaching!

Request: We want your suggestions. If you have questions or see a way to improve this book, please write. Thank you.

George Manning
Kent Curtis
Northern Kentucky University
Highland Heights, Ky. 41076

ACKNOWLEDGMENTS

The Human Side of Work is written by many people. It is the result of countless hours and endless effort from colleagues, students, and others who have helped in some important way. From initial draft to final form, many hands bring these books to life. To each we are grateful.

For this book, recognition is given to the following scientists and authors whose ideas and findings provide theoretical framework and important factual data:

Robert Blake	Michael Hart	Norman Maier
Richard Christie	Stanley Herman	William Menninger
Ernest Dale	Eugene Jennings	R. M. Stogdill
Gary Dressler	Michael Korenvich	Robert Townsend
Fred Fiedler	Harry Levinson	Auren Uris
Marvin Gregory	Gordon Lippitt	Clifton Williams

Appreciation goes to the following colleagues and supporters for substantive help in research, manuscript review, preparation, and advice:

Mike Adams	Bill LeMaster	Jas S. Sekhon
Larry Albice	Cynthia McDaniel	Bill Stewart
Comptyn Allen	Steve McMillen	Cliff Stone
Jack Burleson	Austin Mann	Roger Sweeney
Ken Carter	Naomi Miller	Ralph Tesseneer
Mary Curtis	Ralph O'Brien	Rebecca Tranter
Dave Davis	John Osmanski	Earl Walz
George Doughty	Jim Patton	Jerry Warner
Charlotte Galloway	Mike Quaranta	Susan Wehrmeyer
Carl Goodin	Michelle Robertson	Mary Anne Williams
Jim Kerr	Jerry Roell	Rick Wolfe
Charles Leffler	Vince Schulte	

We want to thank J. Ellen Gerken for many of the figures, illustrations, and photographs.

George Manning
Kent Curtis

CONTENTS

**PART ONE   THE IGNITION KEY, THE GOLDEN KEY, AND THE
SKELETON KEY**   **5**

Introduction   6
What Is Leadership?   6
The Importance of Leadership   7
How Many Leaders Are There?   9
Exercise: Examples of Leadership   10
Nature versus Nurture   11
Leadership in the Work Setting   13
Nine Keys of Leadership   14
The Ignition Key—The Motive to Lead   14
Exercise: Eagles, Beavers, and Bunnies—Social Motives in
    the Work Setting   15
The Golden Key—Leadership by Character   22
The Skeleton Key—The Art of Persuasion   24
Recommended Resources   30
Reference Notes   30
Study Quiz   33
Discussion Questions and Activities   37

PART TWO   THE COMBINATION LOCK AND THE FRONT DOOR KEY   39

The Combination Lock—The Relationship Between Leader,
    Follower, and Situation   40
Exercise: Nine Leadership Qualities: How Do You Rate?   44
Exercise: Interpersonal Trust Scale   45
Exercise: What Type of Leader Are You?   51
Exercise: What Type of Follower Are You?   53
The Front Door Key—The Power of Office   58
Recommended Resources   68
Reference Notes   68
Study Quiz   71
Discussion Questions and Activities   73

PART THREE   THE VAULT KEY AND THE MULTIPLICATION KEY   75

The Vault Key—Leadership by Competence   76
Exercise: Leadership Report Card   77
The Multiplication Key—Effective Delegation   86
Exercise: Delegation Diagnosis   87
Recommended Resources   91
Reference Notes   91
Study Quiz   93
Discussion Questions and Activities   95

PART FOUR   THE MASTER KEY AND THE SCORE KEY   97

The Master Key—Leaders Who Can, Teach   98
Exercise: Numbers Never Lie   100
The Score Key—Effective Discipline   115
Applying the Nine Keys of Leadership   119
Exercise: Personal Analysis of Leadership—Nine Keys to
    Success   121
Conclusion   125
Recommended Resources   126
Reference Notes   126
Study Quiz   129
Discussion Questions and Activities   133

READINGS   135

Boss: Richard J. Daley of Chicago   136
What Makes a Top Executive?   141
How the Boss Stays in Touch with the Troops   149
The Manager's Job: Folklore and Fact   154
Pygmalion in Management   173
Managers Can Drive Their Subordinates Mad   187

CASES   201

What Happened When I Gave Up the Good Life
    and Became President   202
A Different Style of Leadership   210
Mr. Black, Ms. Blue, and Mr. White   214
The Full Court Press   216
The Forklift Fiasco   221

APPLICATION   223

Train the Trainer   224

**APPENDIX A BACKGROUND INFORMATION, TEACHING
SUGGESTIONS, AND TESTING AND GRADING**   269

          Audience   270
          Content and Style   270
          Testing and Review Process   271
          Teaching Formats   273

APPENDIX B   ADDITIONAL REFERENCES   279

APPENDIX C   SUGGESTED FILMS   283

**APPENDIX D   PARTS ONE, TWO, THREE, AND FOUR STUDY
QUIZ ANSWERS**   289

**APPENDIX E   THE RELATIONSHIP OF THE QUIZ QUESTIONS
AND THE DISCUSSION AND ACTIVITIES TO
THE PART OBJECTIVES**   291

Leadership

lead · er · ship   (lēd-ər-ship), noun, 1. showing the way or directing the course of action. 2. influencing or causing to follow by words and deeds. 3. guiding the behavior of others through ideas, strength, or heroic feats. 4. the position or function of one who leads: The king led his people. 5. the ability to lead: She displayed leadership skill.

The best way of educating princes is to teach them to become intimate with all sorts and conditions of men; their commonest handicap is that they do not know their people. People are always masked in their company because they are the masters. They meet many subjects, but no real people. Hence, bad choice of favourites and ministers, that dims the fame of kings and ruins their subjects. Teach a prince to be sober, chaste, pious, generous, and you will teach him how to love his people and his kingly dignity; and you will implant in him every virtue at the same time.

— *Vauvenargues*

Source: Maxims and Reflections of Luc de Clapiers, the Marquis of Vauvenargues, *trans. F.G. Stevens (London: Humphrey Milford, 1940), 255, 257.*

PART ONE

The Ignition Key, the Golden Key, and the Skeleton Key

Learning Objectives

After completing Part One, you will better understand:

1. the definition of leadership;

2. the importance of leadership;

3. how nature (qualities of the person) and nurture (environmental factors) influence the leadership process;

4. the motives a person may have for exercising leadership;

5. how the character of the leader influences the behavior of followers;

6. the correct principles for giving orders.

INTRODUCTION

The success of any work group or organization depends on leadership. This is true for both public and private organizations, whether large or small. People in leadership positions have responsibility for making decisions and accomplishing results. Yet, leaders will be unsuccessful without the support of followers. The saying, "No man is an island," is especially true of the individual who leads.

Excellence in leadership requires the ability to attract capable people, to motivate them to put forth their best efforts, and to solve problems that arise. These are difficult tasks, helping explain why effective leadership is rare and why we respect those who excel. To personalize the subject: have you ever been the victim of a poor leader? How do you feel about the good leaders you have known? If you have experienced both, you know firsthand the importance of this subject. No other factor is more critical for employee morale and job performance.

This book presents an understanding of the nature and dynamics of effective leadership. The approach is interactive, requiring reader participation. Both new and experienced leaders will enjoy completing the exercises and discussing ways to apply the concepts, principles, and techniques on the job. If you are in a leadership position now, or if you expect to be in the future, you will want to do all you can to master the nine keys of leadership success.

WHAT IS LEADERSHIP?

Leadership means leaving a mark. It is initiating and guiding and the result is change. The product is a new character or direction that otherwise would never be. By ideas and deeds, leaders show the way and influence the behavior of others.[1]

To understand the importance of ideas, consider the legend of King Arthur, who lead the Knights of the Round Table with his vision of chivalry:

> . . . My teacher Merlyn, who always remembered things that haven't happened better than things that have, told me once that a few hundred years from now it will be discovered that the world is round — round like the table at which we sat with such high hope and noble purpose. If you do what I ask, perhaps people will remember how we of Camelot went questing for right and honor and justice. Perhaps one day men will sit around this world as we did once at our table, and go questing once more . . . for right . . . honor . . . and justice.[2]

To understand the importance of deeds, consider the storyteller Homer's account of Achilles, who led Greek warriors by his heroic feats:

> . . . So saying, he plunged once more into the fight and man after man fell before his sword and before his spear. He raged among the Trojans like a whirlwind that drives the flames this way and that when there is a forest fire along the dry slopes of the mountains.[3]

The leader who has influenced the world more than all of the kings and all of the armies combined was Jesus, whose ideas guide so many and who taught by his deeds:

> . . . Jesus' actions belong with his preaching totally. Jesus did not simply model what he understood as true openness for others; his behavior empowered and encouraged to true love for their neighbors those who themselves were at the point of giving up.[4]

THE IMPORTANCE OF LEADERSHIP

Upon every wave of political history has been a Caesar, an Elizabeth, a Napoleon, or a Hitler. In every lull, leadership has been absent. Consider the period of approximately A.D. 800 to 1000:

> . . . Europe lapsed into utter decentralization, and lost for centuries the administrative unity that the reign of Charles the Great promised. A heavy blow was dealt at the slowly developing culture that the eighth century produced. It was not without justice that the ninth and tenth centuries have been called the "the Dark Ages." The internal history of continental Europe became a dismal record of tiresome local feuds and private wars.[5]

Leadership is important, not only in government, but in other areas of life. Religious beliefs and social conduct have been influenced by reformers such as Martin Luther King and Susan B. Anthony:

> Martin Luther King said, "I have a dream. It is a dream deeply rooted in the American dream. I have a dream that one day in the red hills of Georgia, sons of former slaveowners will be able to sit down together at the table of brotherhood."[6]

> Susan B. Anthony was a passionate democrat, who saw "the vote" as the symbol of women's emancipation and independence as well as the indispensable condition of a true government. In her old age, still voteless, she conceded, "The world has never witnessed a greater revolution than in the status of women during the past half century."[7]

The fates of nations have been determined by military figures such as Alexander the Great and Joan of Arc:

> Alexander the Great opened a new era in the history of the world and, by his life's work, determined its development for many centuries. The permanent result of his life was the development of Greek civilization into a civilization that was world wide.[8]

ILLUS. 1.1

"I have a dream. . . ."

UPI/BETTMANN NEWSPHOTOS

Joan of Arc organized an army of 4,000 at Tours for the relief of Orleans. This was Joan of Arc's army, an army led by a dressed-up peasant girl ignorant in the art of war. Her very presence that April 28, 1429, inflamed soldiers and civilians with a spirit of daring, and when the storming of the fortress started, the soldiers followed her.[9]

Civilization has been shaped by philosophers such as John Stuart Mill and Adam Smith:

John Stuart Mill was one of England's greatest philosophers, hardly surpassed by thinkers of the highest order. Mill taught that a popular representative government (democracy) inevitably makes for progress.[10]

Adam Smith proclaimed in one of the earliest statements of his position: "Little else is requisite to carry a state to the highest degree of opulence from the lowest barbarism, but peace, easy taxes, and a tolerable administration of justice, all the rest being brought on by the natural cause of things (free enterprise)."[11]

There are many ways to lead, and indeed we are influenced by some people even centuries after they are gone. Some are heroes, devoted to great causes and noble works; some are teachers, the rule breakers and value creators; and some are rulers, motivated principally to dominate others and to exercise power.[12] Consider how the ideas and deeds of the teachers, heroes, and rulers in Figure 1.1 have influenced the world.

FIGURE 1.1

Influential People of History

Teachers	Heroes	Rulers
Aristotle	Beethoven	Alexander the Great
Buddha	Columbus	Charlemagne
Confucius	Edison	Elizabeth I
Jesus	Einstein	Genghis Khan
Luther	Galileo	Hitler
Marx	Michelangelo	Isabella I
Moses	Newton	Julius Caesar
Muhammad	Pasteur	Lenin
Plato	Washington	Mao Tse-tung
St. Paul	Wright Brothers	Napoleon

Source: Michael H. Hart, The 100: A Ranking of the Most Influential Persons in History *(New York: Hart Publishing Co., Inc., 1978)*.

HOW MANY LEADERS ARE THERE?

Are we led by a few, or are there many who lead? The 42nd edition of *Who's Who in America* (1982–83) contains entries for 75,000 people. Each of these individuals, by ideas or deeds, has influenced the behavior of others; each has been teacher, hero, or ruler.

On a different scale, leadership is continually provided by the multitude of people who influence their families, friends, work groups, and organizations. These are parents, supervisors, presidents, and other leadership figures. Think of your own experiences. Have you not at some time provided leadership to others, either by ideas or by the example you set? Think about this question as you complete the following exercise on Examples of Leadership.

EXAMPLES OF LEADERSHIP

Ideas

My ideas have influenced others in the following situations (explain):

Work: _____

_____

_____

School: _____

_____

_____

Home: _____

_____

_____

Other: _____

_____

_____

Deeds

By my actions, I have influenced the following people and events (explain):

_____

_____

_____

_____

_____

_____

_____

NATURE VERSUS NURTURE

A student showed his father his report card containing five F's. He said, "Dad, it's either heredity or environment. What do you think?"

Is leadership the product of nature or nurture? Which is more important — the individual or the environment? Historically, leadership has been attributed to the individual. This view is sometimes called the "great man theory." Throughout history, people have believed that certain individuals possess special qualifications allowing them to rise above the masses, to assume responsibility, to exert power, and to become leaders.[13] Reflecting this view, the Scottish philosopher and historian Thomas Carlyle believed that among the undistinguished masses are people of light and learning, individuals superior in power, courage, and understanding. Carlyle saw the history of the human race as the biographies of these leaders, its great men and women: "Their moral character may be something less than perfect; their courage may not be the essential ingredient; yet, they are superior. They are followed, admired, and obeyed to the point of worship."[14] The American industrialist Henry Ford reflected this belief when he wrote, "The question, 'Who ought to be boss?' is like asking, 'Who ought to be the tenor in the quartet?' Obviously, the one who can sing tenor."[15]

More recently, leadership has been viewed as an acquired competency, the product of many forces, not the least of which is circumstance. In this sense, leadership is seen as a social phenomenon, not a personal trait. This school of thought helps explain why leaders who are successful in one situation (for example, building a bridge) may not be successful in another (such as directing a play or a research team).

The Case for Nature

Ralph M. Stogdill, one of the most distinguished scholars on leadership, has found certain traits of the individual that correlate with leadership. Stogdill writes:

> The leader is characterized by: a strong drive for responsibility and task completion; vigor and persistence in pursuit of goals; venturesomeness and originality in problem-solving; drive to exercise initiative in social situations; self-confidence and sense of personal identity; willingness to accept consequences of decision and action; readiness to absorb interpersonal stress; willingness to tolerate frustration and delay; ability to influence other persons' behavior; and capacity to structure social interaction systems to the purpose at hand.
>
> It can be concluded that the cluster of characteristics listed above differentiate leaders from followers, effective from ineffective leaders, and higher echelon from lower echelon leaders. In other words, different strata of leaders and followers can be described in terms of the extent to which they exhibit these characteristics. These characteristics considered individually hold little diagnostic or predictive significance. In

combination, it would appear that they interact to generate personality dynamics advantageous to the person seeking the responsibilities of leadership.[16]

The Case for Nurture

The elements of circumstance and chance seem to play a part in determining leadership. The same individual may exert leadership in one time and place and not in another. Stogdill explains:

> It should be noted that to a large extent our conceptions of characteristics of leadership are culturally determined. The ancient Egyptians attributed three qualities of divinity to their king. They said of him, "Authoritative utterance is in thy mouth, perception is in thy heart, and thy tongue is the shrine of justice." This statement would suggest that the Egyptians were demanding of their leader the qualities of authority, discrimination, and just behavior.
>
> An analysis of Greek concepts of leadership, as exemplified by different leaders in Homer's *Iliad*, showed four aspects were valued: (1) justice and judgment—Agamemnon; (2) wisdom and counsel—Nestor; (3) shrewdness and cunning—Odysseus; and (4) valor and action—Achilles. All of these qualities were admired by the Greeks. Shrewdness and cunning are not as highly regarded in our contemporary society as they once were (although justice, judgment, wisdom, counsel, valor, and action remain in high esteem).
>
> Thus, the patterns of behavior regarded as acceptable in leaders differ from time to time and from one culture to another.[17]

Probably the most convincing support for leadership as a social phenomenon is the fact that throughout history male leaders have outnumbered female leaders to such a significant degree. Even the definition of the word is a social phenomenon. Consider the case of "President" Mrs. Wilson, leader in all but name. Woodrow, however, is the one history credits as leader, as president, even during incapacitating illness.

Evidence shows that both nature—qualities of the person—and nurture—environmental factors—are important elements in the leadership equation. Leadership results from the inextricable interaction between the two. Findings from sociobiological studies of other animal species support this view. Biologist Richard Borowsky has discovered spontaneous growth among male fish. Young males remain small and sexually underdeveloped until the adult population in the group is reduced. Then, size and sexual maturation accelerate dramatically. Clearly, biological and sociological systems are closely related.[18]

Similar signs of sudden maturation are found in human beings. Spontaneous leaders may emerge in social crises after filling essentially anonymous roles for years. Consider the transformation of Poland's Lech Walesa from shipyard worker to national labor leader during the 1980s. Some people seem to have innate abilities that unfold under certain conditions—external circumstances and internal qualities interact to create a sudden and dramatic spurt of performance.

LEADERSHIP IN THE WORK SETTING

Leadership is a vital factor influencing the success of the work group and organization. Think of the problems that can occur in any work setting:

- communication breakdown
- equipment breakdown
- lack of teamwork
- walkouts and strikes
- wage problems
- quality problems
- employee inefficiency
- work-related injury

Now think of the ability required of those individuals whose responsibility it is to solve these and a multitude of other work-related problems. Leadership is an important and difficult task; it is the cornerstone of organizational effectiveness.

Leadership has many facets. Our discussion focuses on nine keys to leadership success.

ILLUS. 1.2

People provide leadership in all types of settings.

NINE KEYS OF LEADERSHIP

If people cannot decide which course of action to take, or if they are not making satisfactory progress along a chosen path, breakdown occurs. Breakdown can be traced to deficiency in one or more of nine keys to leadership:

- The ignition key—the motive to lead
- The golden key—leadership by character
- The skeleton key—the art of persuasion
- The combination lock—the relationship between leader, follower, and situation
- The front door key—the power of office
- The vault key—leadership by competence
- The multiplication key—effective delegation
- The master key—leaders who can, teach
- The score key—effective discipline

The following pages discuss each of these keys. Also included are questionnaires and learning exercises to personalize the concepts, along with principles and techniques to improve leadership effectiveness. (Note that the nine keys of leadership begin in Part One and continue through Parts Two, Three, and Four.)

THE IGNITION KEY—THE MOTIVE TO LEAD

Someone must provide the spark for action; someone must provide the "ignition key." There are three basic motives for leadership: (1) power—the desire to have influence, give orders, and have them carried out; (2) achievement—the need to create and build something of value; and (3) altruism—a heartfelt interest in helping others.

Why would you want to be a leader? What would be your purpose for assuming the challenge of leadership? The following questionnaire helps answer these questions.

EAGLES, BEAVERS, AND BUNNIES—
SOCIAL MOTIVES IN THE WORK SETTING

Directions

This questionnaire consists of 12 statements. There are no right or wrong answers. For each statement, indicate which of the three alternatives—a, b, or c—is most preferred or most important to you by placing a 3 next to it. Place a 2 by your second choice and a 1 by the statement or choice that is least like you. Do not debate too long over any one statement. Your first reaction is desired.

1. In a work situation, I want to:

    _____ a. be in charge
    _____ b. give assistance to my co-workers
    _____ c. come up with new ideas

2. If I have ultimate responsibility for a project, I:

    _____ a. depend on my own expertise to accomplish tasks
    _____ b. delegate work and oversee progress
    _____ c. use teamwork to accomplish tasks

3. My co-workers see me as:

    _____ a. a competent person
    _____ b. a considerate person
    _____ c. a forceful person

4. When I disagree with a decision, I:

    _____ a. voice my disapproval immediately
    _____ b. take into consideration other peoples' feelings and circumstances
    _____ c. suggest alternatives based upon logic

5. In a group discussion:

    _____ a. I encourage others to express themselves
    _____ b. I will change my view only if a better one is suggested
    _____ c. my ideas generally prevail

6. During labor-management disputes, I would:

    _____ a. keep human relations smooth
    _____ b. maintain a position of strength
    _____ c. work for a compromise

7. I am most satisfied with my job when I:

    _____ a. see progress being made
    _____ b. have a strong voice in determining policy
    _____ c. work with others to achieve results

8. When disagreements arise, I usually:

    _____ a. yield a point to avoid conflict
    _____ b. stick to my guns
    _____ c. use reasoning to seek the best solution

9. As a supervisor, I would:

    _____ a. permit flexibility, as long as the job gets done
    _____ b. recognize that workers have good days and bad days
    _____ c. insist on compliance with my rules and directions

10. As a member of the Board of Directors dealing with a problem, I would most likely:

    _____ a. try to get my ideas adopted
    _____ b. solicit ideas from all members
    _____ c. review the facts

11. When hiring a new employee, I would:

    _____ a. expect future loyalty to me
    _____ b. hire the person who is technically best qualified
    _____ c. take into consideration future relations with co-workers

12. I am most happy in my work if I:

    _____ a. am the decision maker
    _____ b. work with good friends and colleagues
    _____ c. make significant achievements

_____

Source: Jack E. Burleson, Northern Kentucky University, 1977; based on David A. Kolb, Irvin M. Rubin, and James McIntyre, Organizational Psychology: An Experiential Approach, *2d ed. (Englewood Cliffs, N.J.: Prentice-Hall, Inc., 1974), 53,68,69.*

SCORING

Step 1

Scoring is done across the page, from left to right. For each question, put your *a*, *b*, and *c* score in the appropriate columns. Note that *a*, *b*, and *c* scores do not remain in the same column. Continue until all scores are filled in, and then total the columns.

Column I	Column II	Column III
1. a _____	1. c _____	1. b _____
2. b _____	2. a _____	2. c _____
3. c _____	3. a _____	3. b _____
4. a _____	4. c _____	4. b _____
5. c _____	5. b _____	5. a _____
6. b _____	6. c _____	6. a _____
7. b _____	7. a _____	7. c _____
8. b _____	8. c _____	8. a _____
9. c _____	9. a _____	9. b _____
10. a _____	10. c _____	10. b _____
11. a _____	11. b _____	11. c _____
12. a _____	12. c _____	12. b _____
Total _____	Total _____	Total _____

Grand total should be 72 _____

Step 2

Mark the total scores for each column in the appropriate places in Figure 1.3. Shade in the areas as shown in the example, Figure 1.2.

INTERPRETATION

A high score in Column I indicates social motives that are power oriented. A power-oriented person strives for leadership because of the authority it brings. This person is like the eagle whose goal is to dominate. Historical examples are Winston Churchill and Elizabeth I, who are recognized as outstanding leaders because of their mastery of power

FIGURE 1.2

Example

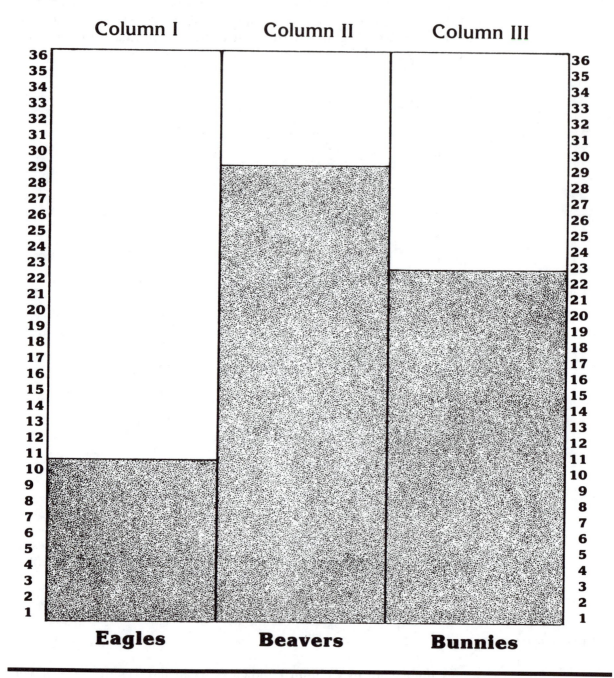

FIGURE 1.3

Your Social Motives

Column I	Column II	Column III

36			36
35			35
34			34
33			33
32			32
31			31
30			30
29			29
28			28
27			27
26			26
25			25
24			24
23			23
22			22
21			21
20			20
19			19
18			18
17			17
16			16
15			15
14			14
13			13
12			12
11			11
10			10
9			9
8			8
7			7
6			6
5			5
4			4
3			3
2			2
1			1

Eagles **Beavers** **Bunnies**

politics. Strength, assertiveness, and dominance are characteristics of the eagle. Positions involving the expression of power are manager, supervisor, and political office holder.

A high score in Column II indicates achievement-oriented social motives. Like the beaver, this type of leader wants to create and build. Madam Curie and Charles Kettering are good examples of achievement-oriented people, each succeeding in making valuable contributions to mankind. Adjectives used to describe beavers are: successful, competent, skillful, and productive. Achievement-oriented people are often found in occupations such as science, business, and the arts.

A high score in Column III indicates altruism — a strong concern for human welfare. Such individuals are people caring and human serving. This type of leader is likely to have traits similar to Florence Nightingale and Albert Schweitzer. These are the bunnies of society. Common characteristics of humanistic leaders are helpfulness, unselfishness, and consideration. Occupations such as teaching and counseling allow the expression of this social motive.

ILLUS. 1.3–1.5

Three kinds of orientation: power, achievement, and service.

UPI/BETTMANN NEWSPHOTOS

Memorex Corporation

There are three important points to remember about scores on this questionnaire:

- Although it is normal for everyone to have some of each social motive, a person usually will prefer one or two over the others. Preference depends on the values (power, achievement, or altruism) promoted by one's culture and on personal traits and experiences.

- People exert leadership in order to satisfy one or a combination of these three motives. All leadership can be said to be motivated by power, achievement, or altruism.

- As either leader or subordinate, a person will be most happy and productive in a job that allows the expression of personal social motives. If an individual's work precludes this, morale and productivity can be expected to go down.

Winston Churchill was most pleased when he could influence events by his powerful will; during these times he felt fulfilled. Churchill wrote, "I have a tendency, against which I should, perhaps, be on my guard, to swim against the stream."

Charles Kettering, the engineering genius, needed to achieve to be happy. His work was a form of self-expression, and he was dissatisfied if he could not experiment and invent. Early, he began advising people in industry:

> . . . I am not pleading with you to make changes, I am telling you that you have to make them — not because I say so, but because Father Time will take care of you if you do not change. Consequently, you need a procurement department for new ideas.

Physician and humanitarian Albert Schweitzer was dedicated to serving others. If he were deprived of this opportunity, the purpose of his life, as he viewed it, would not be achieved. Schweitzer wrote:

> . . . Example is not the main thing in influencing others. It is the only thing. Hope is renewed each time that you see a person you know who is deeply involved in the struggle of life helping another person.[19]

To understand the role of social motives at work, imagine three supervisors given the task of building a house. The achievement-oriented leader obtains satisfaction from creating the house. Building a sound structure and completing the task on time is rewarding. The altruistic leader enjoys working with his crew. He is concerned with human relations and strives to create a spirit of teamwork. Also, he is pleased to think of how much the home will mean to the family who lives in it. The power-oriented manager focuses on how to organize the production of the house. He feels comfortable being in charge and enjoys being recognized as the powerful figure who causes the house to be produced.

In evaluating yourself, are you an eagle, beaver, or bunny? Does your job allow the expression of your social motives?

THE GOLDEN KEY—
LEADERSHIP BY CHARACTER

Some people are able to inspire others and bring forth loyalty. A person who has such a personality is said to have character. In our society, such words as *honor, integrity,* and *courage* are used to define character. These are desirable characteristics that merit the respect and confidence of others.

Psychologist David McClelland describes the influence of the golden key—leadership by character:

> We set out to find exactly, by experiment, what kinds of thoughts the members of an audience had when exposed to a charismatic leader. They were apparently strengthened and uplifted by the experience; they felt more powerful, rather than less powerful or submissive. This suggests that the traditional way of explaining the influence of leaders on followers has not been entirely correct. The leader does not force followers to submit and go along by the sheer overwhelming magic of personality and persuasive powers. In fact, the leader is influential by strengthening and inspiring the audience. The leader arouses confidence in followers, and the followers feel better able to accomplish whatever goals they share with the leader.[20]

In every walk of life, an individual with character may emerge. When this happens, the person is recognized as a leader. The following account by Willie Davis shows how Vince Lombardi exercised tremendous influence in the field of sports because of his charismatic personality. Men played their hearts out for Lombardi for one primary purpose—their goal was to please him, to be equal to their understanding of his character.

He Made Me Feel Important

Football is a game of emotion, and what the old man excels at is motivation. I maintain that there are two driving forces in football; one is anger and the other is fear, and he capitalized on both of them. Either he got us so mad we wanted to prove something to him, or we were fearful of being singled out as the one guy who didn't do the job.

In the first place, he worked so hard that I always felt the old man was really putting more into the game on a day-to-day basis than I was. I felt obligated to put something extra into it on Sunday; I had to, just to be even with him. Another thing was the way he made you a believer. He told you what the other team was going to do, and he told you what you had to do to beat them, and invariably he was right. He made us believe that all we had to do was follow his theories on how to get ready for each game and we'd win.

I knew we were going to win every game we played. Even if we were behind by two touchdowns in the fourth quarter, I just believed that somehow we were going to pull it out. I didn't know exactly how or when, but I knew that sooner or later, we'd get the break we needed—the interception, or the fumble, or something. And the more important it was for us to win, the more certain I was we would win.

Probably the best job I can remember of him motivating us was when we played the Los Angeles Rams the next-to-last game of 1967. We had already clinched our divisional title, and the game didn't mean anything to us, and he was worried about us just going through the motions. Before the game, he was trembling like a leaf. I could see his leg shaking. "I wish I didn't have to ask you boys to go out there today and do this job," he said. "I wish I could go out and do it myself. Boy, this is one game I'd really like to be playing in. This is a game that you're playing for your pride." He went on like that until he got me so worked up that if he hadn't opened the locker-room door quick, I was going to make a hole in it, I was so eager. And we played a helluva game. We had nothing to gain, and the Rams were fighting for their lives, and they just did manage to beat us. They won by three points when they blocked a punt right near the end.

How about the day we beat the Rams, 6–3, in Milwaukee in 1965? We'd broken a two-game losing streak, and we were all kind of happy and clowning around, and he came in and you saw his face and you knew nothing was funny anymore. He kicked a bench and hurt his foot, and he had to take something out on somebody, so he started challenging us. "Nobody wants to pay the price," he said. "I'm the only one here who's willing to pay the price. You guys don't care. You don't want to win."

We were stunned. Nobody knew what to do, and, finally, Forrest Gregg stood up and said, "My God, I want to win," and then somebody else said, "Yeah, I want to win," and pretty soon there were forty guys standing, all of us shouting, "I want to win." If we had played any football team in the world during the next two hours, we'd have beaten them by ten touchdowns. The old man had us feeling so ashamed and angry. That was his greatest asset—his ability to motivate people.

He never got me too upset personally. Of course, I had pretty thick skin by the time I got to Green Bay. Paul Brown had chewed on me so much in Cleveland that when I got to the Packers, Vince was a welcome sight. Vince and Paul Brown were similar in the way they could cut you with words and make you want to rise up and prove something to them.

I think Vince got on me sharp maybe twice in eight years. I remember once, after the Colts had been hooking me on every sweep, he ate me up, and Max McGee said, "Well, I've seen everything: Vince got on Willie Davis."

Maybe he wasn't as tough on me as he was on some people, but, I'll tell you, I hated to have him tell me I was fat. I hated to have him tell me I didn't have the desire anymore. He'd just say those things to the whole team—"You're all fat; you don't want to win anymore"—and I'd get so angry I couldn't wait till I got out on the field.

I guess maybe my worst days in football were the days I tried to negotiate my contracts with the old man. I'd get myself all worked up before I went in to see him. I'd drive up from my home in Chicago, and all the way, I'd keep building up my anger, telling myself I was going to draw a hard line and get just as much money as I deserved.

One year, I walked into his office feeling cocky. You know, "Roll out the cash, Jack, I got no time for small change." All he had to do was say one harsh word, and I was really going to let him have it. I never got a word in. As soon as he saw me, he jumped up and began hugging me and patting me and telling me, "Willie, Willie, Willie, it's so great to see you. You're the best trade I ever made. You're a leader. We couldn't have won without you, Willie. You had a beautiful year. And, Willie, I need your help. You see, I've got this budget problem . . . ."

He got me so off-balance, I started feeling sorry for him. He had me thinking, "Yeah, he's right, he's gotta save some money for the Kramers and the Greggs and the Jordans," and the next thing I knew, I was saying, "Yes, sir, that's fine with me," and I ended up signing for about half of what I was going to demand." When I got out of that office and started driving back to Chicago, I was so mad at myself, I was about to drive off the highway.

The next year, finally, I got him. I went into his office and I said, "Coach, you're quite a guy. I got to be very frank, Coach, I just can't argue with you. You know, you just overwhelm me. So I've jotted down a few things I want to tell you." And I handed him a letter I'd written.

He started reading the letter — and I'd put a lot of stuff in it, like how I felt about the fans and what he'd done for me and how many years I had left — and, at first, he gave me that "heh. . .heh. . .heh. . ." of his. Then, when he got around to how much money I wanted, he put his frown on me. He looked up at me and said, "I can't argue with what you have here, Willie, but I can't pay you that much money."

"Well, Coach," I said, "I really feel that way."

He thought it over a little and said, "I'll tell you what I'll give you," and named a figure not too much below what I was willing to settle for. "You'd be one of the highest-paid linemen in the whole league," he whispered, like he was afraid somebody might hear him.

"Look, Coach," I said, "I really thought hard about this, and I've got to have a thousand dollars more than that. It's only a thousand dollars, but it's the difference between me driving back to Chicago wanting to go head-on into somebody. It's really what I feel I'm worth."

"If it's that important to you," he said, 'you've got it."

I felt good. I had my letter in my hand and I started to walk out, and he said, "Hey, wait a minute. Let me have that letter. Let me keep it. I don't want you giving it to anybody else."[21]

Whatever the arena — sports, education, business, or science — those who lead should possess the "golden key." The following statement by leader and businessman Clarence Francis is a guide for those who would exercise leadership by character:

> You can buy a person's time. You can buy a person's presence at a given place. You can buy a measured number of skilled muscular motions per hour or day. But you cannot buy enthusiasm. You cannot buy initiative. You cannot buy loyalty. You cannot buy the devotion of hearts, minds, and souls. You have to earn these things. To do this the leader must believe that the greatest assets are human assets, and that the improvement of their value is both a matter of material advantage and moral obligation. The leader must believe that workers must be treated as honorable individuals, justly rewarded, encouraged in their own progress, fully informed, and properly assigned, and that their lives and work must be given meaning and dignity on and off the job. If a leader has supervision of so much as one person, he must try to honor these principles in practice.[22]

Do you know someone who has the "golden key" of leadership? If so, how would you describe this person? What qualities inspire others and generate loyalty? Do you, yourself, lead by character?

THE SKELETON KEY — THE ART OF PERSUASION

A carpenter must know and use tools skillfully to erect a beautiful and enduring structure. Similarly, a leader must understand people and know how to motivate them in order to be successful. Management consultant Fred Fiedler writes, "All leadership is manipulative; that is the name of the game. Leadership is the use of power and influence in order to accomplish a task."

The "skeleton key" is the art of persuasion. This art requires ability in four important areas:

- *Understanding:* Leaders must understand why people do what they do. They must understand human motivation, social values, and different types of personalities.

- *Sensitivity:* The ability to see things from the other person's view and "walk a mile in the other person's shoes" is an important ingredient of the skeleton key.

- *Listening:* Leadership requires interest in others and the ability to listen effectively.

- *Speaking:* Vocabulary, clarity, and eloquence are needed to persuade others to take action. Consider the oratory skills of Franklin Roosevelt during the Great Depression, Winston Churchill during World War II, and John Kennedy in the 1960s.

ILLUS. 1.6

Effective leaders use the power of persuasion to accomplish their goals.

Lyndon Johnson was a master of the art of persuasion. Johnson recognized that people usually do what they do for their own reasons. He was sensitive to the other person's view, had keen listening skills, and accomplished his goals by helping others achieve theirs. As the following illustrates, Johnson could usually convince people to do what he wanted.

The Politics of Seduction

From facts, gossip, observation — a multitude of disparate elements — Lyndon Johnson shaped a composite mental portrait of every senator: his strengths and his weaknesses; his place in the political spectrum; his aspirations in the Senate, and perhaps, beyond the Senate; how far he could be pushed, in what direction, and by what means; how he liked his liquor; how he felt about his wife and his family; and, most important, how he felt about himself. For Johnson understood that the most important decision each senator made, often obscurely, was what kind of senator he wanted to be; whether he wanted to be a national leader in education, a regional leader in civil rights, a social magnate in Washington, an agent of the oil industry, a wheel horse of the party, or a President of the United States.

Johnson would, for instance, explain to a senator that, "Although five other senators are clamoring for this one remaining seat on the congressional delegation to Tokyo, I just might be able to swing it for you since I know how much you really want it. It'll be tough, but let me see what I can do." The joys of visiting Tokyo may never have occurred to the senator, but he was unlikely to deny Johnson's description of his desire — after all, it might be interesting, a relaxing change, even fun; and perhaps some of the businesses in his state had expressed concern about Japanese competition.

Johnson's capacities for control and domination found their consummate manifestation during his private meetings with individual senators. Face to face, behind office doors, Johnson could strike a different pose, a different form of behavior and argument. He would try to make each senator feel that his support in some particular matter was the critical element that would affect the well-being of the nation, the Senate, and the party leader; and would also serve the practical and political interests of the senator. From his own insistent energy, Johnson would create an illusion that the outcome, and thus the responsibility, rested on the decision of this one senator.

Then too, Johnson was that rare American man who felt free to display intimacy with another man, through expressions of feeling and also in physical closeness. In an empty room he would stand or sit next to a man as if all that were available was a three foot space. He could flatter men with sentiments of love and touch their bodies with gestures of affection. The intimacy was all the more excusable because it seemed genuine and without menace. Yet it was also the product of meticulous calculation. And it worked. To the ardor and the bearing of this extraordinary leader, the ordinary senator would almost invariably succumb.[23]

In order to exercise the "skeleton key," a leader should consider each person as an individual, learn what motivates that person, and then act to satisfy personal needs while at the same time accomplishing the goal. This process requires understanding, sensitivity, effective listening, and persuasive speaking skills.

George Washington is recognized as one of our great presidents for good reason. Not only is he considered the father of our country, but he had leadership abilities that were clearly recognizable.

George Washington had a great and powerful mind, and he was honest in important matters. Above all, he carried the mark of a leader in setting standards and living up to those standards—a persuasive form of leadership indeed. His bearing and his ability to command respect made him a persuasive leader by example, the most rare yet the most lasting form of persuasion.

How to Give Orders

Giving orders effectively is one of the most important skills of persuasion. The following is a list of important principles for giving orders:

- *Consider the availability of the employee's time and whether this is the ideal person to do the job.* If the employee's schedule is heavily loaded, explain the priority level of the work. A common mistake is for the leader to assign a job to the one who can get it done, even if this is the same person over and over again. This practice creates three problems: (a) the overworked employee becomes resentful; (b) the overworked employee does not know the priority of many assignments; and (c) the abilities of underworked employees are wasted or never developed.

ILLUS. 1.7

Washington had traits that made him a persuasive leader.

THE BETTMANN ARCHIVE, INC.

- *Use orders as a means of developing subordinates.* If a task does not have to be done perfectly or within a certain time period, try giving it to an employee who has never done it before. Besides showing you have faith in the employee, you will be developing another person who will be familiar with the job if the regular performer is not available.

- *Know exactly what you want to communicate before giving an order.* Indecision and confusion on the leader's part create doubt and lack of confidence in employees. If you are giving a speech to your subordinates, prepare and practice it so that what you say will be clear and understandable. If you are going to have a conference with your employees, make notes of the important points you want to cover and refer to them, if needed, during the meeting.

- *Ask rather than tell, but leave no doubt that you expect compliance.* This shows both courtesy and respect. There is an old adage, "You can get more bears with honey than you can with vinegar." You can usually obtain more cooperation by asking for assistance than by commanding others to do a job.

- *Use the correct language for the subordinate's training level.* Recognize the fact that many subordinates will not understand your words and terms as readily as you do. Most occupations and jobs have abbreviations, slang words, and technical language that the new or untrained person will not understand. What does this mean to a new employee—"One BLT without, rush!"—particularly if the person is from a foreign country? For such a person, merely understanding the English language may be difficult, even without acronyms.

  On the other hand, don't talk on a level below your employees' understanding. They may feel you are treating them like children or inferior people. This causes morale and performance problems as surely as does talking over their heads.

- *If many duties or steps are involved in an order, follow oral communication with a memo and keep a copy.* Keeping records of important conferences, orders, and rules can be helpful. As a reference, a memo (short and to the point) can be an excellent memory aid. However, don't become memo crazy; this encourages defensive behavior and wastes time, paper, and storage space.

- *Present orders in logical sequence and clear, concise language.* People remember things best that are clearly stated. If you skip around and are vague, subordinates will miss the point of your message or will easily forget it.

- *Be considerate but never apologetic for asking someone to do a job.* Can you imagine a waterline breaking on a cold, snowy night and Bill, the foreman, saying to Joe, the laborer: "Joe, I feel so sorry for you having to go down in that hole in this freezing weather—it's going to be like ice! Boy, am I glad I don't have to go. . .brrrr!"

If Joe wasn't feeling sorry for himself before Bill started talking, he would be now. A better way for Bill to make the request would be: "Joe, I have some dry clothes for you in the truck, and a thermos of coffee will be ready when you come up. Good luck." The rule is: no apologies, just consideration.

- *Talk deliberately and authoritatively, but avoid shouting across a room or making an unnecessary show of power.* Save your power until it is needed. You reduce effectiveness and put people on the defensive if you are constantly forceful. We have all heard the statement, "She doesn't raise her voice very often, but when she does, everyone listens."

- *Take responsibility for the orders you give.* Avoid quoting others to gain compliance or to relieve yourself of personal responsibility. Have you ever heard this: "Don't blame me. The boss says we have to do it"? If you do not take personal responsibility for the orders you give, the results will be: (a) loss of respect from your subordinates, (b) loss of confidence from your supervisor, and (c) reduced commitment to follow your orders.

  Responsibility is both the reward and price of leadership. We should remember Harry Truman's advice regarding tough leadership situations: "If you can't stand the heat, get out of the kitchen."

- *Give subordinates the opportunity to ask questions and express opinions.* This is a vital point because: (a) employees may be confused by an order, and questions can help clarify the instructions; (b) employees may have information or know something you do not; (c) when you encourage questions and self-expression, you demonstrate respect for employees; and (d) when you allow the opportunity to ask questions and express opinions, you will be rewarded with increased creativity and commitment from your subordinates.

- *Follow up to make sure orders are being carried out properly, and modify them if the situation warrants.* Some leaders say: "I don't have time to follow up; I am too busy giving orders." The folly here is that unless there is follow up, an inappropriate order may be repeated. Without follow-up, one never learns from experience.

  A leader who has the attitude, "Right or wrong, that is my decision," does three things if the decision is wrong: (a) loses the opportunity to correct the mistake; (b) loses the respect of subordinates who are concerned about the quality of work; and (c) sets an example of egotism and closed mindedness.[24]

As you consider the "skeleton key," do you need to improve your persuasive skills? If so, which is your weakest area — understanding people, sensitivity, listening effectiveness, speaking skills, or giving orders? Take steps to improve. Courses in psychology, human relations, communications, and supervision are recommended.

RECOMMENDED RESOURCES

The following readings, case, and films are suggested for greater insight into the material in Part One:

Readings — Boss: Richard J. Daley of Chicago
What Makes a Top Executive?

Case — What Happened When I Gave Up the Good Life and Became President

Films — A Passion for Excellence
Up the Organization
A New Look at Motivation—Affiliation, Power, Achievement

REFERENCE NOTES

1 Eugene E. Jennings, *An Anatomy of Leadership: Princes, Heroes, and Supermen,* (New York: McGraw-Hill, Inc., 1960), 30.

2 Geoffry Ashe, *Camelot and the Vision of Albion* (London: Hinemann, 1977), 134.

3 Rex Warner, *Greeks and Trojans* (London: MacGibbon and Kee, Ltd., 1951), 136.

4 Herbert Braun, *Jesus of Nazareth: The Man and His Time*, trans. Everett R. Kalin (Philadelphia: Fortress Press, 1979), 115.

5 Sir Charles Oman, *The Dark Ages: 476–918* (London: Rivingstons, 1962), 512.

6 From an address by Rev. Martin Luther King, Jr., Lincoln Memorial, Washington, D. C., 28 August 1963.

7 Katherine Anthony, *Susan B. Anthony* (Garden City, N.Y.: Doubleday & Company, Inc., 1954), vi, viii.

8 Ulrich Wikken, *Alexander the Great* (New York: W.W. Norton Co., Inc., 1967), 3.

9 Ingvald Ralchem, *Joan of Arc* (Bergen: Scandinavian University Books, 1971), 13.

10 Karl Britton, *Philosophy and the Meaning of Life* (London/New York: Cambridge University Press, 1969), 93.

11 Donald Winch, *Adam Smith's Politics* (Cambridge/New York: Cambridge University Press, 1978), 4, as reported by Dugald Stewart, *Account of the Life and Writings of Adam Smith*, in his *Collected Works*, ed. Sir William Hamilton, 1858, vol. X, 68.

12 Jennings, *An Anatomy of Leadership*, 1.

13 Jennings, *An Anatomy of Leadership*, 71.

14 Jennings, *An Anatomy of Leadership*, 71; Thomas Carlyle, *Heroes, Hero Worship and the Heroic in History*, ed. Henry Morley (London: Cassell, 1901).

15 Henry Ford in John Bartlett, Anna Sprague DeWolf, and Laura Bartlett Donaldson, *Familiar Quotations*, ed. Emily Morrison Beck (Boston: Little, Brown & Company, 1982), 253.

16 R.M. Stogdill, *Handbook of Leadership*, rev. and exp. Bernard M. Bass (New York: The Free Press, 1981), 81.

17 Stogdill, *Handbook of Leadership*, 5.

18 Harry Levinson, *Executive* (Cambridge: Harvard University Press, 1981), 207; Dava Sobel, "Findings," *Harvard Magazine* 81, no. 3 (January/February 1979): 15.

19 Erica Anderson, *The World of Albert Schweitzer*, text and captions by Eugena Exina (New York: Harper & Brothers, 1955), 138.

20 David C. McClelland, *Power: The Inner Experience* (New York: Irvington/Halstead Press, 1975); David C. McClelland, "Business Drive and National Achievement," *Harvard Business Review* 40, no. 4 (July–August, 1962): 99–112; and David C. McClelland, "That Urge to Achieve," *Think* 32, no. 6 (November–December, 1966).

21 Jerry Kramer, ed., *Lombardi: Winning Is the Only Thing* (New York: Thomas Y. Crowell Company, 1976).

22 Clarence Francis, "Hippocratic Oath for Executives," in John R. Sargent, *What Every Executive Should Know about the Art of Leadership* (Chicago: Dartnell Corp., 1964), 24.

23 Doris Kearns, *Lyndon Johnson and the American Dream* (New York: Harper & Row, Publishers, Inc., 1976).

24 Ernest Dale, *Management Theory and Practice*, 3d ed. (New York: McGraw-Hill, Inc., 1973).

STUDY QUIZ

As a test of your understanding and the extent to which you have achieved the objectives in Part One, complete the following questions. See Appendix D for the answer key.

1. If a person's work prevents the satisfaction of personal social motives, morale and productivity ultimately will decrease.

   a. true
   b. false

2. Breakdown in the work setting can result from leadership deficiency. Examples include all except:

   a. communication breakdown
   b. lack of teamwork
   c. acts of nature
   d. quality problems
   e. employee inefficiency

3. Giving orders is one of the most important skills of the

   a. skeleton key
   b. master key
   c. front door key
   d. ignition key

4. Rules for giving orders include:

   a. before giving an order, consider the availability of the employee's time and whether this is the ideal person to do the job
   b. be sure you know exactly what you want to communicate before you give an order
   c. if several different duties or steps are involved in an order, follow oral communication with a written memo.
   d. present your orders in logical sequence and in clear, concise language
   e. all of the above

5. Either by _____ or _____, leaders show the way and influence the behavior of others.

   a. ideas, deeds
   b. humor, study
   c. fear, force
   d. books, speeches

6. In giving an order, use the correct language level for the subordinate's
   _____.

   a. training level
   b. ethnic background
   c. personality type
   d. age group

7. In giving an order, be considerate, but never be _____ when
   asking someone to do a job.

   a. detailed
   b. articulate
   c. apologetic
   d. assertive

8. Which one of the following is not a characteristic of leadership?

   a. honor
   b. integrity
   c. secularism
   d. courage

9. Both nature and _____ have a role in the leadership
   equation.

   a. nurture
   b. agriculture
   c. water
   d. trees

10. All of the following are basic leadership motives except

    a. power
    b. altruism
    c. achievement
    d. autism

11. According to Fred Fiedler, all leadership is

    a. benign
    b. subsequent
    c. egotistic
    d. manipulative

12. In the passage "He Made Me Feel Important," Vince Lombardi in-
    fluenced his players because of his

    a. size
    b. character
    c. intelligence
    d. insecurity

13. Giving orders is one of the most important skills of which of the following keys?

    a. skeleton key
    b. master key
    c. front door key
    d. ignition key

14. The three basic motives underlying the desire of a person to be a leader are

    a. power, recognition, altruism
    b. altruism, achievement, power
    c. success, acknowledgment, prestige
    d. achievement, power, success

15. A person who is power oriented strives for

    a. authority
    b. fear
    c. achievement
    d. acceptance

16. The Greek warrior Achilles led by

    a. ideas
    b. deeds

17. The three basic types of leaders are

    a. heroes, rulers, teachers
    b. Democrats, Republicans, independents
    c. progressives, traditionalists, moderates

18. Ruler-type leaders include

    a. Buddha, Marx, Aristotle
    b. Newton, Michelangelo, Edison
    c. Caesar, Napoleon, Lenin

19. Elizabeth I was a _____ leader.

    a. power-oriented
    b. achievement-oriented
    c. altruistic-oriented

20. Albert Schweitzer was a _____ leader.

    a. power-oriented
    b. achievement-oriented
    c. altruistic-oriented

21. The reason leaders should give subordinates the chance to ask questions is

    a. employees may be confused
    b. employees may have important information
    c. to show respect for employee opinions
    d. all of the above

———————————

DISCUSSION QUESTIONS AND ACTIVITIES

The following questions and activities help personalize the subject. They are appropriate for classroom exercises and homework assignments.

1. Relate an incident you witnessed in which leadership was important. Describe the leader's ideas and actions.

   _____

   _____

   _____

2. Why would you want to be a leader: power, achievement, or affiliation? Do your work and your personal life allow full expression of your social motives?

   _____

   _____

   _____

3. In small groups, discuss which is more important, nature or nurture. Are leaders born or made?

4. Discuss the role of persuasion in the leadership process. How important are oral skills and personal charm? Do you know a leader who is masterful at talking people into things?

5. Discuss a true-life example of how a leader's character influenced the behavior of followers.

PART TWO

The Combination Lock and the Front Door Key

Learning Objectives

After completing Part Two, you will better understand:

1. qualities of leaders, characteristics of followers, and the nature of situations, as these influence the leadership process;

2. formal authority and the use of power.

THE COMBINATION LOCK — THE RELATIONSHIP BETWEEN LEADER, FOLLOWER, AND SITUATION

The "combination lock" has three important elements: (1) qualities of leaders, (2) characteristics of followers, (3) and the nature of the situation. No single element explains why leadership takes place. Leadership results when the ideas and deeds of the leader match the needs and expectations of the followers in a particular situation.

The relationship between General George Patton, the American Third Army, and the demands of World War II resulted in leadership; however, the same General Patton probably would not have as much influence on the membership and goals of a PTA meeting today. Even if there was agreement about goals, disagreement over style probably would interfere with the leadership process. Similarly, the relationship between Cesar Chavez, California's migrant farm workers, and the economic conditions of the 1960s resulted in leadership, but Chavez probably would not have as much success as the board chairman of a Fortune 500 company today.

ILLUS. 2.1

General Patton's leadership reflected the coming together of ideas and deeds to match the needs of the situation.

THE BETTMANN ARCHIVE, INC.

The story of Hitler, the German people, and World War II shows the importance of the "combination lock."

> Hitler generated his power through the skillful use of suggestion, collective hypnosis, and every kind of subconscious motivation that the crowd was predisposed to unleash. In this way, the people sought out Hitler just as much as Hitler sought them out. Rather than saying that Hitler manipulated the people as an artist molds clay, certain traits in Hitler gave him the opportunity to appeal to the psychological condition of the people.
>
> Seen in this light, Hitler was not the great beginner, but merely the executor of the people's wishes. He was able to feel the character and direction of the people and to make them more conscious of it, thereby generating power that he was able to exploit. This greatness is not due to his personal strength. Isolated from his crowd, Hitler would be without potency.
>
> Hitler was personally weak as an individual, but as one who sensed the character and direction of the group he became the embodiment of power. No doubt his greatness came through his claiming for himself what actually was the condition and achievement of many.[1]

Ultimately, the leader, the followers, and the situation must match for leadership to take place.

Qualities of Leaders

Certain qualities potentially belong to everyone, but some people possess these qualities to an exceptional degree. The following is a discussion of qualities that mark a leader and help influence the leadership process.[2]

Vision A vision of what should or could be is a basic force enabling the leader to recognize what must be done and to do it. Vision inspires others and causes the leader to accept the duties of leadership, whether pleasant or unpleasant. The statesman, Adlai Stevenson, wrote:

> . . .I want somebody on that hilltop or its equivalent who can be thinking and looking far ahead, and who can prod me into doing the things that it would be easier not to do. Don't try to think of things that are politically shrewd. Try to think of the next generation.[3]

A sense of vision is especially powerful when it embodies a common cause—overcoming tyranny, stamping out hunger, or improving the human condition.

If you are the leader of a work group or organization, you should ask, "Do I have a plan? What is my vision of what this department or organization should be?"

Ability The leader must know the job—or invite loss of respect. Subordinates seldom respect the individual who constantly must rely on others when making decisions, giving guidance, or solving problems. Although subordinates usually show a great deal of patience with a new leader, they will lose faith in someone who fails to gain an understanding of the job within a reasonable period of time. Also, the leader must keep job knowledge current. Failure to keep up leads to lack of confidence and loss of employee support.

Leaders should ask, "How competent am I? Am I current in my field? Do I set an example and serve as a resource for my subordinates because I keep job knowledge current?"

Enthusiasm Genuine enthusiasm is an important trait of a good leader. Enthusiasm is a form of persuasiveness that causes others to become interested and willing to accept what the leader is attempting to accomplish. Enthusiasm, like other human emotions — laughter, joy, happiness — is contagious. Enthusiasm shown by a leader generates enthusiasm in followers.

If you are a leader, you must ask, "Do I care personally and deeply about what I am doing? Do I show this to my subordinates? Does my enthusiasm ignite others to take action?"

Stability The leader must understand her or his own world and how it relates to the world of others. One cannot solve the equation of others when preoccupied with the equation of self. Empathy for subordinates cannot be developed if the leader is emotionally involved with personal problems. A display of emotional instability places the leader in a precarious position with regard to subordinates; they will question the leader's objectivity and judgment. Leaving personal problems at home allows the leader to think more clearly and to perform more effectively on the job.

The leader must ask, "Do I possess objectivity? Do I convey stability to my subordinates? Do they trust that personal problems will not interfere with my judgment?"

Concern for Others The leader must not look down on others or treat them as machines — replaceable and interchangeable. The leader must be sincerely and deeply concerned about the welfare of subordinates. The leader must also possess selflessness to the extent that, whenever possible, employee interests are considered first. Loyalty to followers generates loyalty to the leader; and when tasks become truly difficult, loyalty "carries the day."

Leaders must question, "Do I truly care about my subordinates as people, or do I view them more as tools to meet my goals? If I value my subordinates, do they know it?"

Self-confidence Self-confidence gives the leader inner strength to overcome difficult tasks. Subordinates quickly sense a leader's self-confidence, and this results in increased employee commitment and performance. On the other hand, if leaders lack self-confidence, employees may question their authority and even may disobey their orders.

A leader must ask, "What is my self-confidence level? Do I demonstrate confidence by my actions?"

Persistence According to Niccolò Machiavelli, "There is nothing more difficult to take in hand, more perilous to conduct, or more uncertain as to success, than to take the lead in the introduction of a new order of things."[4] The leader must have persistence to stick with difficult tasks until they are completed. Israeli Prime Minister Golda Meir referred to this when she said, "Nothing in life just happens. It isn't enough to just believe in something. You have to have the stamina to meet obstacles and overcome them, to struggle."

If you are the leader, ask, "Do I have self-drive and unflagging persistence to overcome adversity even when others lose their strength and their will?"

Vitality Even if the spirit is willing, physical and emotional strength are needed to exert leadership. The leader should ask, "Am I fit for the tasks of leadership? Am I hardy in body? Do I have sufficient energy?"

Charisma Charisma is a special personal quality to generate others' interest and to cause them to follow. Optimism, forthrightness, and a sense of adventure are traits found in charismatic leaders. These are the qualities that unleash the potential of others and bring forth their energies.

As leader, ask yourself, "Do I possess a positive outlook, directness in my dealings, and excitement in my demeanor?"

ILLUS. 2.2

Charismatic leaders have a positive outlook, directness, and excitement.

© Jack W. Dykinga

How do you rate on the nine qualities of leadership: vision, ability, enthusiasm, emotional stability, concern for others, self-confidence, persistence to see tasks through to completion, physical vitality, and personal charisma? Do you have the qualities that inspire others to follow? The following exercise will help you evaluate yourself.

NINE LEADERSHIP QUALITIES: HOW DO YOU RATE?

Directions

Evaluate yourself on the nine leadership qualities by circling a number from 1 to 10 (1 is low, 10 is high.)

Vision: a sense of what could and should be

| 1 | 2 | 3 | 4 | 5 | 6 | 7 | 8 | 9 | 10 |

Ability: job knowledge and expertise

| 1 | 2 | 3 | 4 | 5 | 6 | 7 | 8 | 9 | 10 |

Enthusiasm: ability to motivate others and to bring out their best

| 1 | 2 | 3 | 4 | 5 | 6 | 7 | 8 | 9 | 10 |

Stability: emotional adjustment and objectivity

| 1 | 2 | 3 | 4 | 5 | 6 | 7 | 8 | 9 | 10 |

Concern for Others: loyalty to employees and an interest in their welfare

| 1 | 2 | 3 | 4 | 5 | 6 | 7 | 8 | 9 | 10 |

Self-confidence: inner strength that generates employee trust

| 1 | 2 | 3 | 4 | 5 | 6 | 7 | 8 | 9 | 10 |

Persistence: ability to see tough tasks through to completion

| 1 | 2 | 3 | 4 | 5 | 6 | 7 | 8 | 9 | 10 |

Vitality: physical and emotional strength

| 1 | 2 | 3 | 4 | 5 | 6 | 7 | 8 | 9 | 10 |

Charisma: magnetic ability to invigorate people and to lead them without controlling them

1	2	3	4	5	6	7	8	9	10

SCORING AND INTERPRETATION

Total your score and add 10 points.

Score	Evaluation
100–90	Excellent; exceptional
89–70	High; very good
69–50	Average; needs improvement
49–below	Low; much work needed

Characteristics of Followers

Characteristics of followers that influence the leadership process are respect for authority and interpersonal trust. People who respect authority figures and have a trusting nature are more easily led than people who disregard authorities and are suspicious of others.

The following questionnaire shows your susceptibility to follow, based on the trust you have in others.

INTERPERSONAL TRUST SCALE

Directions

The following is a survey of a number of work and social questions. Answer each one based on your own experience and judgment in dealing with people.

Many views are represented in this survey. You may find yourself agreeing strongly with some of the statements, disagreeing with others, and perhaps undecided about others. Whether you agree or disagree with any statement, you can be sure that many people feel the same as you do.

Answer each statement by circling the response showing how much you agree or disagree.

Example: Science has its place, but there are many important things that can never possibly be understood.

  a. Strongly disagree
  b. Disagree
  c. Undecided
  ⓓ Agree
  e. Strongly agree

1. The best way to handle people is to tell them what they want to hear.

   a. Strongly disagree
   b. Disagree
   c. Undecided
   d. Agree
   e. Strongly agree

2. It is hard to get ahead without cutting corners here and there.

   a. Strongly disagree
   b. Disagree
   c. Undecided
   d. Agree
   e. Strongly agree

3. Anyone who completely trusts someone else is asking for trouble.

   a. Strongly disagree
   b. Disagree
   c. Undecided
   d. Agree
   e. Strongly agree

4. When you ask someone to do something for you, it is best to give the real reasons for wanting it rather than giving reasons that might carry more weight.

   a. Strongly disagree
   b. Disagree
   c. Undecided
   d. Agree
   e. Strongly agree

5. It is safest to assume that all people have a vicious streak, and it will come out when they are given a chance.

   a. Strongly disagree
   b. Disagree
   c. Undecided
   d. Agree
   e. Strongly agree

6. One should take action only when sure it is morally right.

   a. Strongly disagree
   b. Disagree
   c. Undecided
   d. Agree
   e. Strongly agree

7. Most people are basically good and kind.

   a. Strongly disagree
   b. Disagree
   c. Undecided
   d. Agree
   e. Strongly agree

8. There is no valid reason for lying to someone else.

   a. Strongly disagree
   b. Disagree
   c. Undecided
   d. Agree
   e. Strongly agree

9. Most people forget more easily the death of their father than the loss of their property.

   a. Strongly disagree
   b. Disagree
   c. Undecided
   d. Agree
   e. Strongly agree

10. Generally speaking, people won't work hard unless they are forced to do so.

   a. Strongly disagree
   b. Disagree
   c. Undecided
   d. Agree
   e. Strongly agree

Source: "A Test: Are You Machiavellian?" in Richard Christie, "The Machiavellians Among Us," Psychology Today *(November 1970): 82–83, 85–86.* Reprinted with permission.

SCORING

Step 1

Using the following key, circle your score for each item of the questionnaire:

1.			2.			3.			4.		
	a	5		a	5		a	5		a	1
	b	4		b	4		b	4		b	2
	c	3		c	3		c	3		c	3
	d	2		d	2		d	2		d	4
	e	1		e	1		e	1		e	5

5.	a	5		6.	a	1		7.	a	1		8.	a	1
	b	4			b	2			b	2			b	2
	c	3			c	3			c	3			c	3
	d	2			d	4			d	4			d	4
	e	1			e	5			e	5			e	5
9.	a	5		10.	a	5								
	b	4			b	4								
	c	3			c	3								
	d	2			d	2								
	e	1			e	1								

Step 2

Add up your scores and divide the total by ten.

Total score _____ ÷ 10 = _____

INTERPRETATION

Scores on the Interpersonal Trust Scale (see Figure 2.1) show your tendency to trust people. Typically, the higher the score on the scale (1 to 5), the more trust you have in the inherent decency of others. A high score may reflect susceptibility to suggestion from others. On the other hand, the lower the score on the scale, the less trusting you would be expected to be of others. A low score may reflect a tendency to manipulate others in accomplishing goals.

FIGURE 2.1

Interpersonal Trust Scale

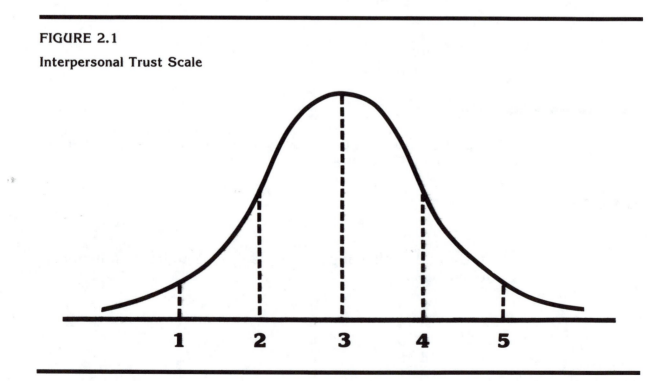

Scores	Characteristics
1.0–2.0	This person believes that most people seek personal advantage, even at the expense of others; given this, the best course of action is self-protection. The 1.0–2.0 may manipulate others in interpersonal relations and avoid making personal commitments. Such a person is difficult to con and is often difficult to lead.
2.0–3.0	This person is generally suspicious of the motives of others and tends toward self-reliance rather than seeking assistance or direction. The 2.0–3.0 will usually act independently, rather than ask for help or delegate, believing the best way to get something done is to do it oneself.
3.0–4.0	This person has confidence in the basic decency of others, combined with an evaluation of the merits of the situation. The 3.0–4.0 will usually trust others temporarily, yet reserve final judgment.
4.0–5.0	This person believes that people are essentially good and therefore readily trusts others. Such a person may not look below the surface of things. The 4.0–5.0 is easily persuaded and should be encouraged to look at all sides of an argument before making a decision.

In reviewing your interpersonal trust scores, what is your tendency? Do you lean toward suspicion and self-reliance? Do you tend to be trusting and suggestible? Or are you somewhere in the middle? Given your level of trust, are you difficult or easy to lead?

Attitudes toward authority have been changing in Western society, and effective leadership today requires adjustment to the ideas and expectations of a new generation of followers. In the past, the traditional leader in the work setting typically was a taskmaster who ruled with a strong arm and forced employees to obey or face the consequences. If employees failed to show respect or follow orders, they were threatened with dismissal or other punishment.

Over the years, employees have developed defenses to protect themselves. They have organized unions to represent their interests, and labor legislation has been created to protect workers from arbitrary firing or mistreatment. In addition, management has learned that people who feel oppressed usually respond in negative ways — slowing down production, producing poor quality work, and being uncooperative.[5]

Today, enlightened leaders do not use the power tactics of the past. Modern managers find that the practice of threatening subordinates is usually counterproductive. Instead, leaders view their task as one of motivating employees to do their best. In doing this, leaders function as facilitators and teachers as opposed to enforcers and disciplinarians, believing that respect should be earned, not demanded.[6]

Nature of the Situation

In the work setting, the type of work to be done influences the leadership process. Leadership studies show that, in general, when the work to be done is clear-cut, routine, and monotonous, a humanistic orientation is best. If the work duties are defined loosely and without much structure, a task orientation is needed.[7]

Studies also show that the size of an organization demands different leadership skills. A small organization of a few hundred employees needs a leader who is primarily a salesperson and production manager. Outside the organization, the leader is the organization's chief advocate, personally meeting with many clients and winning their loyalty. On the inside, the leader organizes the work, assigns tasks, and evaluates subordinates' progress.[8]

In contrast, the leader of a large organization devotes efforts primarily to two concerns: the organization's public image and its investment and growth plans. Leaders of large organizations think in broad terms about the community and the market place, considering how the organization can be placed best in both.[9]

Emotional factors such as confusion, anxiety, and despair can also influence the leadership process. Consider pre-war Germany, where the inactivity of the people seemed intolerable:

> The streets of German towns were full of millions of unemployed waiting for the dole, which was scarcely sufficient to provide for the indispensable needs of daily life. These observations were common to everyone who lived in Germany during the years preceding Hitler's advent to power. The lack of such an important educational factor as compulsory military service on the one hand, and the plague of unemployment on the other, produced their inevitable consequences in the slope of a deplorable moral relaxation and in a not less deplorable decrease of patriotism.[10]

In these circumstances, which were ripe for leadership, Adolf Hitler came to power.

Given the factors just discussed — qualities of the leader, characteristics of the followers, and the nature of the situation — what form of leadership meets the preference of most leaders, the needs of most followers, and the requirements of most situations today? What is the "combination lock"? Businessman and author Robert Townsend answers:

> . . . As for the best leader, the people do not notice his existence. The next best, the people fear. And the next, the people hate. When the best leader's work is done, the people say, "We did it ourselves."[11]

For the "combination lock" to work, the leader must embrace democratic ideals, followers must be both motivated and capable, and the situation must allow sufficient time for discussion and consensus. Not all leaders do, not all followers are, and not every situation does. The "combination lock" of leadership changes from leader to leader, follower to follower, and situation to situation.

Because there is no universal "combination lock," leadership is more art than science and more skill than knowledge. Above all, leadership is difficult. Management consultant and educator Douglas McGregor, creator of the term "Theory X, Theory Y" describes how difficult leadership can be:

No Easy Task

I believed (before coming to Antioch) that a leader could operate successfully as a kind of advisor to his organization. I thought I could avoid being a "boss." Unconsciously, I suspect, I hoped to duck the unpleasant necessity of making difficult decisions, of taking the responsibility for one course of action among many uncertain alternatives, of making mistakes and taking the consequences. I thought that maybe I could operate so that everyone would like me — that "good human relations" would eliminate all discord and argument.

I couldn't have been more wrong. It took a couple of years, but I finally began to realize that a leader cannot avoid the exercise of authority anymore than he can avoid responsibility for what happens to his organization. In fact, it is a major function of the top manager to take on his own shoulders the responsibility for resolving the uncertainties that are always involved in important decisions.

Moreover, since no important decision ever pleases everyone in an organization, the leader must also absorb the displeasure, and sometimes severe hostility, of those who would have taken a different course.[12]

An important factor in the "combination lock" is leader/follower compatibility in the decision-making process. The following exercise is designed to evaluate preferred styles of leading and following: directive, participative, or free rein.

WHAT TYPE OF LEADER ARE YOU?

Directions

Answer the following questions, keeping in mind what you have done, or think you would do, in the situations described.

	Yes	No
1. Do you enjoy the authority leadership brings?	____	____
2. Generally, do you think it is worth the time and effort for a supervisor to explain the reasons for a decision or policy before putting the policy into effect?	____	____
3. Do you tend to prefer the planning functions of leadership, as opposed to working directly with your subordinates?	____	____

4. A stranger comes into your work area, and you know the person is a new employee. Would you first ask, "What is your name?", rather than introduce yourself? ____ ____

5. Do you keep your subordinates totally up-to-date on developments affecting the work group? ____ ____

6. Do you find that in giving out assignments, you tend to state the goals, and leave the methods up to your subordinates? ____ ____

7. Do you think leaders should keep aloof from subordinates, because in the long run familiarity breeds lessened respect? ____ ____

8. It comes time to decide about a company event. You have heard that the majority prefer to have it on Wednesday, but you are pretty sure Thursday would be better for all concerned. Would you put the question to a vote rather than make the decision yourself? ____ ____

9. If you had your way, would you make communications an employee-initiated affair, with personal consultation held only at their request? ____ ____

10. Do you find it fairly easy to give low ratings on employee evaluation forms? ____ ____

11. Do you feel that you should be friendly with your employees? ____ ____

12. After considerable time, you determine the answer to a tough problem. You pass along the solution to your subordinates who poke it full of holes. Would you be annoyed that the problem is still unsolved, rather than become upset with the employees? ____ ____

13. Do you agree that one of the best ways to avoid problems of discipline is to provide adequate punishment for violation of rules? ____ ____

14. Your way of handling a situation is being criticized by your employees. Would you try to sell your viewpoint, rather than make it clear that, as the supervisor, your decisions are final? ____ ____

15. Do you generally leave it up to your subordinates to contact you, as far as informal day-to-day communications are concerned? ____ ____

16. Do you feel that everyone in your work group should have a certain amount of personal loyalty to you? ____ ____

17. Do you favor the practice of using task force teams and committees, rather than making decisions alone? ____ ____

18. Some experts say differences of opinion within work groups are healthy; others feel they indicate basic flaws in the management process. Do you agree with the first view? ____ ____

SCORING

On the scoring matrix below, place a check mark (✔) next to each question you answered Yes. Add up the checks for each column and put the totals in the appropriate spaces.

Scoring Matrix

1. _____	2. _____	3. _____
4. _____	5. _____	6. _____
7. _____	8. _____	9. _____
10. _____	11. _____	12. _____
13. _____	14. _____	15. _____
16. _____	17. _____	18. _____

Directive total _____   Participative total _____   Free-rein total _____

WHAT TYPE OF FOLLOWER ARE YOU?

Directions

Answer the following questions, keeping in mind what you have done, or think you would do, in the situations described.

	Yes	No
1. When assigned a task, do you like to have the details spelled out thoroughly?	___	___
2. Do you think that most supervisors are bossier than they need to be?	___	___
3. Would you say that personal initiative is one of your stronger points?	___	___
4. Do you feel that a supervisor should avoid getting personally involved with subordinates?	___	___
5. In general, would you prefer working with others, as opposed to working alone?	___	___
6. Do you tend to prefer the pleasures of solitude (reading, writing, thinking) more than the pleasures of being with others (parties, get-togethers, etc.)?	___	___
7. Do you tend to be loyal toward those who supervise you?	___	___
8. Do you often lend a helping hand to others in your work group?	___	___
9. When you work on a project, do you prefer using your own ideas, as opposed to your supervisor's ideas to solve problems?	___	___
10. Would you prefer a supervisor who is knowledgeable over one who comes to you to solve problems?	___	___
11. Do you feel it is appropriate for a supervisor to be friendlier with some employees than with others?	___	___

12. Would you prefer assuming full responsibility for the outcome of your work, rather than sharing the responsibility with others? ____ ____

13. Do you think that having men and women in the same work group creates more problems than having all men or all women? ____ ____

14. Do you think a supervisor should discuss new procedures with employees before implementing them? ____ ____

15. Do you insist upon doing what you, yourself, feel is right or important? ____ ____

16. Would you agree that a supervisor who could not keep your loyalty should not be supervisor? ____ ____

17. Would you be upset with a supervisor who fails to have regular staff meetings? ____ ____

18. Do rules and prescribed guidelines inhibit your creativity? ____ ____

SCORING

On the scoring matrix below, place a check mark (✔) next to each question you answered Yes. Add up the checks for each column and put the totals in the appropriate spaces.

Scoring Matrix

1. ____	2. ____	3. ____
4. ____	5. ____	6. ____
7. ____	8. ____	9. ____
10. ____	11. ____	12. ____
13. ____	14. ____	15. ____
16. ____	17. ____	18. ____

Directive total ____   Participative total ____   Free-rein total ____

Source: Naomi Miller, Northern Kentucky University, 1981; based on Auren Uris, "Techniques of Leading – Techniques of Following," in Techniques of Leadership *(New York: McGraw-Hill, Inc., 1953), 49–52, 78–89. Reprinted with permission.*

INTERPRETATION

Your scores show preferred styles of leading and following. Your highest scores indicate your most preferred styles. A description of each style is presented in Figure 2.2.

Figure 2.3 shows the different emphasis in the use of power for each of the three styles.

FIGURE 2.2

Continuum of Leading and Following Styles

DIRECTIVE STYLE		**PARTICIPATIVE STYLE**		**FREE—REIN STYLE**	
Maximum Use of Authority by the Leader				Maximum Area of Freedom of the Subordinate	
Leader decides what is to be done and how it is to be done, and presents the decision to subordinates, allowing no questions or opposing points of view.	Leader attempts to convince subordinates of the "rightness" of decisions.	Leader announces principles and sets forth methods of decision making, yet permits ideas, questions, and discussion from subordinates.	Leader presents a problem, asks for subordinates' ideas, and makes final decision based upon their input.	Leader presents problems with some boundaries and lets subordinates make final decisions.	Leader gives subordinates as much freedom as he has to define problems and make decisions.
DIRECTIVE STYLE (Leader-centered decision making)		**PARTICIPATIVE STYLE** (Leader-and-subordinate-shared decision making)		**FREE—REIN STYLE** (Subordinate-centered decision making)	

Source: *Robert Tannenbaum and Warren H. Schmidt, "How to Choose a Leadership Pattern,"* Harvard Business Review, 36, no. 2 (March–April 1958), 96.

FIGURE 2.3

Emphasis in the Use of Power

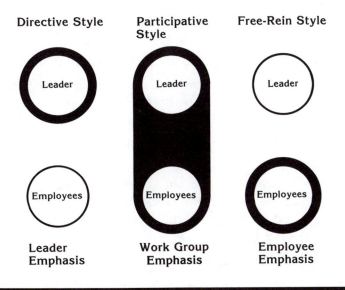

Source: *Keith Davis,* Human Behavior at Work: Organizational Behavior *(New York: McGraw-Hill, Inc., 1981), 136.*

There are eight points to remember about styles of leading and styles of following:

1. Styles of leading and following are usually the same. Confusion results when this is not the case. General George Patton was a directive leader and a free-rein follower, causing mixed signals and much controversy in his relations with commanders and subordinates.

2. Styles of leading and following are shaped by experience. People develop preferred styles by modeling after others, through formal training, and from personal experiences.

3. Leaders have been successful along all points of the continuum: George Washington was directive in his style; both Thomas Jefferson and Andrew Jackson chose participative leadership; Dwight Eisenhower preferred the free-rein style.

4. There is no universally effective style of leading and following. Sometimes it is best for the leader to tell subordinates what to do; sometimes it is best for leaders and subordinates to make decisions together; and sometimes it is best for the subordinates to direct themselves. The best style of leadership depends on factors of the leader, factors of the followers, and the nature of the situation.

Important factors of the leader include:

- *Personal preference:* Some leaders want the formal structure of the directive style; others enjoy the give-and-take of the participative style; others prefer individualism and free-rein leadership.

- *Versatility:* Some leaders have little trouble shifting styles to meet the needs of different subordinates and demands of different situations; others are less flexible.

- *Assessment of competence:* If a decision is important, and the leader has little confidence in the judgment of subordinates, the leader is more likely to be directive.

Important factors of followers include:

- *Need for structure:* Some subordinates want clear guidelines and step-by-step procedures; others want free rein and few rules.

- *Knowledge and interest:* Usually, the higher the knowledge and interest level of the subordinate, the more appropriate free rein is as a style of leading.

- *Leadership expectations:* Some subordinates want the leader to make decisions and supervise closely; others respond best to team effort and participative management; others need a high degree of personal freedom.

Important factors of the situation include:

- *Nature of the work:* Precision work, such as performing an operation, may require directive leadership; creative work, such as developing a new product, may need free-rein leadership.

- *Time pressure:* Generally, the greater the urgency, the more appropriate is leader-centered as opposed to subordinate-centered decision making.

5. Leaders and followers who are constantly effective are sensitive to the various needs of others and the demands of the situation. The most versatile people behave comfortably on all points of the continuum. Such individuals have range. Imagine the range required of a directive leader to meet the needs of a free-rein subordinate.

6. Confusion and frustration usually result if someone behaves on a different point of the continuum than others expect. Examples are: the usually participative leader who acts in a directive manner; followers who have historically responded to directive leadership but now demand freedom.

7. If styles of leading and styles of following conflict, extra patience and communication are needed.

- *Decision making:* Directive leaders may be upset by free-rein followers who insist on challenging decisions and behaving independently.
- *Goal setting:* Directive followers may be upset by free-rein leaders who provide few details on how to do a job.
- *Communication:* Participative followers usually are upset by a leader who fails to have staff meetings, closes the "open door," and shows little concern for people's feelings.

8. Different types of followers relate to different styles of leadership.

- *Directive:* Directive followers usually do their best work when job duties are spelled out and direct orders are given.
- *Participative:* Participative followers want open communication and active involvement in the decision-making process. They usually perform well on task forces, committees, and other work teams.
- *Free rein:* Free-rein followers usually do their best work on special assignments and independent projects. They respond best to individual treatment and personal freedom.

To understand the importance of leader/follower compatibility, consider your own experience. Have you ever had a leader who missed the mark in meeting your needs? Do you, yourself, have the range to meet the needs of all three styles—directive, participative, and free rein?

ILLUS. 2.3

Both responsibility and power come with the office of leadership.

Janice Jones
VICE-PRESIDENT

THE FRONT DOOR KEY—
THE POWER OF OFFICE

Leadership is needed in all areas of society and at all levels of responsibility. Titles of leadership include president, chief, captain, manager, director, and supervisor. Both responsibility and power come with the office of leadership. Meeting the responsibility of the position without abusing its power is the "front door key." As the following parable shows, this is not an easy task.

The Cloak of Omnipotence: A Parable*

In the forest about a mile or so from Organizationville, there once lived a lion whose name was Lionel. From the time he was a cub, Lionel had been an outstanding lion. He was strong, quick, and intelligent, and very well liked by the other animals in the forest.

Lionel's parents were very proud of him and often remarked to each other, "Lionel is a natural leader. He will go far when he grows up and will do important things."

*Source: Herman and Korenich, AUTHENTIC MANAGEMENT, © 1977, Addison-Wesley Publishing Company, Inc. Reading, Massachusetts. pp. 225–236. Reprinted with permission.

Lionel played and studied hard at Lion Elementary School. He was happy and free. Being around him was very pleasant for others. Even when all the young animals played touch football and Lionel would block them quite hard, they would all laugh and get up and play some more. The other animals knew that Lionel was kind and had a good heart, so none feared him despite his great strength.

One day, Lionel's mother happened to come by the playground just as Lionel was making a particularly spectacular block in which he knocked down Willie Lion with his shoulder, Charlie Bear with his hind quarters, and even brushed Ronald Zebra out of the play with his tail. Lionel's teammates congratulated him, and even the animals on the other team slapped him on the shanks and said, "Well done." But Lionel's mother gasped with alarm and called Lionel to her.

"Lionel," she said in a worried tone, "I am concerned about the way you are playing. You must realize that you are bigger and stronger than some of the other animals, and you might hurt them if you play too hard."

"But Mother," said Lionel, who was puzzled, "the other animals play as hard as they can, too, and sometimes they knock me down, or sometimes they dodge around me."

"Still and all," said his mother, "I am worried and I do wish you would be more careful. I don't know what I would say to their mothers if you hurt any of the cubs. You wouldn't want others to think of you as a bully would you, Lionel?"

"No, Mother," said Lionel, though he wasn't quite sure what a bully was. "That's a good cub," Lionel's mother said, smiling. "Now you can go back and play with your friends and I will get your favorite dinner at the market. Remember, always be considerate of other animals' feelings and they will like you."

"Yes, Mother," Lionel said, and he returned to the game.

As he played, Lionel tried to remember his mother's advice. He held back his strength when he blocked, and he even slowed down a bit when he ran. He still played pretty well, but not as well as before and somehow in this game and those that followed, he never had quite as much fun. Still and all, life was happy for Lionel in his cubhood and he had few cares or worries.

Time passed, and one day when Lionel was almost full-grown his father called him into the den for a talk.

"Son," said Lionel's father, "the time has come for us to discuss your future. Your mother and I are very proud of you, but now we should give serious consideration to your higher education and career."

Lionel listened politely to his father, but felt a small twinge of sadness, for he knew he would miss being a cub. "Your mother and I," continued his father "feel that, with your potential, you should attend Animal University and perhaps major in leadership. How would you like to do that, son?"

"It sounds okay, I guess," replied Lionel, with a shuffle of his rear paws and a quick glance outdoors where Charlie Bear and Ronald Zebra were chasing each other in a rousing game of tag.

Lionel's father cleared his throat to reclaim his son's attention. "Attending Animal University and preparing yourself for leadership is an honor, Son, and it is also a heavy responsibility." Lionel's father stroked his whiskers slowly and looked very serious. "One day, you will probably be responsible for leading many of your fellow animals in important activities. Animals like Charlie Bear and Ronald Zebra will turn to you for direction and advice. So it is important that you study hard and listen carefully to your professors so that you are prepared for this."

"Yes, sir," said Lionel quietly, and being a well-brought-up young lion, he heeded his father's advice and headed for Animal University.

Animal U. was an interesting place, and by and large, Lionel enjoyed his time there. He studied hard, met some pretty girl animals, learned to drink beer, sang songs with words he wouldn't have mentioned around his parents, and even tried out for the Animal U. football team. In this endeavor Lionel quickly discovered, somewhat to his surprise, that when he held back his strength in making a block, many other animals ran right over him.

As the years went by, Lionel made good progress in his studies. He learned many useful things about leadership, such as how to think about what needs to be done in the future, how to arrange where other animals should stand and how they should move in order to be most efficient, how to get someone else to do something that you want to get done but haven't time to do yourself, how to keep track of what has been done and subtract it from what was supposed to be done, and finally, how to write reports about all of these things.

When Lionel was a senior, he signed up for a special course called "Animal Relations in Leadership" that was taught by a very famous professor, Dr. Sherwood Giraffe. In Dr. Giraffe's class, Lionel heard again what he heard from his father—that leadership was a very important responsibility.

He learned too about Animal Psychology and how other animals' feelings could be hurt if the leader was harsh with them.

He learned that a leader ought to ask other animals for their opinions before giving his own, because other animals were likely to be overly influenced by what the leader said.

He learned that while animals respected and admired their leaders, they also feared them because they tended to think about leaders as they had their fathers when they were cubs. So a leader had to be careful not to use authority in a way that would injure, frighten, or upset followers.

He learned that a leader ought to always appear confident and not reveal to others any doubt, confusion, or uncertainty, because they might lose confidence in the leader and begin to feel these unhappy feelings too.

He learned that a leader needed to think cautiously before speaking or acting, because a leader's words and deeds carry so much weight.

And he learned, finally, that being a leader is supposed to be a lonely job.

These were serious lessons indeed, Lionel thought, but heeding his father's advice, he learned them well.

When spring came, Lionel graduated from Animal University and returned again to the forest about a mile or so from Organizationville to find a place where he might put to use the valuable training he had received. He had little difficulty in finding employment. In fact Lionel's first job was in a medium-sized meadow as a junior leadership trainee and firstline supervisor over his three old chums, Willie Lion, Charlie Bear, and Ronald Zebra, who had taken two years of technical training in strip painting and touch-up work at a local trade school.

The reunion of Lionel and his friends was a happy one, and their work together in the meadow as leader and followers was happy and satisfying to them all; though if the truth were to be told, Willie, Charlie, and Ronald knew far more about what had to done and how to do it than Lionel did. But they were loving and patient with him, and as time went by, Lionel learned quickly and did quite well as a junior leadership trainee.

One day, however, at lunchtime, the four friends were reviewing their cubdom and decided to reenact Lionel's spectacular block in their most remembered touch-football game. Just at that instant Herbert Hedgehog, Lionel's own leader and an important officer in the meadow enterprise, happened by. Later that day he called Lionel aside.

"Lionel," said Mr. Hedgehog, smiling not unkindly, "I could not help but notice your behavior with your subordinates earlier this afternoon."

"Yes, sir?" asked Lionel, who was puzzled.

"Well," said Mr. Hedgehog, as he smiled again, even more kindly, "It's not that you, as a junior leadership trainee, are actually any better than the other animals in the meadow; rather, let us say that your heavier responsibilities place special obligations on you."

"Obligations?" asked Lionel, even more puzzled.

"Yes, Lionel, obligations that may be hampered by too close and too familiar association with those at lower echelons in the organization."

"I'm sorry, sir," said Lionel, "but I don't understand."

"No," said Mr. Hedgehog, "I can see that you don't. Perhaps I can explain. We who are leaders have heavy responsibility. The others look to us when they are unsure, so we must always act sure or they will worry and be anxious. They admire and respect us, but they also fear us, so we must be careful and considerate of them and try not to use our superior position and authority in ways that would injure them. A leader, in all respects, Lionel, must speak and act more cautiously than other animals, and," Mr. Hedgehog's face grew very serious, "too close and familiar association with those at lower echelons may distract us from our responsibility to them. Leadership," Mr. Hedgehog sighed, "is a lonely job. Do you understand that, Lionel?"

"Yes, sir," said Lionel, and he remembered Dr. Sherwood Giraffe's lectures.

"My suggestion is that you find a way to separate yourself a bit further from those in the lower echelons. I say this for your own good, Lionel," and Mr. Hedgehog smiled his most kindly smile of all. "For if you do what is required of you and meet your leadership responsibilities and obligations, I think you have a promising future."

"Thank you, sir," said Lionel. That evening he stayed awake late pondering on a way to separate himself a bit further from Willie Lion, Charlie Bear, and Ronald Zebra.

Finally, in the early morning hours, it came to him. Lionel decided to buy a cloak. And he did.

It was a light-weight cloak of light blue cotton that could be swung to and fro easily, so whenever Lionel felt himself getting too close to Willie, Charlie, or Ronald, or them getting too close to him, he could easily swish it over and hide a bit of himself from them.

The cloak worked quite well and Mr. Hedgehog was especially pleased. In fact, he put in a word for Lionel with one of the top leaders of the meadow. Lionel's performance had already been noted by the high echelon and so, in a short while, Lionel was promoted. To take his place, Lionel recommended Charlie Bear, and while there were some in the animal recruiting department who suggested a candidate be found from outside the meadow, Lionel's recommendation was finally accepted.

In his new position, Lionel's leadership responsibilities not only included Charlie Bear but four other first-line animal supervisors as well. Lionel realized he was now in middle-management, and one of the first things he did was to buy a new cloak. It was of medium weight and medium blue and considerably more substantial than his first one. In dealing with his new and heavier responsibilities, Lionel used his heavier cape more frequently too.

He would use it when he wanted things changed, but was unwilling to express his dissatisfaction with the way they were presently being done.

For instance, if one of his first-line supervisors made a proposal to him, Lionel might say, "Very nice, very nice," then swish would go the cloak and Lionel would continue, "but don't you think we might possibly want to do that just a bit differently? Not that there's anything wrong with your idea, of course."

He would use it when he was disappointed, or impatient, or irritated with the way another animal was doing his job. "Mmmm," Lionel would mutter under his breath, but realizing that in his terribly powerful position his criticism might hurt the lower-echelon animal, he would say no more. Instead, swish would go his cloak, and later he might mention his displeasure to the other animal's supervisor.

He would use it, too, when he was worried or uncertain, but did not want to reveal his feelings to others. Or when he feared he had made a mistake. Or when he was unsure of his point of view. In each case, swish would go Lionel's cloak.

And so the days in the meadow went by, and as Lionel was a strong, intelligent, and competent lion, he was more and more frequently noticed by all. Soon many spoke of Lionel as an up-and-coming animal with obvious high-echelon leadership potential. Not only did they speak of him that way, but a few could be seen emulating Lionel's style. They would talk as he did or stand as he did. And then, most strikingly of all, some would appear in the meadow wearing brand-new blue cloaks.

Gradually more and more blue-cloaked animals were to be seen, standing or pacing to and fro in the grass. In the practice of swishing their new cloaks, some were awkward at first and got themselves only partially covered, or perhaps forgot to swish at all. But others, Mr. Hedgehog especially, swished as well as Lionel or maybe even better.

As the cloaks increased in number, other things began to change in the meadow. It was quieter and fewer animals smiled — and even fewer laughed out loud. More reports were written than ever before, and memos, too. As the higher-echelon animals became more cautious for the sake of the lower-echelon animals, so did the lower-echelon animals become more cautious for their own sake. Animals whispered a good deal more than they had.

Still, work at the meadow went well enough (though there seemed to be fewer new ideas than before), and Lionel continued to rise in the ranks of the meadow organization until he did, indeed, become one of the high-echelon leaders.

When Lionel's old friends, Willie Lion, Charlie Bear, and Ronald Zebra, heard of Lionel's high promotion, they were all very pleased and decided to have a party for him. They asked Lionel who he would like them to invite, but Lionel could only think of Herbert Hedgehog and a few others.

"Leadership," Lionel sighed, "is a lonely job." Nevertheless, plans for Lionel's party proceeded and Mr. Hedgehog, since he was closest to Lionel's echelon, was given responsibility for buying a suitable gift.

On the evening of the party, the animals met at a local watering hole and when Lionel appeared, his old friends were pleased to see that he was not wearing his cloak. And so the festivities proceeded in a boisterous and happy way reminiscent of their early cub days. In fact, at one point during the party, after much coaxing, Lionel was persuaded to demonstrate again his famous three-man block; and while it did not work as well as it originally had (Lionel had put on some weight since then and his tail was not quite as quick as it once was), it didn't turn out too badly either. All in all, there was a good deal of laughing and carousing until the moment came for the high point of the evening, the presentation of Lionel's gift.

Herbert Hedgehog rose and cleared his throat. "Ahem," he began, "My dear colleagues and associates, we gather here today to honor our illustrious colleague, Lionel Lion. I am certain that we are all proud of the manner in which Lionel has met the heavy challenges and responsibilities of his leadership position." Mr. Hedgehog paused and waited for applause and the other animals tapped their paws.

Then Mr. Hedgehog continued, "Yes, as those of you who have enjoyed his leadership can well attest, Lionel has been an inspiration in meeting the obligations of a true leader. His extreme patience and forbearance are renowned. Never have we known him to roar in anger at a subordinate animal. Always he has been a considerate and thoughtful leader. He has been a steadfast beacon guiding others through both smooth and rocky waters. Calm, detached, and confident, he has not faltered in difficult moments when lesser animals might have given way to anxiety or passion." Mr. Hedgehog glanced around and noticed that others seemed to be getting a bit restless. Only Lionel himself seemed to be paying full attention, with a very serious expression on his face.

"In conclusion, dear colleagues," Hedgehog continued, "on behalf of us all, I should like to present this small token of our high esteem to a most respected leader, Lionel Lion."

Mr. Hedgehog passed a large white box tied neatly with a narrow ribbon to Lionel, who slowly opened it. Inside was a new cloak—but a cloak such as none he had ever seen. It was of the darkest blue imaginable, and of the thickest and heaviest wool. And unlike any other cloak Lionel had ever worn, it had a large dark-lined hood.

"Try it on, Lionel," Mr. Hedgehog urged. Lionel swung the cloak on and began to pace slowly back and forth. It was a very large cloak and almost completely covered him.

"Gosh," said Ronald Zebra, "I can hardly see you at all, Lionel."

"Maybe you ought to get a smaller size, Lionel," laughed Willie Lion. "If you tried to throw a block in that, it would probably get tangled in your paws, and you know you're not as well balanced as you were when you were a cub."

Most of the other animals at the party laughed at Willie Lion's remark, but not Mr. Hedgehog, and when Lionel noticed Mr. Hedgehog wasn't laughing, he didn't laugh either. Instead, he tossed his shoulders and the heavy hood fell in place over his head and face. Lionel said something then, but his voice was muffled by the hood, so none of the other animals heard what it was. With his hood and cloak covering him, Lionel was practically invisible, and no one ventured to ask him to repeat his words. There was not very much laughter or fun afterward either, so the party soon came to an end.

Lionel wore his new cloak almost every day in the meadow, and he often wore the hood as well. The other animals remarked to each other how impressive it was and noted, too, how difficult it was to see Lionel anymore. Cloaks, and even cloaks with hoods, became more and more fashionable among the leadership animals in the meadow, until just about all wore them. All, that is, except Charlie Bear, who continued to prance around the meadow, usually quite cheerfully, without covering himself at all. It was this fact that caused Lionel one late afternoon to call Charlie aside for a talk.

"Charlie," said Lionel, whose hood now lay back against his large shoulders, "you and I have known each other for a long time."

"We sure have," smiled Charlie Bear.

"Yes," said Lionel, tugging a wrinkle from his cloak. "Well, there is something I have been meaning to have a word with you about."

"Yes, Lionel?"

"Well, Charlie, as you may know, I recommended you to be my replacement when you first became a supervisor." Lionel padded a few paces to his left, and then to his right, then to his left again. "I thought that you had a promising future before you. Although you had not attended Animal University, my belief was that you were not just a run-of-the-mill animal, but a bear with potential." Lionel hunched his cloak up just the slightest bit around his shoulders. "I still believe that to be the case, Charles (it was the first time Charlie Bear could remember that Lionel had ever called him Charles), but I must admit I am somewhat disappointed in your progress."

"I'm sorry you're not happy, Lionel," said Charlie.

"Happiness is not the point," said Lionel. "Leadership is a heavy responsibility and happiness is a luxury few of us leaders can afford. We do, after all, have our first obligation to those who look up to us for guidance and direction. And that obligation may be hampered if our relations with our subordinates are too friendly and familiar."

"Do you mean Willie Lion and Ronald Zebra?" asked Charlie Bear.

"Charles, as you well know, I have only the highest regard for Lion and Zebra. However, for their sakes as well as your own, it would be better if you could maintain a somewhat greater distance between yourself and them, as is more appropriate for those at different echelons in the meadow organization." Lionel did some more pacing, then stopped before Charlie Bear. "I would like to ask you something Charlie."

"Okay," said Charlie Bear, who noticed Lionel was calling him Charlie again and felt a little, though not much, better.

"Why don't you wear a cloak? Almost all of the leadership animals do, you know." Lionel smoothed down the heavy cloth of his own cloak.

"Well," said Charlie, "mostly because I'm not cold, and besides I think a cloak would get in my way."

Lionel sighed heavily, "I'm afraid you don't understand, Charlie. This cloak I wear is not for comfort. In fact, there are many times when it is heavy and uncomfortable, times when I wish I could take it off entirely." Lionel seemed suddenly very weary and weighed down beneath his dark blue cloak.

"Then why do you wear it?" asked Charlie. "I wear it," Lionel replied, "for the sake of the other animals, to protect them from my power—the power of my position as their leader. That is my obligation. Now do you understand, Charlie?"

"No," said Charlie Bear, "I don't."

Lionel frowned. "Don't you realize how frightened the other animals would be if I got angry and I didn't cover it with my cloak?"

"Well," said Charlie, "some might be, but others wouldn't. Actually, I think I get more frightened, or at least nervous, when you cover yourself up."

"You still don't understand," said Lionel who was beginning to feel annoyed. "Can't you imagine how upset and worried the others would be if they were to see that I was upset and worried sometimes, if I didn't hide my feelings beneath my cloak?"

"Well, maybe they would be," said Charlie Bear, "but that doesn't seem so bad to me. There are a lot of other worries they have to deal with when they are away from the meadow, you know. Any animal with a mate and cubs knows plenty about upsets and worries, I'll tell you." Charlie Bear chuckled.

"I can see," said Lionel, "that I'm not getting through to you, Charles." He hunched his muscles and the hood of his dark cloak began to rise above his shoulders.

"I'm sorry, Lionel," said Charlie, but I just don't agree with you about this cloak business. In fact, if its not comfortable for you, I can't see why you don't just take it off."

With one quick, sharp motion, Lionel turned away and flipped his hood into place. It completely covered his head and face. Not even a whisker showed. Charlie heard his voice, but it was too muffled by the hood for Charlie to make out any words. But Charlie Bear did not go away.

Instead he said, "Lionel, I can't make out what you mean. Your hood is in the way."

Lionel Lion was furious. With an even quicker and sharper motion than he had made to flip his hood down, he jerked it back up. "I said," he roared, "that I am very upset by your lack of understanding of basic leadership principles."

"Well," growled Charlie Bear, as he reared up on his hind legs to his full awesome height, "I am upset too. And I don't believe in your basic leadership principles at all. You are a strong animal, Lionel, but mostly I remember that from the days we played touch-football together. Since you took to wearing cloaks, I haven't seen much of your strength. I think you're a smart lion too, but you can make mistakes. And when you do, that doesn't make me think the meadow is going to turn brown and die all of a sudden."

"But, you don't understand the responsibilities a leader . . .," Lionel hesitated, trying to find words. His cloak had slipped badly during Charlie's surprising speech, and now it only barely covered his rump.

"I wish," growled Charlie, but with a bit less anger, "that you would stop telling me that I don't understand. And I also wish you would stop protecting me from yourself, because I can protect myself if I need to. I'm not as helpless as you think I am. And when you hide under that big blue cloak of yours, I can't see who you are, and I can't tell how you feel or what you want." Charlie Bear's voice grew softer and gentler. "What's worse is that when you're under that cloak, I can't be your friend."

"But Herbert Hedgehog taught me those leadership principles, Charlie," said Lionel, who was considerably less sure of the principles himself now.

"Well," said Charlie Bear, "I think they are hogwash."

"Maybe they are," said Lionel, "maybe they're hedgehogwash, in fact." And he laughed, and Charlie Bear laughed, and in a moment the two old friends reached out and clasped each other's paws warmly.

In the days that followed in the meadow, Charlie Bear did not begin to wear a cloak. Nor did Lionel immediately discard his. Rather, he began to experiment a bit in wearing it somewhat less often. For example, when he was not satisfied with the way an animal was doing his job, sometimes Lionel would tell him so. The other animal might be surprised and a little upset at first, but if he and Lionel kept talking they could usually work it out. A few times, the other animals even thanked Lionel for his advice. And sometimes, especially with the leadership animals Lionel most often worked with, he would not cover over disappointment or impatience or irritation when he felt them. Lionel discovered to his surprise that few of them were seriously hurt, and some even argued back, as Charlie Bear had done when they thought they were right. And Lionel, as well as the others, often found their arguments stimulating, and exciting, and sometimes even funny.

After a time, Lionel wore his cloak far less, too, when he was worried or unsure of himself, or even when he feared he had made a mistake. But he discovered that the other animals did not crumble, nor did they even seem terribly shocked when he was confused or uncertain. Instead, some made suggestions that actually helped.

Finally, there came a time when Lionel hardly ever wore his cloak at all, although he kept it nearby in case of emergency. But then he knew he was using it for his own sake, not to protect others from him. And in time, Lionel found that others gradually began to give up wearing their cloaks, too, though they did so considerably more slowly than they had taken on the habit of wearing cloaks. And some—in fact, Mr. Hedgehog—never did give up their cloaks at all.

Even so, anyone passing by the meadow on an afternoon would probably have noticed that there were more smiles among the animals, and louder talking, and a good deal more laughing; and all that seemed very good.

Lionel was a good leader. He wanted to do the right thing if he could just discover it. His dilemma was how to have good relations with his followers while meeting the responsibilities of leadership. He discovered the answer was to have open, honest communication with the other animals.

Lionel learned that, along with approval, a leader should express disapproval; otherwise, subordinates may not know when they are doing something wrong. In the long run, a worker is more distressed not knowing if his performance is meeting expectations than being corrected once in a while.

Lionel also learned that a leader does not have to end friendships with subordinates in order to be effective. To the contrary, knowing that the leader is interested and cares about their welfare results in a relaxed, supportive atmosphere, and this increases the morale and productivity of most employees.

The best advice for leaders who wish to avoid the cloak of omnipotence and want to unlock the front door of leadership is presented in the following poem:

Power In

Power may be felt as power-over,
And if so it will be oppressive,
Oppressive to its victim-prisoner,
   and
Oppressive to its wielder-jailer;
For the jailer is not much less
   the prisoner than the prisoner.

Power-over must be held tightly
   and
Carefully with tense alert.
It must be handled, manipulated
   outside the self, now constricted,
   now relaxed a little.
Power-over therefore is not strength,
   but a binding.

Power-over ma
  or greedily;
But it is not lo

Power-in is lov
Power-in is stre
  great joy.
It is easy amus
  love.
Power-in is pot
And if I have it
  even in great
That does not p

Rather,
If I am easy wit
  help you to b
And what two c
  with easy pow
We could free the world."

Tyrannical power, or power-over, causes stress, resentment, and low morale. Power-in, on the other hand, is a relaxed and open approach to authority that results in good human relations and maximum productivity.

The "front door key" is important at every level of responsibility. An organization with two or more levels of leadership will be only as effective as its weakest leadership link. Consider an organization with three levels — first-line supervision, midlevel management, and top management. Even if leadership is effective at the first two levels, poor performance in top management will harm the success of the organization. Similarly, if top management and first-line supervisors are competent, deficiency in midmanagement practices, such as failure to communicate information upward, or failure to communicate orders downward, will reduce the effectiveness of the organization. Finally, excellence at the top and in the middle will be negated by poor leadership practices of first-line supervisors, where the actual production of goods and services takes place. Poor first-line supervision lowers the morale and productivity of the majority of workers.

The goal should be for leaders at all levels of responsibility to possess the "front door key" Can you imagine how successful an organization would be if all the people in all the leadership positions were truly leaders and not bosses?

The Difference Between a Boss and a Leader

The boss drives employees; the leader coaches them.
The boss depends on authority; the leader on good will.
The boss inspires fear; the leader generates enthusiasm.
The boss says "I"; the leader says "We."
The boss places the blame for the breakdown; the leader fixes the breakdown;
The boss knows how it is done; the leader shows how it is done.

boss uses people; the leader develops people.
boss takes credit; the leader gives credit.
he boss commands; the leader asks.
The boss says "Go"; the leader says "Let's go."[14]

Overall, a leader's use of fear and overbearance is only effective for a short period of time. After a while, dissatisfaction and resentment cause employees to rebel or escape. A true leader achieves maximum performance by using good human relations principles.

Have you ever experienced the *boss-versus-leader* syndrome? Have you ever witnessed the *power-over* phenomenon? Have you ever seen the problem of the "*cloak of omnipotence*"? If you have, you know the importance of humility, respect for others, and two-way communication. You know the importance of the "front door key."

RECOMMENDED RESOURCES

The following reading, case, and films are suggested for greater insight into the material in Part Two:

Reading — How the Boss Stays in Touch with the Troops

Case — A Different Style of Leadership

Films — Leadership: Style or Circumstance?
Theory X and Theory Y: The Work of Douglas McGregor, Part I and Part II
The Grid Approach to Conflict Solving
The Managerial Grid in Action

REFERENCE NOTES

1   Eugene E. Jennings, *An Anatomy of Leadership: Princes, Heroes, and Supermen* (New York: McGraw-Hill, Inc., 1960), 13.

2   William L. Edmonson, Island Creek Coal Company; "Leadership in the Air Force," Maxwell Air Force Base, Alabama, October 1974.

3   Adlai E. Stevenson in Will Forpe and John C. McCollister, *The Sunshine Book: Expressions of Love, Hope, and Inspiration* (Middle Village, N.Y.: Jonathan David Publishers, 1979), 19.

4   Niccolò Machiavelli, *The Prince*, Chapter 6, 1532.

5   William C. Menninger and Harry Levinson, *Human Understanding in Industry* (Chicago: Science Research Associates, 1956), 6-7.

6   Menninger and Levinson, *Human Understanding in Industry*, 6-7.

7   Joan Biaoni, based on Andrew D. Szilagyi and Marc J. Wallace, *Organizational Behavior and Performance* (Santa Monica, Calif.: Goodyear, 1977).

8   Ithiel de Sola Pool, "The Head of the Company: Conceptions of Role and Identity," *Behavioral Science* 9, no. 2 (April 1964): 147–155.

9   de Sola Pool, "The Head of the Company," 147–155.

10 Jennings, *An Anatomy of Leadership*, 13, 131–134.

11 Robert Townsend, *Up the Organization* (New York: Alfred A. Knopf Inc., 1970).

12 Douglas McGregor in Sargent, *What Every Executive Should Know about the Art of Leadership* (Chicago: Dartnell Corp., 1964), 13.

13 Stanley M. Herman and Michael Korenich, *Authentic Management: A Gestalt Orientation to Organizations and Their Development* (Reading, Mass.: Addison-Wesley Publishing Co., Inc., 1977), 114.

14 Dave Davis, "Management Style and Effect," ATE Management and Service Company, 1983.

STUDY QUIZ

As a test of your understanding and the extent to which you have achieved the objectives in Part Two, complete the following questions. See Appendix D for the answer key.

1. The nature of the situation can have significant influence on the leadership process.

   a. true
   b. false

2. Some people are more trusting and therefore more easily led than others.

   a. true
   b. false

3. When an activity is perceived as _____, conditions are ripe for the exercise of leadership.

   a. excusable
   b. intolerable
   c. appropriate
   d. ideal

4. Both responsibility and _____ come with the leadership position.

   a. confusion
   b. dependence
   c. wealth
   d. power

5. Tyrannical power, or power-over, causes:

   a. stress, resentment, and low morale
   b. rebellion, resentment, and high productivity
   c. relaxation, concern, and high morale
   d. stress, resentment, and high morale

6. Select the answer that best describes the quality of the leader, characteristic of the follower, and nature of the situation most conducive to leadership taking place.

   a. selfishness, mistrust, emergency
   b. intelligence, experience, despair
   c. humanism, anger, routine
   d. self-confidence, obedience, confusion

7. The ingredient that constitutes the "front door key" is:
   a. meeting the responsibility of office without abusing its power
   b. giving orders on time
   c. job knowledge and experience
   d. persuading others to take action

8. Key factors in the "combination-lock" include:
   a. time, space, energy
   b. qualities of leaders, characteristics of followers, nature of situation
   c. ability, experience, training

9. All of the following are important qualities of leadership except:
   a. ability
   b. stability
   c. persistence
   d. charisma
   e. seniority

10. The three styles of leadership are:
    a. high, low, middle
    b. directive, participative, free rein
    c. traditional, modern, new wave

DISCUSSION QUESTIONS AND ACTIVITIES

The following questions and activities help personalize the subject. They are appropriate for classroom exercises and homework assignments.

1. Do you possess the qualities of leadership—vision, ability, enthusiasm, and so forth? Discuss.

   _____

   _____

   _____

2. How susceptible to leadership are you? Are you basically a trusting person or a suspicious person when it comes to following others?

   _____

   _____

   _____

3. In what type of situation would you prefer to lead—crisis or routine? Would you be a better field commander or a better administrative officer?

   _____

   _____

   _____

4. Divide into groups to discuss the use and abuse of power. Is it true that power corrupts and absolute power corrupts absolutely? Cite examples of leaders who became better people because of the responsibility of leadership.

5. Debate the theory that Americans by nature do not like to be led, that it goes against the spirit of rugged individualism.

PART THREE

The Vault Key and the Multiplication Key

Learning Objectives

After completing Part Three, you will better understand:

1. the principles of effective supervision;
2. the rules for effective delegation.

THE VAULT KEY — LEADERSHIP
BY COMPETENCE

Certain principles of leadership have maximum positive influence on followers. In the field of sports, consider Alonzo Stagg, Knute Rockne, Eddie Robinson, and Paul "Bear" Bryant. Although their styles were different, each followed universal principles of leadership that brought out the best in the pride and performance of their subordinates. These principles constitute the "vault key" of leadership — leadership by competence. They apply at all levels of leadership and in all fields of work.

For an evaluation of your competence as a leader (or an evaluation of your leader's competence), complete the following Leadership Report Card and read the discussion that follows each question. Note that this

ILLUS. 3.1

You must practice the principles of effective leadership, not just know what they are.

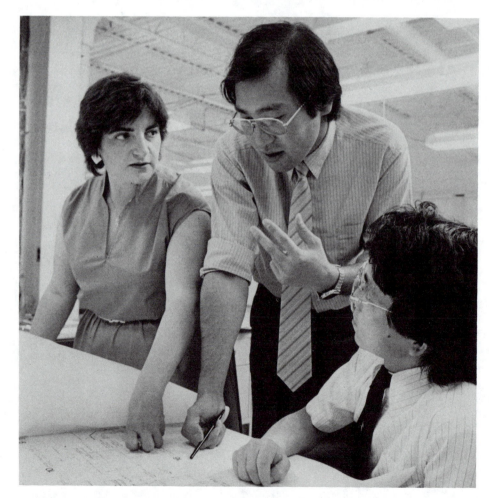

questionnaire is an assessment of leadership actions, as opposed to personality traits. Followers are unable to read the minds of their leaders and can only go by what they see them do; therefore, it is important to consider how well you are *practicing* the principles of effective leadership.

LEADERSHIP REPORT CARD

Directions

Circle the appropriate number for each question and read the accompanying rationale. If you are evaluating your leader, substitute *he* or *she* for *I*, and *his* or *her* for *my*.

A. I have a clear understanding of my responsibilities in order of priority.

1. I haven't the foggiest
2. Things are vague
3. There is some confusion
4. Generally speaking, yes
5. Exactly

Rationale:

- If the leader is confused about personal goals and duties, how can the leader guide the behavior of subordinates? The leader won't know in which direction to lead them.

B. All of my people know what their job duties are in order of priority.

1. None do
2. Many do not
3. Usually
4. Almost all do
5. All do

Rationale:

- Job expectations must be understood and agreed on by every subordinate for maximum job satisfaction and productivity.

- Not knowing what is expected of you is a major cause of stress at work.

C. The jobs my people have are satisfying to them.

1. Not really
2. Some are
3. So so
4. More than most
5. Definitely yes

Rationale:

- A person's work is an important part of personal identity in Western society.

- Work must be personally satisfying if high morale and productivity are to be achieved.

D. My people know whether they are doing a good job or need to improve.

1. No, it's best they don't
2. Some do
3. I try to get to most of them
4. Practically all do
5. Yes, it's rare they don't

Rationale:

- Not knowing how you are doing causes worry and anxiety and dissipates energy.

E. I recognize and reward good performance.

1. The paycheck is enough
2. Sometimes
3. More often than not
4. Almost always
5. Always

Rationale:

- Appreciation for a job well done reinforces good work.

- Ignoring a job well done reduces commitment. The employee begins to think: "If they don't care, why should I?" People need psychic, social, and economic reinforcement at work.

- The best leaders look for the opportunity to recognize employees. When they see them doing something right, they express appreciation immediately.

F. I have criticized an employee in the presence of others.

1. I believe in making an example
2. Occasionally
3. Almost never
4. Once
5. Never, not once

Rationale:

- Public criticism embarrasses, alienates, and ultimately outrages not only the employee being chastised, but all who are present.

- As Ralph Waldo Emerson said, "Criticism should not be querulous and wasting, all knife and root-puller; but guiding, instructive, and inspiring; a south wind, not an east wind."[1]

G. I care about the personal well-being of my people, and they know it.

    1. Honestly, no
    2. Some of them, yes
    3. Usually
    4. Almost all of them, yes
    5. Totally

Rationale:

- People resent being treated as unimportant; they want others to care about them and show respect for them.

- If the leader does not show concern for subordinates, they will either worry unnecessarily, or reduce allegiance to the leader. In either case, energy, time, and commitment are diverted from the work at hand.

H. I have policies and procedures for employee development and cross-training.

    1. There is no need for this
    2. I plan to someday
    3. On occasion, for some employees
    4. Yes, generally speaking
    5. It is a major commitment I have

Rationale:

- Employee training does six important things: builds skills, raises morale, cuts avoidable turnover and absenteeism, raises loyalty, reduces mistakes, and increases productivity.

I. I have given assignments to people without first considering the availability of their time and the competence they possess.

    1. Often
    2. Occasionally
    3. Rarely
    4. I almost never do this
    5. Never

Rationale:

- Assigning work that is over a subordinate's level of skill creates undue stress and is likely to result in a costly error.

- Assigning more work to a subordinate than is possible to accomplish in the time available creates frustration, low morale, resentment, and lower performance in the long run.

J. I have been accused of favoritism regarding some of my employees.

1. Often
2. More than most
3. At times
4. Rarely
5. Never

Rationale:

- The values of equality and fair treatment are widely shared in Western society; favoritism runs directly counter to these values.

K. I take personal responsibility for the orders I give and never quote a superior to gain compliance.

1. Never
2. Rarely
3. Usually
4. Almost always
5. Always

Rationale:

- Leaders who violate this principle lose the respect of their subordinates, upper management, and ultimately themselves as they become merely "paper leaders."

L. I do not promise what cannot be delivered, and I deliver on all promises made.

1. I have dropped the ball often
2. I have failed occasionally
3. Usually
4. Almost without exception
5. Always

Rationale:

- Broken promises lower employee confidence and respect for the leader.

- Disappointments deflate employee morale and performance, especially when they come from the leader.

M. My people understand the reasoning behind policies and procedures.

1. Rarely
2. Occasionally
3. Sometimes
4. Usually
5. Always

Rationale:

- Not knowing the purpose of a policy or procedure often results in mistakes.

- The following story shows the importance of understanding *why:*

    > The members of a crew on a submarine were about to take battle stations, and the ship's Captain was worried about a young seaman whose job it was to close the watertight doors between certain compartments. The young man didn't seem to realize the purpose of his job, so the Captain undertook to impress him. He told him that if he failed his job, the ship would be lost. Not only that, some of the men aboard were specialists and it cost thousands to train each of them; they might be drowned. The Captain stated: "So you see how important it is that you do your job . . . this is a very expensive ship, and these men are very valuable." The young crewman replied: "Yes sir, and then there's me too." The Captain stopped worrying.[2]

- Uncertainty about policies can lead to paralysis.

N. The rules we live by are discussed to see if revisions are needed.

1. Rarely
2. Sometimes
3. Usually
4. Almost always
5. Always

Rationale:

- People are more likely to follow a rule they help set.

- People need to know the appropriate limits of behavior and guidelines for conduct.

- Rules should be periodically reviewed for appropriateness; some rules may no longer be necessary or desirable.

O. I encourage my people to express disagreement with my views if I'm dealing in a controversial area.

1. Never
2. Rarely
3. Sometimes
4. Fairly often
5. Always

Rationale:

- People have the need to express themselves on emotional issues without fear of reprisal.

- Good ideas can come from constructive disagreement.

- Remember Harry Truman's advice: "I want people around me who will tell me the truth as they see it. You cannot operate if you have people around you who put you on a pedestal and tell you everything you do is right. Because that can't be possible."

P. My people know and feel free to use the right of appeal, formal and informal.

1. There is no procedure for appeal
2. There is a procedure, but it is not widely known
3. Some do
4. Most do
5. All do

Rationale:

- Not all decisions are good ones, and some should be reversed.

- Every rule must have an exception, and a review or appeal process can facilitate this.

- An appeal process is a defense against arbitrary and capricious treatment, and it meets the need for fair play.

Q. The last time I listened closely to a suggestion from my people was:

1. I can't remember
2. Two months ago
3. A month ago
4. Last week
5. Within the last two days

Rationale:

- Not listening shows disrespect, and people "turn off" when they do not feel respected.

- Important information and ideas may be lost unless two-way communication prevails.

- Ben Jonson's words make the point well: "Very few men are wise by their own counsel; or learned by their own teaching. For he that was only taught by himself, had a fool to be his [teacher]."[3]

R. I encourage my people to participate in decisions affecting them unless compelling reasons prevent it.

1. Rarely
2. Sometimes
3. Usually
4. Almost always
5. Always

Rationale:

- Democracy is a political value taught in our society. It should come as no surprise when employees want to be involved in decisions that affect them.

- Participation leads to understanding; understanding leads to commitment; and commitment leads to loyalty.

S. I have mastered both the job knowledge and technical skills of my work.

1. I am totally out of my element
2. I need much improvement
3. I am okay
4. I am very good
5. Excellent

Rationale:

- Job knowledge helps the leader gain the respect and loyalty of subordinates.

- Job expertise helps solve critical problems.

T. I have lost control of my emotions or faculties in the presence of my people.

1. Often
2. Occasionally
3. Rarely
4. Almost never
5. Never

Rationale:

- Emotional stability in the leader can be an anchor of strength for subordinates.

- Past a certain point, as emotionality increases, objectivity and the ability to make good judgments decrease.

U. I set a good example for my people in the use of my time at work.

1. If they did what I do, we'd be in trouble
2. I waste pretty much time
3. Sometimes yes, sometimes no
4. Usually
5. I wish they would use me as a model

Rationale:

- Because people are influenced primarily by the example the leader sets, leaders must follow effective time management practices.

- Effective time management results in efficiency and smooth operations in the work setting.

Source: Steve McMillen and Steve Martin, Northern Kentucky University, 1984.

SCORING

Add up the numbers you circled for all 21 questions and place your total score here: _____.

INTERPRETATION

Scores 95–105

You should go to the head of the class. Your leadership practices can serve as a model for others. Your behavior concerning employee communication, rewards, decision making, assignment of work, and the example you set are ideal.

Scores 84–94

You are on solid footing as a leader. You understand and employ the basic principles of effective supervision, regardless of the level and field of leadership. As such, your subordinates should be happy under your direction, and the quality of their work can be expected to be high.

Scores 63–83

You are doing some things right, and you are making mistakes in other areas. You are neither all good, nor all bad in your leadership practices. Go back to the test and see where your strengths are and capitalize on these. Also, work diligently to raise your low scores. For example: Do you have two-way communication with your subordinates? Are you following the principles of effective motivation? Are you setting a good example by your own work habits and the use of your time?

Scores 62 and Lower

Either because of lack of training, lack of application, or lack of aptitude, you are not practicing the principles of good leadership. To diagnose the problem, answer these three questions: (1) Have you been "reading the wrong book" or "following the wrong models" of leadership? (2) Do you know the right answers but have been inattentive to practicing them? (3) Are you cut out for leadership, or do you feel more comfortable working alone—being responsible for your own work, as opposed to assigning, coordinating, teaching, and facilitating the work of others?

Whatever the cause of your low scores, for the benefit of your subordinates and the quality of work of your group, you should address the problem and solve it. The best way to do this is to read the rationale for the correct answers and then make every effort to exhibit the correct behavior on the job.

There is a concept: work — play — hell. The theory is that any person's morale can be diagnosed according to the percentage of time spent on the job in each of these states. Imagine your own job. What percentage of your time is spent in work (drudgery)? What percentage is spent in play (enjoyable, uplifting activities — jobs can be enjoyable)? What percentage in hell (pain — boredom, conflict, anxiety)? See Figure 3.1.

If more than 20 % of your job life is hell, this is a problem (more than a day a week is spent in pain), and this will show up — in your attitude, performance, relationships, even your health. If less than 20 % of your time is fun, this is a problem (there is not enough joy in your job), and this will show up as your interest goes down and ultimately your performance goes down. In a true sense, the task of leadership is to maximize the play quotient and minimize the hell quotient for all employees.[4] The Leadership Report Card can be used as a tool toward that end. If you are in a leadership position, take your scores seriously and make every effort to work toward the 95–105 level of leadership competence.

FIGURE 3.1

Job Satisfaction

	%
Work	_____
Play	_____
Hell	_____
Total	100%

THE MULTIPLICATION KEY—
EFFECTIVE DELEGATION

Does the following scenario sound familiar? The leader starts a job, gives it to an employee for the difficult and boring parts, takes it back to add the finishing touches, presents the completed project to upper management, takes the credit. The employee loses interest, feels used, becomes frustrated, quits.

There are many reasons leaders fail to delegate. Some do not know how. Others do not think their subordinates will do the job as well as they, themselves, will. Others do not trust their subordinates to follow through. Still others fail to delegate because they fear their subordinates will show them up by doing a better job.

Regardless of the reason, failure to delegate should be corrected: (1) delegation gives the leader time to carry out important responsibilities in the areas of planning, coordination, problem solving, and employee development; (2) delegation gives subordinates a sense of accomplishment and job satisfaction and helps prepare them for more difficult tasks and additional responsibility. Employees who are bored and underused come alive when whole and important jobs are delegated to them.

Delegation is the key to multiplying the effectiveness of the leader and the work group. You can test your delegation strengths and weaknesses by completing the following questionnaire.

ILLUS. 3.2

Ability and willingness to delegate is a mark of good leadership.

DELEGATION DIAGNOSIS

Directions

Answer Yes or No for each of the following questions. Do not debate too long over any one question. Go with your first reaction.

	Yes	No
1. Do you spend more time than you should doing work your subordinates could do?	___	___
2. Do you often find yourself working while your subordinates are idle?	___	___
3. Do you feel you should be able to personally answer any question about any project in your area?	___	___
4. Is your "in box" usually full?	___	___
5. Do your subordinates take initiative to solve problems without your direction?	___	___
6. Does your operation function smoothly when you are absent?	___	___
7. Do you spend more time working on details than you do planning and supervising?	___	___
8. Do your subordinates feel they have sufficient authority over personnel, finances, facilities, and other resources for which they are responsible?	___	___
9. Have you bypassed your subordinates by making decisions that were part of their jobs?	___	___
10. If you were incapacitated for an extended period of time, is there someone trained who could take your place?	___	___
11. Is there usually a big pile of work requiring your action when you return from an absence?	___	___
12. Have you ever assigned a job to a subordinate primarily because it was distasteful to you?	___	___
13. Do you know the interests and goals of every person reporting to you?	___	___
14. Do you make it a habit to follow up on jobs you delegate?	___	___
15. Do you delegate complete projects as opposed to individual tasks whenever possible?	___	___
16. Are your subordinates trained to maximum potential?	___	___
17. Do you find it difficult to ask others to do things?	___	___
18. Do you trust your employees to do their best in your absence?	___	___
19. Are your subordinates performing below their capabilities?	___	___

20. Do you always give credit for a job well done? ____ ____

21. Do subordinates refer more work to you than you delegate to them? ____ ____

22. Do you support your subordinates when their authority is questioned? ____ ____

23. Do you personally do those assignments only you could or should do? ____ ____

24. Does work pile up at any one point in your operation? ____ ____

25. Do all subordinates know what is expected of them in order of priority? ____ ____

Source: *Gene Archbold and Steve McMillen, based on* Delegation Concepts *(Grandville, Mich: Time Management Center, 1977); and John McKinney,* Time Management *(New York: Penton Learning, Inc., 1977).*

SCORING

Give yourself one point for each Yes answer for numbers 5, 6, 8, 10, 13, 14, 15, 16, 18, 20, 22, 23, and 25; and give one point for each No answer for items 1, 2, 3, 4, 7, 9, 11, 12, 17, 19, 21, and 24. Place your total score here: _____.

INTERPRETATION

Scores 20–25

You follow excellent delegation practices that help the efficiency and morale of your work group. These skills maximize your effectiveness as a leader and help develop the full potential of your subordinates.

Scores 15–19

Your score is okay, but nothing special if you are striving for excellence in leadership skills. To clear up the deficiency, review the questions you missed and take appropriate steps so that you will not repeat these delegation mistakes.

Scores 14 and Below

Delegation weakness is reducing your effectiveness as a leader. The overall performance of your work group is lower than it should be because you are either unable or unwilling to relinquish power to others. In addition, delegation mistakes may cause dissatisfaction among subordinates. At the least, they will not develop job interest and important skills unless you improve in this area. Remember Andrew Carnegie's admonition: "It marks a big step in a supervisor's development when he comes to realize that other people can be called on to help him do a better job than he can do alone."

Rules for Effective Delegation

The following 21 rules for effective delegation constitute the "multiplication key" for successful leadership.[5] Effective leaders are those who incorporate these rules into their day-to-day work life.

- *Don't delegate the bad jobs, saving the good ones for yourself.* Don't be like the supervisor who always calls on his assistant for the dirty work, late night work, and disciplining, reserving for himself all the easy assignments and the ones that bring reward.

- *Share power with subordinates.* Fight the natural fear, common to all leaders, of losing control. Remember, to hoard your power is to lose it. Only by delegating authority to others will you accomplish more and greater work.

- *Know your subordinates.* Effective delegation requires knowing the aptitudes and interests of all your subordinates. If all else is equal, assign social tasks to employees who enjoy dealing with people, fact finding and report preparation to those who enjoy investigation and writing, hands-on work to employees who like personal involvement, and include idea-oriented employees in brainstorming or in formulating policies.

- *If you delegate work that is not within a subordinate's normal job, be sure to explain why.* If the purpose of an assignment is training, or if an assignment is an emergency, be sure the employee understands the special nature of the task.

- *Delegate work evenly among all subordinates.* Don't overwork some employees while underworking others. This lowers the morale and performance of both the overused and underused workers.

- *Once you have delegated a task, follow up to make sure the job is done properly, being careful not to oversupervise.* Oversupervision encourages dependency in some employees. For others, it results in unnecessary discussion and wasted time. For others, it leads to resentment and conflict.

- *Delegate only if you have confidence that the subordinate is capable of handling the assignment.* Assigning work that is beyond a subordinate's ability causes fear of failure and costly mistakes. Delegate power only when you are sure it will not be abused.

  One way to learn if a subordinate is capable of handling an assignment is to ask. Remember, though, that people tend to overestimate the odds of succeeding at easy tasks (they may say they can do the job in less time than they actually need) and underestimate the ability to succeed at difficult tasks (for fear of failure, they may avoid jobs they are actually capable of performing).

- *Define responsibilities for each subordinate and make this information known to others.* Employees should know job duties in order of priority at all times. Also, employees who work together should know what each other's responsibilities are.

- *Delegate in such a way that a subordinate receives instruction from only one person and is held accountable to only one person.* If this is impossible, be sure each supervisor has the same understanding of what the subordinate is supposed to do, how the work is to be done, and when it is to be completed.

- *When you delegate authority, be sure to back your subordinate if that authority is questioned.* When all else is equal, support your subordinate. If the subordinate has made a mistake, discuss the mistake privately and then let the subordinate personally correct the problem.

- *Let employees know what decisions they have authority to make and delegate decision making to the lowest possible level.* This improves service and efficiency by avoiding referrals through many departments and levels of an organization in order to solve a problem or receive an answer.

- *Delegate with consistency.* Don't go on delegation campaigns, overwhelming subordinates sometimes and underusing them at other times.

- *Delegate whole tasks so that subordinates can see projects through to completion; allow sufficient time to get jobs done.* Avoid the "Zeigarnick Effect," in which employee morale, commitment, and performance deteriorate because the employee is not able to finish a task. Work that has not been started may or may not be a motivator, but unfinished tasks almost always demotivate.[6]

- *Insist on clear communication when delegating work.* The supervisor must be sure the subordinate knows exactly what is expected, in what form, and when it is to be completed. Obtain agreement to provide regular feedback on progress and problems. Follow-up will ensure the success of delegated tasks.

- *Reinforce good performance.* When a subordinate accomplishes an assignment, be sure to recognize, and thus reinforce, good performance.

- *Make good use of questions when delegating work.* Encourage employees to ask questions to clarify assignments. Also, ask subordinates what you can do to help them succeed.

- *When you assign tasks, be sure they can be accomplished.* Impossible tasks demotivate employees. A critical factor in job success is sufficient resources. Are the necessary equipment, manpower, materials, and money available to do the job? If not, making the assignment wastes valuable time and resources that could be used more productively elsewhere.

- *Explain the importance of assignments.* Show employees how assigned tasks can satisfy important individual needs, as well as meet the goals of the organization.

- *Learn to live with work that is not done the way you would do it.* Establish high standards of performance and do not tolerate low-quality work; however, balance this with the fact that no two people are exactly alike, and your subordinate's approach to a task may not be the same as your own.

- *Avoid delegating tasks that are pets, personal, and petty.* Some tasks should not be delegated: (1) Pets: if an assignment is unique to your own interest or skill, you should do it. Perhaps no one else will be able to do it as well. (2) Personal: if a task is private or personal, do it yourself; otherwise, it puts an unfair burden on your subordinate. (3) Petty: if a task is petty, never delegate it. To do so lowers your self-respect and the respect of your subordinates.

- *Follow the three D's for all work — do it, delegate it, or ditch it.* Do assignments yourself; delegate work to competent subordinates as soon as possible; ditch unimportant tasks. In any case, don't let assignments pile up, as they will ultimately reduce the efficiency of your work group.

Applying the 21 rules for effective delegation results in optimum employee development, the best leader/follower relations, and maximum job performance.

RECOMMENDED RESOURCES

The following reading, case, and films are suggested for greater insight into the material in Part Three.

Reading — The Manager's Job: Folklore and Fact

Case — Mr. Black, Ms. Blue, Mr. White

Films — The One-Minute Manager
Delegating

REFERENCE NOTES

1 Ralph Waldo Emerson, *Journals*, in Burton Stevenson, ed., *Home Book of Quotations* (New York: Dodd, Mead & Company, 1967), 338.

2 Marvin G. Gregory, ed., *Bits and Pieces* (Fairfield, N.J.: The Economics Press, 1980), 16–17.

3 Ben Jonson, *Explorata: Consilia*, in Stevenson, *Home Book of Quotations*, p.1969.

4 David Berlo, *The Management of Free People* (in press).

5 Gene Archbold and Steve McMillen, Northern Kentucky University, based on *Delegation Concepts* (Grandville, Mich.: Time Management Center, 1977); and John McKinney, *Time Management* (New York: Penton Learning, Inc., 1977).

6 Norman R.F. Maier, *Psychology in Industrial Organizations*, 4th ed. (Boston: Houghton Mifflin Company, 1973), 437–438.

STUDY QUIZ

As a test of your understanding and the extent to which you have achieved the objectives in Part Three, complete the following questions. See Appendix D for the answer key.

1. What two purposes does effective delegation serve?

   a. gives the leader a chance to see how well subordinates work; gives subordinates a chance to compete with other employees
   b. helps the leader cut down on routine work; helps the subordinate learn self-control
   c. provides more time for the leader to handle important matters; provides less time for employees to waste the company money
   d. gives the leader time to carry out other responsibilities; gives the subordinate a sense of accomplishment and job satisfaction

2. Be certain all subordinates know what decisions that have authority to make, and have decisions made at the _____ possible organizational level.

   a. highest
   b. lowest

3. Delegate ____ tasks so that a subordinate can see a project or assignment through to completion; allow time to get the task done.

   a. whole
   b. partial

4. Which rules apply to effective delegation: *(a)* know your subordinate well; *(b)* use the interrogatory approach when delegating work; *(c)* avoid delegating tasks that are pets, personal, or petty; *(d)* delegate with consistency?

   a. *a, b, c*
   b. *b, c, d*
   c. *a* and *d*
   d. none of the above
   e. all of the above

5. In delegating work, which set of the three D's should you follow?

   a. Delegate it, delegate it, or ditch it
   b. Do it, delegate it, or ditch it
   c. Distribute it, do it, or destroy it
   d. Diminish it, delegate it, or drown it

6. If more than ____% of your job is painful (hell), there is a morale problem.

   a. 5
   b. 10
   c. 15
   d. 20

7. If less than ____% of your job life is enjoyable (fun), there is a morale problem.

   a. 10
   b. 20
   c. 40
   d. 80

8. Delegate work _____ among all employees.

   a. immediately
   b. evenly

9. Avoid delegating tasks that are:

   a. pets, personal, petty
   b. job-related, repetitive, pivotal

10. A person's work is an important part of _____ in Western society.

    a. special concern
    b. personal identity
    c. financial difficulty

11. Employee training:

    a. builds skills
    b. raises morale
    c. cuts turnover
    d. reduces mistakes
    e. increases productivity
    f. all of the above

DISCUSSION QUESTIONS AND ACTIVITIES

The following questions and activities help personalize the subject. They are suitable for classroom exercises and homework assignments.

1. Evaluate yourself. Do you use the principles of good leadership? Describe someone you know who uses the principles of good leadership.

   _____

   _____

   _____

2. Have you ever been the victim of poor leadership? Have you ever had a bad supervisor? Describe conditions under this situation.

   _____

   _____

   _____

3. If you were to improve as a leader, what weakness(es) should you address? Develop a three- to five-step plan to improve.

   _____

   _____

   _____

4. Gather in groups to discuss the role of delegation in the leadership process. Who has worked under a manager with delegation weaknesses? Who has worked under a manager with delegation strengths? Compare and contrast.

5. Debate the theory that most American big businesses and governmental agencies are too bureaucratic, and that managers fail to delegate because of insecurity and lack of training. True or false?

PART FOUR

The Master Key and the Score Key

Learning Objectives

After completing Part Four, you will better understand:

1. the importance of employee training and development;

2. the qualities leaders should possess as teachers;

3. the principles, methods, and techniques for developing others;

4. the principles of effective discipline;

5. how to apply the nine keys of leadership to any situation to achieve success.

THE MASTER KEY—
LEADERS WHO CAN, TEACH

Many leaders view training as the most relevant and rewarding of all their tasks. Effective leaders at all levels of responsibility—chief executive, middle manager, and first-line supervisor—are aware that the failure experienced by Rodger in the following story can occur in the adult world of work as well.

Why Can't Rodger Learn?

When Rodger was first observed in the classroom, he was beginning to fail and to feel defeated, but he was trying. When the observers walked in, he was listening with obvious interest to a story his teacher was reading. He sat quietly for at least 15 minutes. After the story, the teacher wrote some letters of the alphabet on the blackboard and requested that the children copy them on a sheet of paper she passed out. Rodger picked up the crayon and looked at his neighbor's paper to see what he was supposed to do; he then started to write. The teacher moved over to him, took the crayon out of his hand and said firmly and with minor irritation, "Not a crayon, Rodger; use a pencil."

Rodger glanced at the little girl on his right, in obvious embarrassment. He wanted her to like him. He turned back to the teacher and said in a small voice, "I don't have a pencil." The teacher turned to the class and announced, "Some of us are not prepared. Who has a pencil to lend Rodger?" Another child, eager to please the teacher, moved over to Rodger and handed him a pencil. Rodger was looking at the floor in embarrassment but managed to thank him. In a few moments he again tried to find out how to do the assigned task. He watched his neighbor,

ILLUS. 4.1

Training must be relevant to the needs of the workplace.

but the child turned to him and said angrily, "Stop looking. Do your own stuff."

Finding no answer to his dilemma, Rodger decided to escape by going up to sharpen his pencil. Another child was ahead of him, so Rodger waited patiently for his turn. His smallness in comparison to the other children was very evident. Two other children came to sharpen their pencils and pushed Rodger aside. He allowed the intrusion, because what can be done when others are so much bigger and aggressive? Another child came up and also attempted to push Rodger aside. Anger flooded over his face. He had to show them that he had importance too. He attempted to push the intruder away saying, "It's my turn." The teacher noticed Rodger pushing and said angrily, "Rodger, take your seat, immediately." The teacher then glanced over at the observers, grimaced with distaste, and shook her head. She was sure that they shared insight into Rodger's problems.

Rodger walked dejectedly back to his seat. After a few moments of depressed staring at his paper, he leaned toward the girl on his left and whispered desperately, "How do you do it?" The girl frowned and said, "Shh-h," and hit him on the head with her pencil.

The teacher noticed difficulty again and assuming that Rodger was responsible (after all, he is such a problem), said in exasperation, "Rodger, will you please pay attention to your paper!"

Rodger glanced around the room to see if everyone else was looking at him. He stared down at his shoe, his face red. He could have been saying, "What's wrong with me? Why can't I do anything right? Why does everyone hate me?" He still wanted to try; he had not reached the place where complete failure and hostility had taken over. Therefore, he attempted to do something about the hated paper before him. He made some marks; then, as though talking to himself, he said, "Is this good?" He glanced over at the paper of the boy on his right. As if in answer to his own question, he said, "Oh, ugh. Look at his." He wanted to think somebody was doing worse than he was. The boy stuck out his tongue at him, and Rodger turned listlessly back to his paper.

The teacher was coming up the aisle again and paused at Rodger's seat. "Rodger, we are not writing our names, we are just practicing M's." She hurried over to the blackboard without showing him what to do and started moving through the next lesson. Several more letters were presented. Rodger became restless. He didn't understand. He wiggled in his seat and then stood up. The children began to practice the letters again. Rodger became very frustrated as he found he was unable to form them. He let his paper fall to the floor.

"Pass your papers to the end of the table," the teacher said. "Rodger, get your paper," said the little girl next to him, "Rodger, I'm telling. We have to pass them down." The angry voice of the teacher was once again heard. "Rodger, get your paper off the floor." Rodger complied, but he hit the paper with his pencil. He didn't like it. It was no good. He felt badly. He didn't want anyone else to see it.

The teacher gave all the children another piece of paper to continue the letter-making practice. Rodger somehow found new determination and tried again. He followed the teacher's movements in the air, whispering to himself in concentration. The angry little girl leaned over to him and said, "Shh-h," and hit him on the head with her pencil again. Rodger wanted her to like him, so he did nothing. But his frustration had to be expressed. He zoomed his pencil in the air, making a quiet airplane noise. He forgot the task. The teacher scolded him again and wearily exhorted him to pay attention.

The observation lasted only one hour. What happens over time to such a person, who experiences hour after hour of failure? Two months after the initial observation, Rodger refused to try any learning task. He often crawled on the floor like an animal, making odd noises. He could not sit still for more than five minutes, and he hit his peers and yelled at them. His teacher became frantic. His mother was so worried that she came to school often and peered through the window of the schoolroom door. "He cries every day about school. He says everyone hates him," she explained.

Failure and a particular kind of punishment had distorted Rodger. In many schools where administrators and teachers are unaware of the seriousness of allowing a child to fail or of using aversive techniques to change behavior, they still ask about such a child, "Why did it happen?" "Probably the parents," the accusing answer echoes down the school halls.[1]

Effective leaders know that Rodger's failure wasn't necessary, that preventing such failure is important, and that their own ability to teach is often the key. These leaders continually ask: "How can I develop my people most effectively? What is the best approach? When should I listen; when should I be autocratic? When should I demand; when should I ask? If I become too friendly with my subordinates, will I lose their respect? How should I use my power to reward and punish? How can I facilitate both the work and the growth of my subordinates?" Answers to these questions constitute the "master key—leaders who can, teach."

Are leaders who are interested in employee development on the wrong track? Are they overly concerned with a relatively unimportant subject? Are they too employee centered to the detriment of organizational goals? Take the following test to see for yourself the importance of developing others. You will find that training helps both employee morale and job performance.

NUMBERS NEVER LIE

Directions

Your task is to circle the numbers in Figure 4.1, beginning with 1, and proceeding sequentially through 2, 3, 4, and so forth, to 60. Do not skip any numbers. You are to circle as many as possible within a 60-second time limit.

FIGURE 4.1

Numbers Work Sheet

DISCUSSION

Now that you have completed the task, how did you do? How do you feel? Perhaps you did not do as well as you would have liked, and probably you feel frustrated. At this point, you are asked to repeat the task, but this time you will be given the benefit of training.

NUMBERS NEVER LIE (continued)

Further Directions

Step 1. Draw a straight line between the dots at the top and bottom of Figure 4.2.

Step 2. Draw a straight line from the dot at the left side of the figure to the dot on the right side of the figure.

Step 3. You now have four quadrants. Notice that all of the odd numbers are on the left side of the vertical line; the even numbers are on the right side. Notice also that the first five numbers are in the top half of the figure, the next five numbers are in the bottom half of the figure, and so on for every sequence of five numbers up to 60.

Step 4. Your task is to circle the numbers in Figure 4.2, beginning with 1, and proceeding sequentially through 2, 3, 4, and so forth, to 60. Do not skip any numbers. You are to circle as many as possible within a 60-second time limit.

FURTHER DISCUSSION

How did you do this time? How do you feel? Typically, people will do at least 25 percent better — and even as much as 100 percent better. Usually, they feel much less frustrated. Both performance and attitude improve because training has been provided.

Number counting is a simple and insignificant task, but think of the many complex and important jobs performed in the work setting — everything from repairing cars to repairing bodies — and consider the potential for improving the quality of work and quality of work life through proper training. Imagine the benefit we would gain with even a 25-percent improvement in job performance and employee satisfaction.

Enlightened leaders recognize the importance of employee development. Like the productive farmer who plants good seeds and cares for them properly, effective supervisors view employee development as an essential key to success.

Presented in Figure 4.3 is a checklist for orienting new employees, one of the first and most important training functions of the supervisor.

FIGURE 4.2

Numbers Work Sheet

First impressions are lasting. The orientation checklist helps the new employee to get off to a good start. It also gives the employee a positive impression of the company as a good place to work.

The Leader as Teacher

Because developing others is so important, it is no wonder that teaching is called the highest calling, and that so many leaders find training others to be so satisfying. Read carefully the following profile of one of the most influential teachers in history. Remember that Socrates taught Plato, who taught Aristotle, who taught Alexander; and collectively these ancient Greeks taught Western civilization. The ideas and conduct of nearly 1

FIGURE 4.3

Checklist for New Employee
Orientation

This outline should be followed for welcoming and training new employees. The orientation period is important for winning the worker's loyalty, stimulating interest, and helping the employee to be productive. For each new employee, check each item and enter the date as it is completed.

Date Completed

1. Get ready to receive the new employee

   ☐ Review work experience and education. _____

   ☐ Have an up-to-date job description or list of duties and responsibilities available for discussion. _____

   ☐ Have workplace, equipment, and supplies ready. _____

2. Welcome the new employee

   ☐ Explain your relationship to the new employee. _____

   ☐ Assign workplace and equipment. _____

3. Show interest in the employee

   ☐ Discuss the employee's background and interests. _____

   ☐ Inquire about transportation to and from work. _____

   ☐ Inquire about any possible financial difficulties because of pay procedures and suggest local sources of assistance. _____

4. Explain the organization and the work group

   ☐ Describe the mission, goals, activities, and traditions of the organization. _____

   ☐ Review the organization chart. _____

   ☐ Indicate the employee's position in the organization. _____

   ☐ Explain the function of the work group. _____

   ☐ Explain relationship of the employee to others in the work group. _____

FIGURE 4.3—*continued*

5. Introduce employee to co-workers

    ☐ Tell the work group the new employee's duties. _____

    ☐ Explain duties of each co-worker. _____

    ☐ Arrange for a co-worker to take the employee to lunch. _____

6. Show the layout of the work setting and available facilities

    ☐ Explain layout of work area. _____

    ☐ Show elevators, washroom, water fountain, fire exits, and other facilities. _____

7. Explain rules and regulations

    ☐ Hours of work. _____

    ☐ Punctuality and attendance. _____

    ☐ Lunch period. _____

    ☐ Rest periods. _____

    ☐ Use of telephone. _____

    ☐ Personal leave. _____

    ☐ Other rules, practices and procedures (smoking, fire regulations, etc.) _____

8. Instruct employee in job assignment

    ☐ Give step-by-step instruction. _____

    ☐ Explain quality and quantity work standards. _____

    ☐ Assign workplace, tools, and supplies. _____

    ☐ Indicate availability for future assistance. _____

    ☐ Provide learning aids—samples of work, manuals, job aids, procedures, lists of special technical terms, etc. _____

    ☐ Emphasize safe work habits. _____

    ☐ Stress security and safety aspects of job. _____

9. Follow-up

    ☐ Check frequently on progress. _____

    ☐ Encourage questions. _____

    ☐ Make corrections and give encouragement. _____

Source: John E. Osmanski, The New Era Company, Cincinnati, Ohio, 1987. Reprinted with permission.

billion people have been influenced significantly by these great teachers. Leaders who believe in developing others will relate to the story of Socrates.

The Highest Calling

Socrates wrote nothing that was published. Yet we know him as one of the greatest teachers in history, perhaps the greatest of the great men produced by Athens. His name commands admiration, honor, and reverence. It was the aim of Socrates to turn men's minds in the same direction, so that they might have knowledge of goodness. With that knowledge he was sure that men would have no other aim. For his virtue, the Athenians killed him (he took the fatal hemlock) and crowned his life with immortality.

. . . Men and women were his objective; to them he had a mission. He wandered through the streets and down to the market place, or often he would go to the public gymnasium. Then he started business — the business of teaching. He would talk to all people. High and low, great personages and folk of no importance would listen to him and answer, or pretend to answer, the teasing questions by which he made his points. It was his pretense to be the most ignorant man in any discussion. He would use simple illustrations and ask simpler questions — the famous Socratic irony — to draw his hearers to the examination of good. Goodness was his objective. Without goodness a man was nothing. Socrates believed that all men would seek goodness if they had true knowledge of it; that all virtue was the knowledge of goodness; all sin the ignorance of goodness.

. . . Some listened to Socrates for their own ends, to learn his skill in dialectic and his powers of argument and refutation; others to learn from him how to make their lives better. They were a diverse company: Critias, one of the thirty tyrants; Alcibiades the brilliant; vicious Crito; Xenophon; the younger Pericles; Cebes the Theban; Euripedes the playwright; and Plato, the great philosopher; these were some who sat at his feet. The attendance of his "disciples" was casual and voluntary. Socrates founded no formal school of learning. He merely questioned and reasoned and taught, and tried to lead men toward the light. He said, "If I could get to the highest place in Athens, I would lift my voice and say: 'What mean ye, fellow citizens that ye turn every stone to scrape wealth together, and ye take so little care of your children, to whom ye must one day relinquish all?'"

. . . The life of Socrates was a living example of his ideals. His philosophy, as set forth by Plato, marks an epic in human thought. "He brought philosophy down from heaven to earth," wrote Cicero. For Socrates was the founder of moral philosophy. He was not concerned with abstract metaphysics, but with mankind and its conduct. He was scoffed at for taking his examples from common life, but he did so to lead plain men to goodness, truth, and beauty.

. . . When Socrates died, Plato wrote: "This was the end of our friend, a man, as we may say, the best of all his time that we have known, and moreover the most wise and just." It was an epithet as true as it was noble.[2]

Just as there is no single best way to lead, there is no one best way to teach. Each leader brings unique personal experiences and talent to the task of developing others. The following list describes five types of teacher/leaders. Not all types are appropriate for all subordinates in all circumstances.

Types of Teacher/Leaders

Shamans. These teacher/leaders heal through the use of personal power. They focus the attention of their followers on themselves. When this approach is combined with unusual gifts and skills, shamans are charismatic. They have power, energy, and commitment that they use to energize their subordinates.

Priests. These teacher/leaders claim power through office. They are agents of omnipotent authority, and the people who follow them are taught to see themselves as set apart from others. Priests establish structure, order, and continuity — a past program and a plan for the immediate and distant future. The priest operates in a hierarchy with roles and duties in a hierarchical ladder.

Elected leaders. These teacher/leaders undergo trials, self-transformation, training, or some other form of rite to achieve their positions. Elected leaders derive power, not only from their own experience, but also from the mandate of their subordinates. Consent of followers constitutes much of the power of these teacher/leaders.

Missionaries. The missionary teacher/leader is goal directed. Usually the mission involves a utopian view of the future and a program for achieving reforms. The missionary teaches out of personal conviction, believing in certain ideals and seeing it as a duty to pass these ideals to others.

Mystic healers. These teacher/leaders seek the source of illness and health in the follower's personality. Mystic healers try to discover the statue in the marble and seek, like Michelangelo, to find what can be created from the raw material. To be successful, this type of teacher/leader requires unselfish motivation and considerable sensitivity, as well as flexibility to vary treatment according to the nature and needs of subordinates.[3]

As you read about these types of teacher/leaders, can you recognize which type you tend to be? Do you embody more than one type in your approach to leadership?

Much of contemporary leading and teaching incorporates the priestly, elected, and missionary types. The priest teacher brings continuity and hierarchy to the task, as power is delegated by the most powerful and people at each level, division, or unit are differentiated from others. The elected teacher gains leadership position by election; followership is by consent. Missionary leaders can be found in many organizations that have some kind of central mission — economic, religious, political, or otherwise.

Whether a leader is shaman, priest, elected, missionary, or mystic, the leader should possess the following qualities:

- *Knowledge.* Above all, leaders should have knowledge; leaders should know their subject.

- *Enthusiasm.* IQ (intelligence quotient) and PQ (personality quotient) are valuable, but EQ (enthusiasm quotient) is essential. How can a leader expect followers to be enthusiastic about a subject that seems boring or unimportant to the leader?

- *Helpfulness*. Leaders should teach for the benefit of others, not for personal advantage. Their goal should be to share information and help others grow.

- *Appearance*. A favorable appearance is important. People take personal appearance as an unspoken statement of the quality of a person's message.

- *Cheerfulness*. A smile costs little and goes far in creating a teaching relationship. If leaders win the hearts of their subordinates, they will win their minds far more easily.

- *Respect*. Respect for the subordinate is essential. Nothing demonstrates respect so clearly as listening. In his essay, "On Liberty," John Stuart Mill explains the importance of listening: (1) One's ideas may be wrong, in which case presentation of the opposing view should lead to the correct conclusions. (2) Any individual's view on a matter generally contains only a portion of the truth; so the more views considered, the more likely it is the whole truth will appear. (3) If one's conclusions are completely valid and are based on the whole truth, they will withstand the onslaught of opposing arguments and emerge stronger than ever.[4]

- *Communication*. Leaders should know the exact meaning of words and have the ability to speak effectively. They should not talk over subordinates' heads, assuming they know more than their subordinates do; and they should avoid talking down to subordinates, making them feel inferior.

- *Self-control*. The best leaders neither lose self-control (thus reducing the ability to handle problems), nor criticize destructively. If criticism is required, they are tactful, helpful, and constructive.

- *Self-confidence*. Leaders should have self-confidence, based on knowledge and a sense of purpose.

- *Tolerance*. Leaders should be tolerant of different types of subordinates and patient if others are slow to learn.

- *Honesty*. Leaders should be honest. When they do not know something, they should say so.

These eleven characteristics should be used to select new leaders as well as to help experienced leaders develop teaching effectiveness. Consider yourself: which qualities are your strengths, and which qualities should you improve?

Principles of Employee Development

Like the pine tree that is stunted if it grows near the timberline, more fully developed if it grows farther down the mountainside, and tall and green if it grows in the valley, people also experience maximum develop-

ment under proper conditions.[5] Effective employee development includes the following steps and principles:[6]

Step 1: Identifying Training Needs. Training needs equal the total requirements of the job minus present performance. Training needs fall into three categories: skills (such as reading and writing), attitudes (such as cooperation and self-confidence), and knowledge (such as history and science). In general, training needs have been changing over the years because of the changing nature of jobs. As Figure 4.4 shows, there has been an increasing need for employees with strong minds and interpersonal skills.

The training needs of employees may be overlooked because leaders are preoccupied with pressing production problems or are insensitive to the development of others. If this happens, morale goes down, and ultimately so does job performance. Two of the best ways to identify training needs are: (1) to observe employees as they work and (2) to ask them if they think they would benefit from additional training.

Recognizing the need for training is important for the subordinate as well as the leader. Growth and development simply cannot be forced. Not all employees feel a need to improve. Some believe they are fine as they are; others are reconciled to their present performance, thinking they could not improve even if they tried, and it would not be worth the effort. For growth to take place, an interest in learning is needed. Social

FIGURE 4.4

The Changing Nature of Jobs and Training Needs

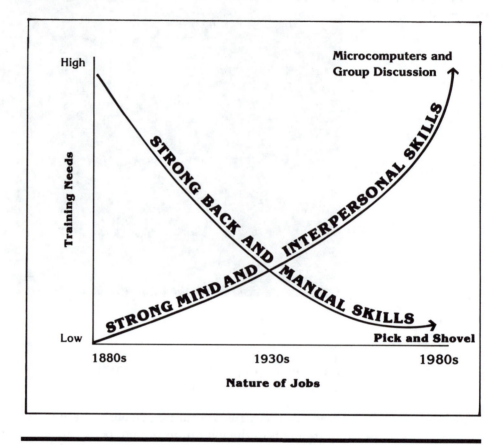

philosopher and management consultant Peter Drucker reflects an openness to change:

> "I'm fifty.
> Here I am fifty years old,
> And I don't know
> What I want to be
> When I grow up."[7]

Step 2: Preparing the Employee to Learn. A person must be ready to learn. Curiosity must be stimulated and interest awakened if employee development is to take place. Before you can learn anything, your attention must be on the subject. If you are emotionally upset, distracted, or uninterested, learning suffers.

Mental, motor, and emotional faculties must be present, and learning should proceed in a step-by-step fashion. One could hardly expect to learn calculus without first learning algebra, and it would be unrealistic to expect to run before first learning to walk. Also, some employees may be "late bloomers"; they may not be ready to grow or achieve full potential until later than others.

Finally, the subject must be relevant to the learner. People will not acquire new skills, attitudes, or knowledge unless they see personal value in them. Consciously or unconsciously, they ask, "What does learning math have to do with me?" "Why do I need to know accounting?" "How does 'Thou shalt not steal' apply to my life?" Conditions that support employee growth are presented below.

Conditions Conducive to Growth

People grow when there is a felt need.
People grow when they are encouraged by someone they respect.
People grow when their plans move from general goals to specific actions.
People grow as they move from a condition of lower to higher self-esteem.
People grow as they move from external to internal commitment.

Leaders can help employees grow by:

- Learning the backgrounds, interests, and skills of employees.

- Putting employees at ease. Most people fear change; therefore, training may need to proceed slowly.

- Explaining the value of growth and development. Many people need encouragement to improve. Leaders should show enthusiasm for the subject and the chances of improvement.

- Creating a learning climate free from interruptions and distractions.

- Having a helpful, friendly attitude toward employees.

- Showing employees how what they are learning can be used; helping employees see practical value in training and development.

- Helping employees experience success — nothing succeeds like success. In one experiment with adults, half the group was told they did well at solving puzzles (seven out of ten correct), while the other half was told they had done poorly (only three out of ten correct). The results presented were fictitious, as both groups had performed equally. Then, the two groups were given ten additional puzzles to solve. The half who had been told they did well in the first round did significantly better in the second round; the half who had been told they did poorly in the first round did significantly worse in the second round. Association with success leads to persistence, motivation, and improved performance.[8]

Step 3: Presenting the Training. Leaders should practice the following concepts, principles, and techniques when they are instructing others:

- *Use the correct medium or combination of techniques for instruction.* Consider whether one-on-one coaching, lectures, group discussion, case studies, role playing, conferences, field trips, panels, programmed learning, films, records, television, reading, or on-the-job training is the best method for developing your subordinates, or whether a combination of approaches would be most appropriate. Remember that different people respond differently to various teaching methods. Remember also that variety can be the spice of training. For a review of the learning effectiveness of different training methods, see Figure 4.5.

• *Use cases, stories, and real-life examples as often as possible.* Most people learn best through personal experience and practical examples. As a rule, the more involved the learner is, the better. Optimum learning involves all of a person's faculties, including mental, emotional, and motor. Consider the following:

> If a person lives with criticism,
>   he learns to condemn.
> If a person lives with hostility,
>   he learns to fight.
> If a person lives with ridicule,
>   he learns to be shy.
> If a person lives with shame,
>   he learns to feel guilty.
> If a person lives with tolerance,
>   he learns to be patient.
> If a person lives with encouragement,
>   he learns self-confidence.
> If a person lives with praise,
>   he learns to appreciate.
> If a person lives with fairness,
>   he learns to be just.
> If a person lives with security,
>   he learns to have faith.
> If a person lives with love,
>   he learns to give love.

—Anonymous

• *Tell and demonstrate carefully and patiently each point you are making.* Present concepts and principles in a well-organized way. If you are illogical, the trainee will have trouble learning. Put emphasis on key points that need to be remembered. Encourage note-taking if the material must be memorized.

• *Encourage questions.* Try to put yourself in the subordinate's position. Would you have any questions?

Step 4: Practicing, Testing, Rewarding, and Referring. These are critical elements in the learning process.

• *Practice.* Practice builds proficiency. Trainees should try new tasks or skills as soon as possible. Most things people learn involve more

FIGURE 4.5

Ratings of Training Directors on Effectiveness of Alternative Methods for Various Training Objectives

TRAINING METHOD	KNOWLEDGE ACQUISITION		CHANGING ATTITUDES		PROBLEM-SOLVING SKILLS		INTERPERSONAL SKILLS		PARTICIPANT ACCEPTANCE		KNOWLEDGE RETENTION	
	Mean	Mean Rank	Mean	Mean Rank	Mean	Mean Rank	Mean	Mean Rank	Mean	Mean Rank	Mean	Mean Rank
Case study	3.56	2	3.43	4	3.69	1	3.02	4	3.80	2	3.48	2
Conference (discussion) method	3.33	3	3.54	3	3.26	4	3.21	3	4.16	1	3.32	5
Lecture (with questions)	2.53	9	2.20	8	2.00	9	1.90	8	2.74	8	2.49	8
Business games	3.00	6	2.73	5	3.58	2	2.50	5	3.78	3	3.26	6
Movie films	3.16	4	2.50	6	2.24	7	2.19	6	3.44	5	2.67	7
Programmed instruction	4.03	1	2.22	7	2.56	6	2.11	7	3.28	7	3.74	1
Role playing	2.93	7	3.56	2	3.27	3	3.68	2	3.56	4	3.37	4
Sensitivity training (T-group)	2.77	8	3.96	1	2.98	5	3.95	1	3.33	6	3.44	3
Television lecture	3.10	5	1.99	9	2.01	8	1.81	9	2.74	9	2.47	9

Source: S.J. Carroll, F.T. Paine, and J.M. Ivancevich, "The Relative Effectiveness of Training Methods: Expert Opinion and Research," Personnel Psychology 25 (1972): 495–509. Reprinted with permission.

than abstract thinking and must be learned with the senses and muscles as well. By actually repairing a car, a person will learn more about automobile maintenance than by merely reading about it. This represents learning by doing.

- *Test.* A leader cannot know for sure what the trainee has learned until the trainee is tested. The best tests are not answered by a simple yes or no; they involve the use of questions and situations that make learners think and put answers into their own words. Only then will the leader know the extent and quality of learning that has taken place.

- *Reward.* Reinforce improvement with reward. Often, a word of praise or smile of recognition is enough to encourage continued employee development. Recognize that plateaus are normal in the learning process. Typically, learning increases sharply at first, then levels off. With continued effort, the learner will experience further growth before reaching another plateau. This growth and leveling process occurs over and over until the learner reaches maximum performance (see Figure 4.6).

FIGURE 4.6

Periods of Learning

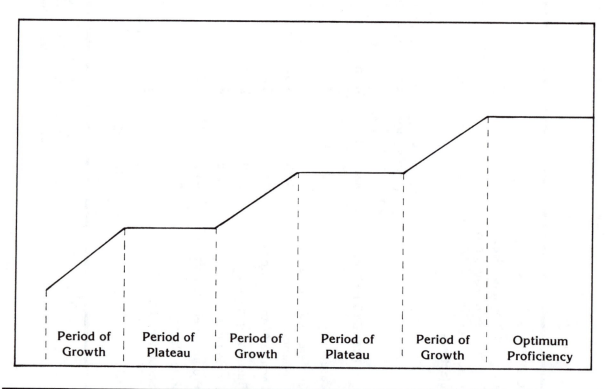

| Period of Growth | Period of Plateau | Period of Growth | Period of Plateau | Period of Growth | Optimum Proficiency |

- *Refer.* The leader should tell the trainee how to get more information, whom to turn to for future help — in essence, where to go for further growth.

To review, the four steps for employee development are: (1) identifying training needs; (2) preparing the employee to learn; (3) presenting the training; and (4) practicing, testing, rewarding, and referring. To understand the importance of employee development as a leadership key, consider the people in your own life who have guided your growth and spurred you to action. These were leaders who possessed the "master key." Leaders who can, teach.

THE SCORE KEY — EFFECTIVE DISCIPLINE

In recent years, there has been a tendency toward permissiveness in employee relations. Lack of discipline results in an untrained, poorly organized, and unproductive work force. Employees need to know what is expected of them, how they are doing, and that they are responsible for their actions.

An unnecessarily rigid environment and excessive discipline, on the other hand, may cause employees to fear or hate authority and to feel anxious or overly guilty about making mistakes. If employees feel that conditions are too restrictive, counterproductive measures such as slowdowns, sabotage, and strikes may result.

Inconsistent discipline should also be avoided because it makes it difficult for employees to understand what behavior is appropriate and what is not allowed. When people are punished one time and ignored or even rewarded the next time for doing the same thing, they become confused. Inevitably, this results in resentment, lowered morale, and reduced productivity.[9]

Three elements are important for effective discipline: (1) defined roles, so employees know what is expected; (2) clear guidelines, so employees understand acceptable behavior; and (3) effective methods and procedures for taking corrective action.[10]

Taking corrective action can be unpleasant and unpopular, but it is necessary because employees may make mistakes that should not be tolerated. Examples include theft, equipment abuse, and safety violations; offenders include first-line workers, middle-level managers, and top executive personnel.

Use of the following principles will help provide effective discipline and corrective action.[11]

- *Establish just and reasonable rules.* As an example, think of civil rules that are just, reasonable, and necessary, such as not driving through a red light or not stealing. Employees need similar guidelines for behavior on the job.

Work rules should be established in such areas as attendance, job performance, safety, security, language, dress, and personal conduct. When possible, employees should be involved in establishing work rules. Committees on safety and quality of work life help serve this purpose.

- *Communicate rules to all employees.* Rules should be thoroughly explained to new employees during orientation and should also be published in an employee handbook or posted on a bulletin board.

  As few rules as possible should be made, and these should be reviewed annually. Changes in rules should be communicated in writing, since people can only be responsible for rules they know about.

- *Provide immediate corrective action.* Some leaders postpone corrective action because carrying it out is uncomfortable or distasteful. Corrective action should be taken as soon as possible after mistakes are made. The practice of storing up observations and complaints and then unloading on an employee in one angry session only alienates subordinates. Immediate correction and penalties (if appropriate) are more acceptable to the offender, and thus more effective. If there is an association between misconduct and swift corrective action, the repetition of the offense is less likely to occur.

- *Create a system of progressive corrective measures for violation of rules.* Fairness requires a progression of penalties — oral warning, written warning, suspension from the job, and discharge. The leader should be sure that a final warning has been issued prior to actual discharge. This progression gives the employee a chance to improve and gives the leader a chance to help the employee.

  If a penalty is necessary, severity should depend on the offense, the employee's previous record, and the corrective value of the penalty. Theft may justify immediate suspension; tardiness may not.

- *Provide an appeal process for corrective action.* An appeal process helps ensure fair treatment for employees. If poor decisions have been made during the corrective process, a procedure for review can help correct a wrong disciplinary action.

- *Preserve human dignity.* Corrective action should take place in private. This reduces defensiveness and the likelihood that other employees may become involved and create an even bigger problem. Meeting privately provides better opportunity to discuss the problem and prevent it from happening again.

  When meeting with an employee, allow time to explain fully. Be a good listener. Ask questions that help the employee clarify actions. Allow for honest mistakes. Everybody makes a mistake sometime.

ILLUS. 4.3

Corrective action must preserve human dignity.

Strike a balance between developing the employee and correcting the problem. Criticize the act, not the employee as a person. Be sure to look at all sides of the problem. If you are in error, admit it. It is possible that the employee is innocent of intentional wrongdoing. If this is so, do not take punitive action but provide training. End corrective action on a positive note. Emphasize cooperation and optimism for future performance.

- *Do not charge a rule violation without first knowing the facts.* In any situation involving disciplinary action, the burden of proof and fairness is on the accuser. Be sure that: (1) the rule is enforced consistently and that this is not an isolated case; (2) the subordinate was informed of the rule; (3) the subordinate broke the rule; (4) it can be proved that the subordinate broke the rule; and (5) corrective measures are fair.

  Effective discipline requires preparation. Preparation accomplishes two purposes: (1) assurance that the action is fair and (2) factual support in case the leader must defend the action. Before taking corrective action, obtain all of the facts.

- *Avoid negative emotions.* Relax before meeting with your subordinate; remain calm. It is difficult to think and to communicate clearly when you are upset or arguing. Never scold or talk down to the subordinate and do not curse or strike the person. Once you have taken corrective action, start over with a clean slate. Do not hold grudges or stereotype the subordinate as a troublemaker.

- *Remember the purpose of corrective action.* The purpose is to prevent future problems, not to punish or obtain revenge. Be sure the employee understands what is wrong and why it is wrong. Be sure the employee understands the rules and the reasons they exist. Ask yourself, "Is this disciplinary action too severe?" If a lesser measure will accomplish the same purpose, use it. Also ask, "Did I clarify the problem, or did I blame the employee?" Finally, ask, "Does this corrective action provide a way to avoid the same situation in the future?"

- *Avoid double standards.* Rules and standards of conduct should be the same for all people in the same occupation and organization, and they should be enforced equally. If this is not the case, disciplinary action is unfair, and when higher management, union arbitrators, or governmental agencies review the decision, the action taken probably will be reversed. Consider the following case:

> Sure, I had a crescent wrench in my lunch box, but I'm no thief. Everybody does it. I could give you dozens of examples, but I won't. One thing I will say is that taking company property is not restricted to hourly employees.
>
> Look at the way management uses company cars and gasoline for personal trips. And in the shops, we're always fixing something for management — using company labor, tools, and parts. I'm always hearing stories from the front office about how managers combine vacations and company-paid business trips, or use their expense accounts for personal entertainment.
>
> I'm willing to live by the same rules everybody else does, but I won't sit still for being singled out. Let's face it: the way most employees think is that as long as you don't overdo it, taking company property is a form of employee benefit — like vacations and insurance.[12]

- *Enforce rules consistently and firmly.* Disciplinary measures should be taken only when they are fair, necessary, procedurally correct, immediate, and constructive. Once these conditions are met, if disciplinary action is in order, the leader should proceed with confidence and firmness and should stick to the decision.

  When a leader backs down on a rule violation, subordinates either think the rule is unimportant or is being applied unfairly. The only time backing down is advised is when a wrong decision has been made. If the leader makes a mistake, the decision must be changed and fairness must prevail.

In summary, employee discipline is an important ingredient for successful leadership. Discipline can be a vehicle for communication and problem solving that helps both employee morale and job performance.

APPLYING THE NINE KEYS
OF LEADERSHIP

We have defined leadership, presented its importance, emphasized the need for effective leadership in the work setting, and discussed the concepts, principles, and techniques of the nine keys of leadership. The following story of the Christian Crusades shows the importance of leadership and the critical role of each of the nine keys.

On November 27, 1095, Pope Urban II delivered a speech in Clermont, France. Whether right or wrong, this speech before a crowd of thousands was one of the most important acts in history. It launched the first Christian Crusade and set the stage for eight major and many minor crusades to follow over a period of roughly 200 years. The contact that resulted between western Europe and the more advanced Byzantine and Islamic cultures helped prepare the way for the Renaissance, which led to the full flowering of Western culture to the present day.

In his powerful address, Pope Urban decried the actions of the Seljuk Turks, who were occupying the Holy Land and harming Christian pilgrims visiting the land of Christ. He called for a great crusade to right this wrong and to recapture the Holy Lands for Christianity. Also, he pointed out that the Holy Lands were rich with gold and other wealth, and it would be the duty of the crusaders to claim these riches. Finally, he told his audience that participation in this crusade would replace all penances and would result in the remission of all sins. He declared: "You, oppressors of orphans and widows. You, murderers and violators of the church. Hasten as you love your souls, under your captain Christ, to the rescue of Jerusalem. All you who are guilty of such sins as exclude you from the kingdom of God, ransom yourselves at this price, for such is the will of God."

By the time Urban II had finished his speech, the crowds were chanting, "Deus le bolt! Deus le bolt!" (God wills it!). These words were to become the battle cry of the great crusades.[13]

Why did the Crusades take place? Why did thousands of people sew white crosses on their shoulders (thus the term Crusader, from the verb meaning "to mark with a cross") and march off in a series of Holy Wars in which thousands of soldiers and civilians would die? The answer is not simple, but applying the nine keys of leadership to Pope Urban's speech at Clermont helps explain how it happened:

- *The motive to lead.* Pope Urban chose to make his speech because of power, achievement, or altruism. Urban elected to act, thus providing the "ignition key."

- *The power of office.* The position of Pope was the only leadership stage from which the great Crusades could be launched. No national king or regional leader could have done it. Only the Pope possessed authority transcending earthly territories and titles. The papal position provided the "front door key."

- *The art of persuasion.* If the Pope's Crusades speech is representative, there is no question that he had mastered the "skeleton key" — he understood the nature and needs of people, and he used this knowledge to spur his followers to action. Specifically, the call to Holy War captured both the noble imagination and the materialistic interests of his audience. The opportunity to do right and simultaneously to fill one's pockets struck a responsive chord throughout all of Europe, which was both very religious and very impoverished at the time.

- *Effective delegation, development, and discipline.* The Pope's speech at Clermont demonstrated the "multiplication key," the "master key," and the "score key." Urban II delegated the Holy War to an army of thousands, drew on the teachings of the church to prepare the Crusaders for their assignment, and relied on religious rewards and punishments to discipline his followers.

- *Leadership by character and competence.* History tells us that Pope Urban II was admired and respected by others. He seems to have possessed both the "golden key" (character) and the "vault key" (competence). As a young man he was chosen to be Archdeacon at Reims, and successively he became Chimiac Monk, Prior, and Cardinal-Bishop. Finally, in A.D. 1088, Odo de Lagery was elected Pope Urban II.

- *The relationship between leader, followers, and situation.* The goals, position, and skills of the Pope meshed positively with the obedience, trust, and interests (selfish and selfless) of his followers, and these fit the dire conditions of Europe at the time. Leadership was effected — and history was shaped — by the elements and interrelationships of the "combination lock."[14]

Just as we have analyzed Urban II's launching of the Great Crusades, so can any act of leadership be evaluated. The ideas and deeds of one person or group will influence the behavior of others to the degree that the nine keys of leadership are present and in force. The success an individual experiences as a supervisor on the job or a parent in the home depends on:

- *The ignition key.* The leader's motives for influencing others — power, achievement, or altruism — including the strength of these motives.

- *The golden key.* The character of the leader — honor, courage, vision, and other related qualities.

- *The skeleton key.* The leader's ability to understand people and to persuade them to do things, including sensitivity to their needs, skill in listening and speaking, and effectiveness in giving orders.

- *The combination lock.* The interaction between leadership qualities (such as self-confidence), characteristics of followers (such as willingness to trust), and the nature of the situation (such as emergencies).

- *The front door key.* The power that comes with the leadership position, combined with the leader's use of power-in as opposed to power-over.

- *The vault key.* The leader's competence in performing leadership functions, such as assigning work, communicating with followers, and rewarding performance.
- *The multiplication key.* The leader's use of the principles and techniques of effective delegation.
- *The master key.* The leader's ability to teach — to develop others and to bring out their best in personal growth and job performance, including the leader's use of learning principles and training techniques.
- *The score key.* The degree of discipline the leader has developed in followers, including the effective use of corrective action.

This model of the leadership process can be used to diagnose past leadership as well as to predict future leadership effectiveness. For a personal evaluation of the nine keys of leadership, complete the following.

PERSONAL ANALYSIS OF LEADERSHIP— NINE KEYS TO SUCCESS

Directions

Complete the following steps.

Step 1. Describe a true-life situation that requires leadership, either in your work or your personal life. Examples include creating a business, raising a family, and leading a work group._____

_____

_____

_____

_____

_____

_____

_____

_____

_____

_____

_____

_____

Step 2. Answer the following questions in detail. Be specific.

The Ignition Key

Why would you want to provide leadership in this situation—for power, achievement, or altruism? How strong is your interest in providing leadership?_____

_____

_____

_____

_____

_____

_____

The Golden Key

What leadership qualities do you possess? Do you have the force of character that makes others want to follow you? Which of your qualities are most important in this instance?_____

_____

_____

_____

_____

_____

_____

The Skeleton Key

Do you understand the needs and goals of the people involved? What are they? What would you say to persuade these people to take action?

_____

_____

_____

_____

_____

_____

_____

The Combination Lock

Are the people and conditions right for you to provide leadership? Explain._____

_____

_____

_____

_____

_____

_____

_____

The Front Door Key

Do you understand the difference between a boss and a leader? Which would you be? Specifically, what would you do?_____

_____

_____

_____

_____

_____

_____

_____

The Vault Key

What principles of leadership would you practice that would help your followers to be effective? List these._____

_____

_____

_____

_____

_____

_____

_____

The Multiplication Key

Are you willing to delegate duties and authority to others? Do you know how? In this instance, whom would you assign to do what? By when? How would you accomplish this?_____

_____

_____

_____

_____

_____

_____

_____

The Master Key

Do you have the ability to train others? What qualities do you possess that will help you in this process? What steps would you take to develop others?_____

_____

_____

_____

_____

_____

_____

_____

The Score Key

Do you understand the principles of effective discipline? Will you be too permissive, too restrictive, too inconsistent, or just right? Who will be most likely to need corrective action? What will you do?_____

_____

_____

_____

_____

_____

_____

Step 3. What is your prediction of the outcome of the situation? To what extent are the nine keys of leadership present in this situation? Whether you would be hero, teacher, or ruler as a leader, how successful will you be in lighting the path and encouraging others to follow? Will your ideas and actions show the way and influence the behavior of others? Explain.

_____

_____

_____

_____

_____

_____

_____

_____

CONCLUSION

Studying leadership leaves one with three impressions: (1) leadership is important; (2) leadership is complex; (3) being a leader isn't easy. Half in jest and half in earnest, the following leader's prayer is offered as a reflection of point three and a fitting thought for those who would be leaders.

A Leader's Prayer

Help me to become the kind of leader my management would like to have me be.

Give me that mysterious something that will enable me at all times to explain policies, rules, regulations, and procedures to my workers, even when they have never been explained to me.

Help me to teach and train the uninterested and unruly, without ever losing my patience and temper.

Give me that love for my fellowman that passes all understanding, so that I may lead the obstinate into paths of righteousness by my own example and my soft persuading voice, instead of busting them in the nose.

Instill tranquility and peace of mind into my inner being, so that no longer will I wake from my restless sleep in the middle of the night, crying out, "What has the boss got that I haven't got, and how did he get it?"

Teach me to smile if it kills me.

Make me a better leader of others by helping me develop greater qualities of understanding, tolerance, sympathy, wisdom, perspective, mind reading, and second sight.

And when Thou has helped me to achieve the high pinnacle my management has prescribed for me, and when I have become the paragon of all supervisory virtue in this earthly world, then, dear Lord, move over.

— Anonymous

We hope you will keep this book handy and refer to it often in your leadership role. What are the qualities of leadership? See pages 41–45. What is the role of leadership style? See pages 51–57. What are the principles of effective supervision? See pages 76–85. How do you give orders? See pages 27–29. What are the rules for effective delegation? See pages 86–91. How do you deal with employee problems? See pages 115–118. Why would you want to be a leader? See page 14–21. We encourage you to use this book as a reference and training guide.

Leadership is an important process with enormous potential to help or harm. Consider your own experiences with the leaders you have known, and think of their impact on their worlds, including how they have affected you. Now consider your own work and life and the occasions you may have to provide leadership to others, the opportunities you will have to light the fire and influence others to take action. During these times, remember to use the nine keys of leadership. Apply the concepts, principles, and techniques you have learned to *be the manager you have always wanted to have.*[15]

RECOMMENDED RESOURCES

The following readings, cases, application, and films are suggested for greater insight into the material in Part Four:

Readings	— Pygmalion in Management Managers Can Drive Their Subordinates Mad
Cases	— The Full Court Press The Forklift Fiasco
Application	— Train the Trainer

Films	— Productivity and the Self-fulfilling Prophecy: The Pygmalion Effect
	  Coaching
	  The Power of Reinforcement
	  Working with Difficult People
	  Resolving Conflicts

REFERENCE NOTES

1 William Stewart, "Developing Others," Department of Adult Technical Education, University of Cincinnati.

2 John Allen, ed., *100 Great Lives* (New York: Journal of Living Publishing Corp., 1944), 20–22, 25.

3 Harry Levinson, *Executive* (Cambridge, Mass.: Harvard University Press, 1981), 150.

4 John Stuart Mill, "On Liberty" in Karl Britton, *Philosophy and the Meaning of Life* (London: Cambridge University Press, 1969), 93.

5 James C. Coleman, *Personality Dynamics and Effective Behavior* (Chicago: Scott, Foresman & Company, 1960), 97–98.

6 *Leadership and Discussion Techniques for Supervisory Personnel* (Columbus, Ohio: Ohio Trade and Industrial Education Service).

7 Peter Drucker in Will Forpe and John C. McCollister, *The Sunshine Book: Expressions of Love, Hope, and Inspiration* (Middle Village, N.Y.: Jonathan David Publishers, 1979), 50.

8 Gordon L. Lippitt, *Organizational Renewal: A Holistic Approach to Organizational Development*, 2d ed. (Englewood Cliffs, N.J.: Prentice-Hall, Inc., 1982), 337.

9 Coleman, *Personality Dynamics*, 102.

10 Coleman, *Personality Dynamics*, 102.

11 Gary Dressler, *Applied Human Relations* (Reston, Va.: Reston, 1983), 49–52; George Odiorne, *How Managers Make Things Happen* (Englewood Cliffs, N.J.: Prentice-Hall, Inc., 1961), 132–143; and J. Clifton Williams, *Human Behavior in Organizations* (Cincinnati: South-Western, 1978), 199–208.

12 Williams, *Human Behavior in Organizations*, 202.

13 Richard A. Newhall, *The Crusades* (Hinsdale, Ill.: Dryden Press, 1963), 40–41.

14 Newhall, *The Crusades*, 40–42, 90–91; and Michael Hart, *The 100: A Ranking of the Most Influential Persons in History* (New York: Hart Publishing/A. & W. Publishers, Inc., 1978), 268–270.

15 Robert Caplon, "Day in the Life of a Manager," IBM-Northern Kentucky University Management Training Program, December 1986.

STUDY QUIZ

As a test of your understanding and the extent to which you have achieved the objectives in Part Four, complete the following questions. See Appendix D for the answer key.

1. The best training method for changing attitudes is

    a. television lecture
    b. sensitivity training (T-group)
    c. programmed instruction

2. The best training method for conveying a large amount of information is

    a. lecture with questions
    b. programmed instruction
    c. television lecture

3. In Western society, the need for strong backs and manual skills is going _____; the need for strong minds and interpersonal skills is going _____.

    a. down, down
    b. up, up
    c. up, down
    d. down, up

4. The best training method for teaching problem-solving skills is

    a. lecture (with questions)
    b. movie/films
    c. case study

5. Types of teacher/leaders include

    a. shamans
    b. priests
    c. elected leaders
    d. missionaries
    e. mystics
    f. all of the above

6. Conditions conducive to employee growth include

    a. felt need
    b. encouragement
    c. plans move from general goals to specific action
    d. self-esteem
    e. all of the above

7. The best training method for interpersonal skills is

    a. lecture (with discussion)
    b. programmed instruction
    c. sensitivity training (T-group)

8. The step(s) for new employee orientation include

    a. getting ready to receive new employee
    b. welcoming new employee
    c. showing interest in new employee
    d. explaining organization and work group
    e. introducing new employee to co-workers
    f. showing layout of work setting
    g. explaining rules and regulations
    h. instructing in job assignment
    i. following up
    j. all of the above

9. There are many different types of leaders, but all should possess which of the following teaching qualities?

    a. experience, tolerance, intelligence
    b. honesty, appearance, quietness
    c. knowledge, self-control, enthusiasm
    d. cheerfulness, happiness, self-confidence

10. Pope Urban II's speech at Clermont is an example of using which of the following keys of leadership?

    a. ignition key, master key
    b. multiplication key, score key
    c. front door key, golden key, vault key
    d. skeleton key, combination key
    e. all of the above

11. The trainee must practice newly acquired skills as soon as possible after training is completed for the learning process to be most effective.

    a. True
    b. False

12. Typically, learning increases sharply, levels off, increases again, plateaus again, and so on, until optimum proficiency has been achieved.

    a. True
    b. False

13. Steps to training others include

    a. identifying training needs
    b. preparing the employee to learn
    c. presenting the course or subject matter
    d. application, follow-up, and reward
    e. all of the above

14. The master key is: leaders who can _____.

    a. do
    b. teach
    c. preach
    d. control

15. All of the following except _____ are important for effective discipline.

    a. adequately defined roles
    b. clear limits
    c. effective methods for corrective actions
    d. swift and severe punishment

16. For effective corrective action, you should not charge a rule violation without first having the

    a. time
    b. facts
    c. education
    d. skills

17. The purpose of discipline is _____ action.

    a. supplementary
    b. positive
    c. corrective
    d. employee

DISCUSSION QUESTIONS AND ACTIVITIES

The following questions and activities help personalize the subject. They are appropriate for classroom exercises and homework assignments.

1. Who was the best boss you ever had? What was it like working under this person? What was this person's attitude toward you and your development?

   _____

   _____

   _____

2. Identify the people in your life who have had a positive impact on you. Discuss the qualities of these people.

   _____

   _____

   _____

3. Have you ever made a mistake or an error in judgment for which you were corrected? Regardless of whether it was done well or poorly, explain how the corrective action was handled.

   _____

   _____

   _____

4. Use small-group discussion to consider the role of discipline in the leadership process. As group members, think of great leaders you have known. How did these leaders approach discipline?

5. Discuss the role of training. Can you think of an incident when a poorly trained employee or work group performed poor-quality work with disastrous consequences? Describe.

6. Discuss the nine keys of leadership as they apply in a true-life situation. What is the prediction for success?

READINGS

Boss: Richard J. Daley of Chicago 136

What Makes a Top Executive? 141

How the Boss Stays in Touch with
the Troops 149

The Manager's Job: Folklore and Fact 154

Pygmalion in Management 173

Managers Can Drive Their Subordinates
Mad 187

Editor's Note: *Some of the facts in the readings chosen for this book may appear to be out of date; however, the articles have been selected because of the overall importance of the subject matter.*

Boss: Richard J. Daley of Chicago

If there is a council meeting, everybody marches downstairs at a few minutes before ten. Bush and the department heads and personal aides form a proud parade. The meeting begins when the seat of the mayor's pants touches the council president's chair, placed beneath the great seal of the city of Chicago and above the heads of the aldermen, who sit in a semi-bowl auditorium.

It is his council, and in all the years it has never once defied him as a body. Keane manages it for him, and most of its members do what they are told. In other eras, the aldermen ran the city and plundered it. In his boyhood they were so constantly on the prowl that they were known as "the Gray Wolves." His council is known as "the Rubber Stamp."

He looks down at them, bestowing a nod or a benign smile on a few favorites, and they smile back gratefully. He seldom nods or smiles at the small minority of white and black independents. The independents anger him more than the Republicans do, because they accuse him of racism, fascism, and of being a dictator. The Republicans bluster about loafing payrollers, crumbling gutters, inflated budgets—traditional, comfortable accusations that don't stir the blood.

That is what Keane is for. When the minority goes on the attack, Keane himself, or one of the administration aldermen he has groomed for the purpose, will rise and answer the criticism by shouting that the critic is a fool, a hypocrite, ignorant, and misguided. Until his death, one alderman could be expected to leap to his feet at every meeting and cry, "God bless our mayor, the greatest mayor in the world."

But sometimes Keane and his trained orators can't shout down the minority, so Daley has to do it himself. If provoked, he'll break into a rambling, ranting speech, waving his arms, shaking his fists, defending his judgment, defending his administration, always with the familiar "It is easy to criticize . . . to find fault . . . but where are your programs . . . where are your ideas. . . ."

If that doesn't shut off the critics, he will declare them to be out of order, threaten to have the sergeant at arms force them into their seats, and invoke Robert's Rules of Order, which, in the heat of debate, he once described as "the greatest book ever written."

Source: Boss: Richard J. Daley of Chicago *by Mike Royko. Copyright* © *1971 by Mike Royko. Reprinted by permission of the publisher, E.P. Dutton, a division of New American Library.*

All else failing, he will look toward a glass booth above the spectator's balcony and make a gesture known only to the man in the booth who operates the sound system that controls the microphones on each alderman's desk. The man in the booth will touch a switch and the offending critic's microphone will go dead and stay dead until he sinks into his chair and closes his mouth.

The meetings are seldom peaceful and orderly. The slightest criticism touches off shrill rebuttal, leading to louder criticism and finally an embarrassingly wild and vicious free-for-all. It can't be true, because Daley is a man who speaks highly of law and order, but sometimes it appears that he enjoys the chaos, and he seldom moves to end it until it has raged out of control.

Every word of criticism must be answered, every complaint must be disproved, every insult must be returned in kind. He doesn't take anything from anybody. While Daley was mediating negotiations between white trade unions and black groups who wanted the unions to accept blacks, a young militant angrily rejected one of his suggestions and concluded, "Up. . . ."

Daley leaped to his feet and answered, "And up. . . ." Would John Lindsay have become so involved? Independent aldermen have been known to come up with a good idea, such as providing food for the city's hungry, or starting day-care centers for children of ghetto women who want to work; Daley will acknowledge it, but in his own way. He'll let Keane appropriate the idea and rewrite and resubmit it as an administration measure. That way, the independent has the satisfaction of seeing his idea reach fruition and the administration has more glory. But most of the independents' proposals are sent to a special subcommittee that exists solely to allow their unwelcome ideas to die.

The council meetings seldom last beyond the lunch hour. Aldermen have much to do. Many are lawyers and have thriving practices, because Chicagoans know that a dumb lawyer who is an alderman can often perform greater legal miracles than a smart lawyer who isn't. . . .

The afternoon work moves with never a minute wasted. The engineers and planners come with their reports on public works projects. Something is always being built, concrete being poured, steel being riveted, contractors being enriched.

"When will it be completed?" he asks.

"Early February."

"It would be a good thing for the people if it could be completed by the end of October."

The engineers say it can be done, but it will mean putting on extra shifts, night work, overtime pay, a much higher cost than was planned.

"It would be a good thing for the people if it could be completed by the end of October."

Of course it would be a good thing for the people. It would also be a good thing for the Democratic candidates who are seeking election in early November to go out and cut a ribbon for a new expressway or a water filtration plant or, if nothing else is handy, another wing at the O'Hare terminal. What ribbons do their opponents cut?

The engineers and planners understand, and they set about getting it finished by October.

On a good afternoon, there will be no neighborhood organizations to see him, because if they get to Daley, it means they have been up the ladder of government and nobody has been able to solve their problem. And that usually means a conflict between the people and somebody else, such as a politician or a business, whom his aides don't want to ruffle. There are many things his department heads can't do. They can't cross swords with ward bosses or politically heavy businessmen. They can't make important decisions. Some can't even make petty decisions. He runs City Hall like a small family business and keeps everybody on a short rein. They do only that which they know is safe and that which he tells them to do. So many things that should logically be solved several rungs below finally come to him.

Because of this, he has many requests from neighborhood people. And when a group is admitted to his office, most of them nervous and wide-eyed, he knows who they are, their leaders, their strength in the community. They have already been checked out by somebody. He must know everything. He doesn't like to be surprised. Just as he knows the name of every new worker, he must know what is going on in the various city offices. If the head of the office doesn't tell him, he has somebody there who will. In the office of other elected officials, he has trusted persons who will keep him informed. Out in the neighborhoods his precinct captains are reporting to the ward committeemen, and they in turn are reporting to him.

His police department's intelligence-gathering division gets bigger and bigger, its network of infiltrators, informers, and spies creating massive files on dissenters, street gangs, political enemies, newsmen, radicals, liberals, and anybody else who might be working against him. He has dumped several party members for violating his personal moral standards. If something is leaked to the press, the bigmouth will be tracked down and punished. Scandals aren't public scandals if you get there before your enemies do.

So when the people come in, he knows what they want and whether it is possible. Not that it means they will get it. That often depends on how they act.

He will come out from behind his desk all smiles and handshakes and charm. Then he returns to his chair and sits very straight, hands folded on his immaculate desk, serious and attentive. To one side will be somebody from the appropriate city department.

Now it's up to the group. If they are respectful, he will express sympathy, ask encouraging questions, and finally tell them that everything possible will be done. And after they leave, he may say, "Take care of it." With that command, the royal seal, anything is possible, anybody's toes can be stepped on.

But if they are pushy, antagonistic, demanding instead of imploring, or bold enough to be critical of him, to tell him how he should do his job, to blame him for their problem, he will rub his hands together, harder and harder. In a long, difficult meeting, his hands will get raw. His voice gets lower, softer, and the corners of his mouth will turn down. At this point, those who know him will back off. They know what's next. But the unfamiliar, the militant, will mistake his lowered voice and nervousness for weakness. Then he'll blow, and it comes in a frantic roar.

"I want you to tell me what to do. You come up with the answers. You come up with the program. Are we perfect? Are you perfect? We all make mistakes. We all have faults. It's easy to criticize. It's easy to find fault. But you tell me what to do. This problem is all over the city. We didn't create these problems. We don't want them. But we are doing what we can. You tell me how to solve them. You give me a program." All of which leaves the petitioners dumb, since most people don't walk around with urban programs in their pockets. It can also leave them right back where they started.

They leave and the favor seekers come in. Half of the people he sees want a favor. They plead for promotions, something for their sons, a chance to do some business with the city, to get somebody in City Hall off their backs, a chance to return from political exile, a boon. They won't get an answer right there and then. It will be considered and he'll let them know. Later, sometimes much later, when he has considered the alternatives and the benefits, word will get back to them. Yes or no. Success or failure. Life or death.

Some jobseekers come directly to him. Complete outsiders, meaning those with no family or political connections, will be sent to see their ward committeemen. That is protocol, and that is what he did to the tall young black man who came to see him a few years ago, bearing a letter from the governor of North Carolina, who wrote that the young black man was a rising political prospect in his state. Daley told him to see his ward committeeman, and if he did some precinct work, rang doorbells, hustled up some votes, there might be a government job for him. Maybe something like taking coins in a tollway booth. The Rev. Jesse Jackson, now the city's leading black civil rights leader, still hasn't stopped smarting over that.

Others come asking him to resolve a problem. He is the city's leading labor mediator and has prevented the kind of strikes that have crippled New York. His father was a union man, and he comes from a union neighborhood, and many of the union leaders were his boyhood friends. He knows what they want. And if it is in the city's treasury, they will get it. If it isn't there, he'll promise to find it. He has ended a teachers' strike by promising that the state legislature would find funds for them, which surprised the Republicans in Springfield, as well as put them on the spot. He is an effective mediator with the management side of labor disputes, because they respect his judgment, and because there are few industries that do not need some favors from City Hall.

QUESTIONS

1. What leadership style do you think works best in public office? Describe a true-life figure who has this style.

   _____

   _____

   _____

2. What style of leadership would you use if you were a mayor, governor, or other elected official? Why?

   _____

   _____

   _____

What Makes a Top Executive?

Senior Executive: At one time, Jim was the leading, perhaps the only, candidate for chief executive officer. And then he ran into something he'd never faced before—an unprofitable operation. He seemed to go on a downward spiral after that, becoming more remote each day, unable to work with key subordinates.

Interviewer: Why do you think he derailed?

Senior Executive: Some of it was bad luck, because the business was going down when he inherited it. Some of it was surrounding himself with specialists, who inevitably wear the blinders of their particular field. And some of it was that he had never learned to delegate. He had no idea of how to lead by listening.

The case of Jim is by no means unusual. Many executives of formidable talent rise to very high levels, yet are denied the ultimate positions. The quick explanations for what might be called their derailment are the ever-popular Peter Principle—they rose past their level of competence—or, more darkly, they possessed some fatal flaw.

The grain of truth in these explanations masks the actual complexity of the process. So we learned from a study that we recently did here at the Center for Creative Leadership, a nonprofit research and educational institution in Greensboro, North Carolina, formed to improve the practice of management.

When we compared 21 derailed executives—successful people who were expected to go even higher in the organization but who reached a plateau late in their careers, were fired, or were forced to retire early—with 20 "arrivers"—those who made it all the way to the top—we found the two groups astonishingly alike. Every one of the 41 executives possessed remarkable strengths, and every one was flawed by one or more significant weaknesses.

Insensitivity to others was cited as a reason for derailment more often than any other flaw. But it was never the only reason. Most often, it was a combination of personal qualities and external circumstances that put an end to an executive's rise. Some of the executives found themselves

Source: Morgan W. McCall, Jr., and Michael M. Lombardo. Reprinted with permission from Psychology Today Magazine. *Copyright © 1983, American Psychological Association.*

in a changed situation, in which strengths that had served them well earlier in their careers became liabilities that threw them off track. Others found that weaknesses they'd had all along, once outweighed by assets, became crucial defects in a new situation requiring particular skills to resolve some particular problem.

Our goal was to find out what makes an effective executive, and our original plan was to concentrate on arrivers. But we soon realized that, paradoxically, we could learn a lot about effectiveness by taking a close look at executives who had failed to live up to their apparent potential.

We and our associate, Ann Morrison, worked with several Fortune-500 corporations to identify "savvy insiders" — people who had seen many top executives come and go and who were intimately familiar with their careers. In each corporation one of us interviewed several insiders, usually a few of the top 10 executives and a few senior "human resources professionals," people who help to decide who moves up. We asked them to tell both a success story and a story of derailment.

FATAL FLAWS

Asked to say what had sealed the fate of the men (they were all men) who fell short of ultimate success, our sources named 65 factors, which we boiled down to 10 categories:

1. Insensitive to others: abrasive, intimidating, bullying style.
2. Cold, aloof, arrogant.
3. Betrayal of trust.
4. Overly ambitious: thinking of next job, playing politics.
5. Specific performance problems with the business.
6. Overmanaging: unable to delegate or build a team.
7. Unable to staff effectively.
8. Unable to think strategically.
9. Unable to adapt to boss with different style.
10. Overdependent on advocate or mentor.

No executive had all the flaws cited; indeed, only two were found in the average derailed executive.

As we have noted, the most frequent cause for derailment was insensitivity to other people. "He wouldn't negotiate; there was no room for countervailing views. He could follow a bull through a china shop and still break the china," one senior executive said of a derailed colleague.

Under stress, some of the derailed managers became abrasive and intimidating. One walked into a subordinate's office, interrupting a meeting and said, "I need to see you." When the subordinate tried to explain that he was occupied, his boss snarled, "I don't give a damn. I said I wanted to see you now."

Others were so brilliant that they became arrogant, intimidating others with their knowledge. Common remarks were: "He made others feel stupid" or "He wouldn't give you the time of day unless you were brilliant too."

In an incredibly complex and confusing job, being able to trust others absolutely is a necessity. Some executives committed what is perhaps management's only unforgivable sin: They betrayed a trust. This rarely had anything to do with honesty, which was a given in almost all cases. Rather, it was a one-upping of others, or a failure to follow through on promises that wreaked havoc in terms of organizational efficiency. One executive didn't implement a decision as he had promised to do, causing conflicts between the marketing and the production divisions that reverberated downward through four levels of frustrated subordinates.

Others, like Cassius, were overly ambitious. They seemed to be always thinking of their next job, they bruised people in their haste, and they spent too much time trying to please upper management. This sometimes led to staying with a single advocate or mentor too long. When the mentor fell from favor, so did they. Even if the mentor remained in power, people questioned the executive's ability to make independent judgments. Could he stand alone? One executive had worked for the same boss for the better part of 15 years, following him from one assignment to another. Then top management changed, and the boss no longer fit in with the plans of the new regime. The executive, having no reputation of his own, was viewed as a clone of his boss and was passed over as well.

A series of performance problems sometimes emerged. Managers failed to meet profit goals, got lazy, or demonstrated that they couldn't handle certain kinds of jobs (usually new ventures or jobs requiring great powers of persuasion). More important in such cases, managers showed that they couldn't change; they failed to admit their problems, covered them up, or tried to blame them on others. One executive flouted senior management by failing to work with a man specifically sent in to fix a profit problem.

After a certain point in their careers, managers must cease to do the work themselves, and must become executives who see that it is done. But some of the men we studied never made this transition, never learning to delegate or to build a team beneath them. Although overmanaging is irritating at any level, it can be fatal at the executive level. When executives meddle, they are meddling not with low-level subordinates but with other executives, most of whom know much more about their particular area of expertise than their boss ever will. One external-affairs executive who knew little about government regulation tried to direct an expert with 30 years' experience. The expert balked, and the executive lost a battle that should never have begun.

Others got along with their staff, but simply picked the wrong people. Sometimes they staffed in their own image, choosing, for instance, an engineer like themselves when a person with marketing experience would have been better suited for the task at hand. Or sometimes they simply picked people who later bombed.

Inability to think strategically — to take a broad, long-term view — was masked by attention to detail and a miring in technical problems, as some executives simply couldn't go from being doers to being planners. Another common failure appeared as a conflict of style with a new boss. One manager who couldn't change from a go-getter to a thinker/planner eventually ran afoul of a slower-paced, more reflective boss. Although the successful managers sometimes had similar problems, they didn't get into wars over them, and rarely let the issues get personal. Derailed managers exhibited a host of unproductive responses — got peevish, tried to shout the boss down, or just sulked.

In summary, we concluded that executives derail for four basic reasons, all connected to the fact that situations change as one ascends the organizational hierarchy:

1. *Strengths become weaknesses.* Loyalty becomes overdependence, narrowness, or cronyism. Ambition is eventually viewed as politicking and destroys an executive's support base.

2. *Deficiencies eventually matter.* If talented enough, a person can get by with insensitivity at lower levels, but not at higher ones, where subordinates and peers are powerful and probably brilliant also. Those who are charming but not brilliant find that the job gets too big and problems too complex to get by on interpersonal skills.

3. *Success goes to their heads.* After being told how good they are for so long, some executives simply lose their humility and become cold and arrogant. Once this happens, their information sources begin to dry up and people no longer wish to work with them.

4. *Events conspire.* A few of the derailed apparently did little wrong. They were done in politically, or by economic upheavals. Essentially, they just weren't lucky.

While conducting the interviews, we heard few stories about water-walkers. In fact, the executive who came closest to fitting that category, the one "natural leader," derailed precisely because everyone assumed that he could do absolutely anything. At higher levels of management, he became lost in detail, concentrated too much on his subordinates, and seemed to lack the intellectual ability to deal with complex issues. Still, no one helped him; it was assumed that he would succeed regardless.

In short, both the arrivers and those who derailed had plenty of warts, although these generally became apparent only late in the men's careers. The events that exposed the flaws were seldom cataclysmic. More often, the flaws themselves had a cumulative impact. As one executive put it, "Careers last such a long time. Leave a trail of mistakes and you eventually find yourself encircled by your past."

In general, the flaws of both the arrivers and the derailed executives showed up when one of five things happened to them: (1) They lost a boss who had covered, or compensated for, their weaknesses. (2) They entered a job for which they were not prepared, either because it entailed much greater responsibility or because it required the executives to perform functions that were new to them. Usually, the difficulties were compounded by the fact that the executives went to work for a new boss whose style was very different from that of his newly promoted subordinate. (3) They left behind a trail of little problems or bruised people, either because they handled them poorly or moved through so quickly that they failed to handle them at all. (4) They moved up during an organizational shake-up and weren't scrutinized until the shake-down period. (5) They entered the executive suite, where getting along with others is critical.

One or more of these events happened to most of the executives, so the event itself was telling only in that its impact began to separate the two groups. How one person dealt with his flaws under stress went a long way toward explaining why some men arrived and some jumped the tracks just short of town. A bit of dialogue from one interview underscores this point:

Senior Executive: Successful people don't like to admit that they make big mistakes, but they make whoppers nevertheless. I've never known a CEO [chief executive officer] who didn't make at least one big one and lots of little ones, but it never hurt them.

Interviewer: Why?

Senior Executive: Because they know how to handle adversity.

Part of handling adversity lies in knowing what *not* to do. As we learned, lots of different management behavioral patterns were acceptable to others. The key was in knowing which one colleagues and superiors would find intolerable.

As we said at the beginning, both groups were amazingly similar: incredibly bright, identified as promising early in their careers, outstanding in their track records, ambitious, willing to sacrifice—and imperfect. A closer look does reveal some differences, however, and at the levels of excellence characteristic of executives, even a small difference is more than sufficient to create winners and losers.

THE ARRIVERS AND THE DERAILED COMPARED

In the first place, derailed executives had a series of successes, but usually in similar kinds of situations. They had turned two businesses around, or managed progressively larger jobs in the same function. By contrast, the arrivers had more diversity in their successes—they had turned a business around *and* successfully moved from line to staff and back, or started a new business from scratch *and* completed a special assignment with distinction. They built plants in the wilderness and the Amazonian jungle, salvaged disastrous operations, resolved all-out wars between corporate divisions without bloodshed. One even built a town.

Derailed managers were often described as moody or volatile under pressure. One could control his temper with top management he sought to impress, but was openly jealous of peers he saw as competitors. His too-frequent angry outbursts eroded the cooperation necessary for success, as peers began to wonder whether he was trying to do them in. In contrast, the arrivers were calm, confident, and predictable. People knew how they would react and could plan their own actions accordingly.

Although neither group made many mistakes, all of the arrivers handled theirs with poise and grace. Almost uniformly, they admitted the mistake, forewarned others so they wouldn't be blind-sided by it, then set about analyzing and fixing it. Also telling were two things the arrivers didn't do: They didn't blame others, and once they had handled the situation, they didn't dwell on it.

Moreover, derailed executives tended to react to failure by going on the defensive, trying to keep it under wraps while they fixed it, or, once the problem was visible, blaming it on someone else.

Although both groups were good at going after problems, arrivers were particularly single-minded. This "What's the problem?" mentality spared them three of the common flaws of the derailed: They were too busy worrying about their present job to appear overly eager for their next position; they demanded excellence from their people in problem-solving; and they developed many contacts, saving themselves from the sole-mentor syndrome. In fact, almost no successful manager reported having a single mentor.

Lastly, the arrivers, perhaps due to the diversity of their backgrounds, had the ability to get along with all types of people. They either possessed or developed the skills required to be outspoken without offending people. They were not seen as charming-but-political or direct-but-tactless, but as direct-and-diplomatic. One arriver disagreed strongly with a business strategy favored by his boss. He presented his objections candidly and gave the reasons for his concerns as well as the alternative he preferred. But when the decision went against him, he put his energy behind making the decision work. When his boss turned out to be wrong, the arriver didn't gloat about it; he let the situation speak for itself without further embarrassing his boss.

One of the senior executives we interviewed made a simple but not simplistic distinction between the two groups. Only two things, he said, differentiated the successful from the derailed: total integrity, and understanding other people.

Integrity seems to have a special meaning to executives. The word does not refer to simple honesty, but embodies a consistency and predictability built over time that says, "I will do exactly what I say I will do when I say I will do it. If I change my mind, I will tell you well in advance so you will not be harmed by my actions." Such a statement is partly a matter of ethics, but, even more, a question of vital practicality. This kind of integrity seems to be the core element in keeping a large, amorphous organization from collapsing in its own confusion.

Two Executives: A Study in Contrast

The two case histories that follow are told in the words of corporate executives who knew them well.

	One who arrived	One who derailed
The man	"He was an intelligent guy with a delightful twinkle in his eye. He could laugh at himself during the toughest of situations."	"He got results, but was awfully insensitive about it. Although he could be charming when he wanted to be, he was mostly knees and elbows."
Notable strengths	"He was a superb negotiator. He could somehow come out of a labor dispute or a dispute among managers with an agreement everyone could live with. I think he did this by getting all around a problem so it didn't get blown. People knew far in advance if something might go wrong."	"He was a superb engineer who came straight up the operations ladder. He had the rare capability of analyzing problems to death, then reconfiguring the pieces into something new."
Flaws	"He was too easy on subordinates and peers at times. Line people wondered whether he was tough enough, and sometimes, why he spent so much time worrying about people."	"When developing something, he gave subordinates more help than they needed, but once a system was set up, he forgot to mind the store. When things went awry, he usually acted like a bully or stonewalled it, once hiring a difficult employee and turning him over to a subordinate. 'It's your problem now,' he told him."
Career	"He was thrown into special assignments — negotiations, dealing with the press, fix-it projects. He always found a way to move things off dead center."	"He rocketed upward through engineering/operations jobs. Once he got high enough, his deficiencies caught up with him. He couldn't handle either the scope of his job or the complexity of new ventures."
And ended up . . .	Senior Vice President	"Passed over, and it's too bad. He was a talented guy and not a bad manager, either. I suppose that his overmanaging, abrasive style never allowed his colleagues to develop and never allowed him to learn from them."

Ability—or inability—to understand other people's perspectives was the most glaring difference between the arrivers and the derailed. Only 25 percent of the derailed were described as having a special ability with people; among arrivers, the figure was 75 percent.

Interestingly, two of the arrivers were cold and asinine when younger, but somehow completely changed their style. "I have no idea how he did it," one executive said. "It was as if he went to bed one night and woke up a different person." In general, a certain awareness of self and willingness to change characterized the arrivers. That same flexibility, of course, is also what is needed to get along with all types of people.

A final word—a lesson, perhaps, to be drawn from our findings. Over the years, "experts" have generated long lists of critical skills in an attempt to define the complete manager. In retrospect it seems obvious that no one, the talented executive included, can possess all of those skills. As we came to realize, executives, like the rest of us, are a patchwork of strengths *and* weaknesses. The reasons that some executives ultimately derailed and others made it all the way up the ladder confirm what we all know but have hesitated to admit: There is no one best way to succeed (or even to fail). The foolproof, step-by-step formula is not just elusive; it is, as Kierkegaard said of truth, like searching a pitch-dark room for a black cat that isn't there.

QUESTIONS

1. Evaluate yourself. Do you possess the critical qualities of a top executive? Cite examples.

   _____

   _____

   _____

2. Consider someone who has held a high leadership position and then derailed. What were the reasons for the failure? Discuss.

   _____

   _____

   _____

How the Boss Stays in Touch
with the Troops

There was a time, not long after World War II, when "communication" was a major preoccupation of top executives everywhere. The need for good communication in business, which today seems almost too obvious to mention, was then an arresting new idea. It was one of a number of ideas whose origins lay in academic research, and whose rapid dissemination gave many executives the sense that management — i.e., what they did all day — was developing into a real science.

In more recent years, a lot of top executives have been discovering that communication is also an art. Today everyone understands clearly that information has to flow in both directions in a large hierarchical organization. And everyone understands that, just as some Harvard Business School professors demonstrated years ago in those famous experiments at Western Electric, employees want a sense of participation — a feeling that they are members of the team. . .

THE ONLY QUESTION IS HOW

Chief executives have, it happens, developed some effective techniques, or gimmicks, for staying in touch. These techniques enable them to extend their reach beyond the dozen or so top managers with whom they deal every day and with whom staying in touch is relatively easy. Inevitably, all this communicating takes up a certain amount of time — it involves an evening now and then, or setting aside a half hour during an already crowded day, or finding a few moments for a chat en route to and from the office. But many chief executives believe that the techniques have become an important part of the job. In addition to providing lower-level executives with that sense of participation, they work in two different ways to strengthen the bottom line.

First, they enable the chief executive to acquire information he mightn't otherwise get. They help him avoid the situation in which everyone but the boss knows that an explosion is coming. "I cannot over-emphasize the importance of getting out of your office and listening to

Source: *Herbert E. Meyer, "How the Boss Stays in Touch with the Troops,"*
Fortune 91 *(June 1975): 152–155. Research Associate: Wilton Woods. Reprinted by permission.*

what the employees are saying," says Richard M. Furlaud, chairman of Squibb Corp. "You listen for optimism, or you listen for a sense of pessimism which may be about something unreported to you. You listen for that quiet panic that can develop when some operation—or some individual—is not doing as well as the official reports would indicate."

Furlaud likes to keep his antennae beamed so as to pick up any changes in staff morale. He wants to be able to spot any decline in morale early, when there's time to get at the root of the problem before profits start to suffer. Why not wait for Squibb's formal reporting system to turn up the problem? Because, Furlaud says, it may take too long.

Chief executives' efforts to stay in touch support the bottom line in another way: by making sure that orders from the top are reaching the troops intact. Once again, Squibb's articulate Mr. Furlaud: "You want to be sure that your objectives are understood. The company has goals, and your objective is to meet those goals. But you don't want to do it by doing anything illegal or immoral. Top management should make sure that guys down the line know what the company's goals are."

DINING OUT ON THE ROAD

One chief executive who works hard and enthusiastically at talking with executives down the line is W. Michael Blumenthal, former professor of economics at Princeton, former Assistant Secretary of State, and now chairman of Bendix Corp. "You can't operate successfully in any organization if you're cut off from your people," says Blumenthal. "You've got to reach out toward them—out beyond the tight little group you work with daily—and let them know they can reach you when they feel they have to."

Blumenthal, who happens to be naturally ebullient and informal, has developed a variety of techniques for giving the troops at Bendix more access to the chief executive. Whenever he's in one of the hundred or so cities in which Bendix operates, Blumenthal makes certain to schedule lunches and dinners with divisional executives at all levels. "The conversations jump all over the place," he says. "One minute we're talking Bendix business, the next minute we're talking politics. Everybody learns."

LOOKING OVER THE OFFICE

When he's at company headquarters in Southfield, Michigan, Blumenthal works hard at staying in touch with lower-level executives. For example, when he writes a memorandum to someone in the same building, Blumenthal likes to deliver the memo himself. Usually, when he finds the recipient in his office, the chairman invites himself in for a chat. "It's a nice way to stay in touch," he explains cheerfully. "I like to see where a guy works—you know, what his desk looks like, and so on. It kind of rounds out my picture of the guy."

Blumenthal says that the actual content of the chat is apt to be of no great import on these occasions. Sometimes the conversation is quite unrelated to business; it may focus on the subordinate's personal life — e.g., his teenage son is just out of high school and trying to decide whether to start college or work for a year.

Sometimes, alternatively, the employee takes advantage of his few minutes with the chairman to tip him off to something that's going on in the company. "You'd be amazed how often I pick up information this way," says Blumenthal. "It's rarely anything earth-shattering. But it's often something I like to know about, something that gives me a feeling for what's going on. . . ."

The chairman of Pfizer Corp., Edmund T. Pratt Jr., has a different way of making off-hours contact. A lifelong tennis buff, Pratt noticed a few years ago that a number of Pfizer's other executives had also begun to play. So he rented time on one of Manhattan's indoor tennis courts, and invited company executives to use it during the reserved evening hours. A round-robin schedule was developed so that everyone, including Pratt, got to play with everyone else.

"Playing tennis with my people gives me a terrific opportunity to find out what's on their minds," Pratt says. "You'd be surprised at how much I learn. Changing in the locker room, or sitting around with the guys afterward, makes for a better atmosphere than the office. Besides, we all need the exercise."

Southland Corp. developed one effective way for the boss to communicate with his subordinates — though it wasn't really the boss's idea. When the executive vice president proposed that an executives' bar and lounge be opened on the top floor of the company's Dallas headquarters building, President Jere W. Thompson was against it at first. "I just didn't see the need for it," he recalls.

But the executive vice president kept pushing, and finally Thompson said to go ahead and build the thing. "It's great," he says now. "I'm a real strong believer in it. The lounge helps us get to know our people individually. Of course, you still have to balance your knowledge of the people against the usual reports of performance. But it gives us another view of the man. . . ."

A WORD WITH THE DESIGNER

Thompson's efforts to stay in touch with Southland's executives go beyond his biweekly foray into the company lounge. He also holds a two-hour, no-agenda staff meeting every other Monday morning to which about fifteen people are invited. Thompson believes these meetings provide a good forum for executives to say whatever is on their minds, about business in general, the company, or the work they're doing. It's also a good chance for everyone to gossip a little.

Meetings without agendas are also used by Richard B. Loynd, president of Eltra Corp., a New York-based producer of electrical products.

Once a month he calls together about fifteen members of the headquarters staff (there are about fifty in all), ranging in rank from vice presidents to junior members of the financial department; secretaries are also included. Out-of-town Eltra executives who happen to be in New York are also invited. Loynd rotates the participants so that everybody gets a chance to attend at least a few times a year.

Communicating with subordinates is an especially difficult task for an executive who has not been promoted from within the company, but who has been brought in from outside. When Anthony J.A. Bryan arrived in Houston to become president of Cameron Iron Works two years ago (after a twenty-five-year career with Monsanto), he worked hard at getting acquainted with the Cameron staff. He scheduled a series of breakfasts and lunches at a restaurant near the company's headquarters, and over a period of fifteen months ate and spoke with more than 2,000 of Cameron's 4,500 Houston employees—including line foremen, engineers, and secretaries, as well as top managers. He told them a little about himself, about his plans for Cameron, and about his personal style of operating. Then he answered questions.

A STRANGER IN THE NIGHT

During the same period, Bryan made constant forays out of his own office and down to Cameron's production areas. Employees say that it was not unusual for them to look up from their work, even during the late night shifts, to see a slim, bespectacled stranger in a dark suit and a hard hat waiting patiently for a chance to shake their hands. Once, before he had an opportunity to introduce himself, the stranger was ordered to leave a restricted area.

Bryan told all of Cameron's employees that their president was available whenever they wanted to speak with him. He meant it, which is fortunate, because many Cameron workers took him at his word. At least twice a week, nowadays, an employee comes up to Bryan's office for a chat with the boss. Sometimes the man has a problem that isn't being satisfactorily handled via the usual channels. Sometimes he has a suggestion to offer, and doesn't quite know whom he should be telling about it. Not long ago an employee came to Bryan with a proposal for a special metal clamp he thought would increase the durability of the safety shoes workers must wear.

Bryan believes the time he puts in talking with company employees is extremely useful. "If one man comes in here with a personal problem of some sort, it's a good bet we have some other people with the same problem. By getting involved in one case, I learn how well, or how poorly, our regular machinery is equipped to deal with it. And our employees get to feel that their ideas, their own contributions to the company's productivity, matter to management."

THE CHAIRMAN TAKES THE LOCAL

Many chief executives have a variety of techniques for exposing themselves, more or less randomly, to the troops. Robert T. Quittmeyer, president of Amstar, leaves about two lunch hours a week unscheduled. On those days he goes to the company cafeteria and sits down with any group of employees, executive or clerical, whose table has an empty chair. Fletcher Byrom, the chairman of Koppers Co., has made it a practice always to take the local elevator, rather than the express, to and from his fifteenth-floor office "on the chance that someone will want to say something to me when he sees me."

Chief executives do a lot of traveling, and many of them are keenly aware of the opportunities to get to know other executives on trips. Ian MacGregor, chairman of AMAX Inc., has a custom of taking along one or two junior executives when he travels on business. "Two days in a plane going to Johannesburg," says MacGregor, "and you get to know a man pretty well."

Obviously, it is possible for chief executives to "overcommunicate." There are situations in which a boss who thinks he's just being friendly can leave a subordinate feeling that he's being watched or that his privacy is being invaded. Still, the desire to be communicated with is a powerful one, and the greater risks for morale would appear to be on the side of seeming unfriendly.

And, of course, the boss learns a lot by being "friendly." "You must discipline yourself to do these things," says Anthony Bryan. "If not, your isolation increases. You may think you know what you're doing, but you don't test yourself sufficiently. That's dangerous."

QUESTIONS

1. What techniques have you seen leaders use to "stay in touch with the troops"?

   _____

   _____

   _____

2. If you were the boss, what techniques would you use to keep communication lines open?

   _____

   _____

   _____

The Manager's Job:
Folklore and Fact

If you ask a manager [Ramond Z. Browski, for instance] what he does, he will most likely tell you that he plans, organizes, coordinates, and controls. Then watch what he does. Don't be surprised if you can't relate what you see to these four words.

When he is called and told that one of his factories has just burned down, and he advises the caller to see whether temporary arrangements can be made to supply customers through a foreign subsidiary, is he planning, organizing, coordinating, or controlling? How about when he presents a gold watch to a retiring employee? Or when he attends a conference to meet people in the trade? Or on returning from that conference, when he tells one of his employees about an interesting product idea he picked up there?

The fact is that these four words, which have dominated management vocabulary since the French industrialist Henri Fayol first introduced them in 1916, tell us little about what managers actually do. At best, they indicate some vague objectives managers have when they work.

The field of management, so devoted to progress and change, has for more than half a century not seriously addressed *the* basic question: What do managers do? Without a proper answer, how can we teach management? How can we design planning or information systems for managers? How can we improve the practice of management at all?

Our ignorance of the nature of managerial work shows up in various ways in the modern organization — in the boast by the successful manager that he never spent a single day in a management training program; in the turnover of corporate planners who never quite understood what it was the manager wanted; in the computer consoles gathering dust in the back room because the managers never used the fancy on-line MIS some analyst thought they needed. Perhaps most important, our ignorance shows up in the inability of our large public organizations to come to grips with some of their most serious policy problems.

Somehow, in the rush to automate production, to use management science in the functional areas of marketing and finance, and to apply the skills of the behavioral scientist to the problem of worker motivation, the manager — that person in charge of the organization or one of its subunits — has been forgotten.

My intention in this article is simple: to break the reader away from Fayol's words and introduce a more supportable, and what I believe to be a more useful, description of managerial work. This description derives from my review and synthesis of the available research on how various managers have spent their time.

In some studies, managers were observed intensively ("shadowed" is the term some of them used); in a number of others, they kept detailed diaries of their activities; in a few studies, their records were analyzed. All kinds of managers were studied — foremen, factory supervisors, staff managers, field sales managers, hospital administrators, presidents of companies and nations, and even street gang leaders. These "managers" worked in the United States, Canada, Sweden, and Great Britain. The following is a brief review of the major studies that I found most useful in developing this description, including my own study of five American chief executive officers.

Research on Managerial Work

Considering its central importance to every aspect of management, there has been surprisingly little research on the manager's work, and virtually no systematic building of knowledge from one group of studies to another. In seeking to describe managerial work, I conducted my own research and also scanned the literature widely to integrate the findings of studies from many diverse sources with my own. These studies focused on two very different aspects of managerial work. Some were concerned with the characteristics of the work — how long managers work, where, at what pace and with what interruptions, with whom they work, and through what media they communicate. Other studies were more concerned with the essential content of the work — what activities the managers actually carry out, and why. Thus, after a meeting, one researcher might note that the manager spent 45 minutes with three government officials in their Washington office, while another might record that the company's stand was presented on some proposed legislation in order to change a regulation.

A few of the studies of managerial work are widely known, but most have remained buried as single journal articles or isolated books. Among the more important ones I cite (with full reference in the footnotes) are the following:

Sune Carlson developed the diary method to study the work characteristics of nine Swedish managing directors. Each kept a detailed log of activities. Carlson's results are reported in his book *Executive Behavior*. A number of British researchers, notably Rosemary Stewart, have subsequently used Carlson's method. In *Managers and Their Jobs*, she describes the study of 160 top and middle managers of British companies during four weeks, with particular attention to the differences in their work.

Leonard Sayles's book *Managerial Behavior* is another important reference. Using a method he refers to as "anthropological," Sayles studied the work content of middle- and lower-level managers in a large U.S.

corporation. Sayles moved freely in the company, collecting whatever information struck him as important.

Perhaps the best-known source is *Presidential Power*, in which Richard Neustadt analyzes the power and managerial behavior of Presidents Roosevelt, Truman, and Eisenhower. Neustadt used secondary sources—documents and interviews with other parties—to generate his data.

Robert H. Guest, in *Personnel*, reports on a study of the foreman's working day. Fifty-six U.S. foremen were observed and each of their activities recorded during one eight-hour shift.

Richard C. Hodgson, Daniel J. Levinson, and Abraham Zaleznik studied a team of three top executives of a U.S. hospital. From that study they wrote *The Executive Role Constellation*. These researchers addressed in particular the way in which work and socioemotional roles were divided among the three managers.

William F. Whyte, from his study of a street gang during the Depression, wrote *Street Corner Society*. His findings about the gang's leadership, which George C. Homans analyzed in *The Human Group*, suggest some interesting similarities of job content between street gang leaders and corporate managers.

My own study involved five American CEOs of middle- to large-sized organizations—a consulting firm, a technology company, a hospital, a consumer goods company, and a school system. Using a method called "structural observation," during one intensive week of observation for each executive I recorded various aspects of every piece of mail and every verbal contact. My method was designed to capture data on both work characteristics and job content. In all, I analyzed 890 pieces of incoming and outgoing mail and 368 verbal contacts.

A synthesis of these findings paints an interesting picture, one as different from Fayol's classical view as a cubist abstract is from a Renaissance painting. In a sense, this picture will be obvious to anyone who has ever spent a day in a manager's office, either in front of the desk or behind it. Yet, at the same time, this picture may turn out to be revolutionary, in that it throws into doubt so much of the folklore that we have accepted about the manager's work.

I first discuss some of this folklore and contrast it with some of the discoveries of systematic research—the hard facts about how managers spend their time. Then I synthesize these research findings in a description of ten roles that seem to describe the essential content of all managers' jobs. In a concluding section, I discuss a number of implications of this synthesis for those trying to achieve more effective management, both in classrooms and in the business world.

SOME FOLKLORE AND FACTS ABOUT MANAGERIAL WORK

There are four myths about the manager's job that do not bear up under careful scrutiny of the facts.

1. *Folklore: The manager is a reflective, systematic planner.* The evidence on this issue is overwhelming, but not a shred of it supports this statement.

Fact: Study after study has shown that managers work at an unrelenting pace, that their activities are characterized by brevity, variety, and discontinuity, and that they are strongly oriented to action and dislike reflective activities. Consider this evidence:

Half the activities engaged in by the five chief executives of my study lasted less than nine minutes, and only 10% exceeded one hour.[1] A study of 56 U.S. foremen found that they averaged 583 activities per eight-hour shift, an average of 1 every 48 seconds.[2] The work pace for both chief executives and foremen was unrelenting. The chief executives met a steady stream of callers and mail from the moment they arrived in the morning until they left in the evening. Coffee breaks and lunches were inevitably work related, and ever-present subordinates seemed to usurp any free moment.

A diary study of 160 British middle and top managers found that they worked for a half hour or more without interruption only about once every two days.[3]

Of the verbal contacts of the chief executives in my study, 93% were arranged on an ad hoc basis. Only 1% of the executives' time was spent in open-ended observational tours. Only 1 out of 368 verbal contacts was unrelated to a specific issue and could be called general planning. Another researcher finds that "in *not one single case* did a manager report the obtaining of important external information from a general conversation or other undirected personal communication."[4]

No study has found important patterns in the way managers schedule their time. They seem to jump from issue to issue, continually responding to the needs of the moment.

Is this the planner that the classical view describes? Hardly. How, then, can we explain this behavior? The manager is simply responding to the pressures of his job. I found that my chief executives terminated many of their own activities, often leaving meetings before the end, and interrupted their desk work to call in subordinates. One president not only placed his desk so that he could look down a long hallway but also left his door open when he was alone — an invitation for subordinates to come in and interrupt him.

Clearly, these managers wanted to encourage the flow of current information. But more significantly, they seemed to be conditioned by their own work loads. They appreciated the opportunity cost of their own time, and they were continually aware of their ever-present obligations — mail to be answered, callers to attend to, and so on. It seems that no matter what is being done, the manager is plagued by the possibilities of what might be done and what must be done.

When it is necessary to plan, the manager seems to do so implicitly in the context of daily actions, not in some abstract process reserved for two weeks in the organization's mountain retreat. The plans of the chief executives I studied seemed to exist only in their heads — as flexible, but often specific, intentions. The traditional literature notwithstanding, the job of managing does not breed reflective planners; the manager is a real-time responder to stimuli, an individual who is conditioned by the job to prefer live to delayed action.

2. *Folklore: The effective manager has no regular duties to perform.* Managers are constantly being told to spend more time planning and delegating, and less time seeing customers and engaging in negotiations. These are not, after all, the true tasks of the manager. To use the popular analogy, the good manager, like the good conductor, carefully orchestrates everything in advance, then sits back to enjoy the fruits of the labor, responding occasionally to an unforeseeable exception.

But here again the pleasant abstraction just does not seem to hold up. We had better take a closer look at those activities managers feel compelled to engage in before we arbitrarily define them away.

Fact: In addition to handling exceptions, managerial work involves performing a number of regular duties, including ritual and ceremony, negotiations, and processing of soft information that links the organization with its environment. Consider some evidence from the research studies:

A study of the work of the presidents of small companies found that they engaged in routine activities because their companies could not afford staff specialists and were so thin on operating personnel that a single absence often required the president to substitute.[5]

One study of field sales managers and another of chief executives suggest that it is a natural part of both jobs to see important customers, assuming the managers wish to keep those customers.[6]

Someone, only half in jest, once described the manager as that person who sees visitors so that everyone else can get their work done. In my study, I found that certain ceremonial duties — meeting visiting dignitaries, giving out gold watches, presiding at Christmas dinners — were an intrinsic part of the chief executive's job.

Studies of managers' information flow suggest that managers play a key role in securing "soft" external information (much of it available only to them because of their status) and in passing it along to their subordinates.

3. *Folklore: The senior manager needs aggregated information, which a formal management information system best provides.* Not too long ago, the words *total information system* were everywhere in the management literature. In keeping with the classical view of the manager as that individual perched on the apex of a regulated, hierarchical system, the literature's manager was to receive all important information from a giant, comprehensive MIS.

But lately, as it has become increasingly evident that these giant MIS systems are not working — that managers are simply not using them — the enthusiasm has waned. A look at how managers actually process information makes the reason quite clear. Managers have five media at their command — documents, telephone calls, scheduled and unscheduled meetings, and observational tours.

Fact: Managers strongly favor the verbal media — namely telephone calls and meetings. The evidence comes from every single study of managerial work. Consider the following:

In two British studies, managers spent an average of 66% and 80% of their time in verbal (oral) communication.[7] In my study of five American chief executives, the figure was 78%.

These five chief executives treated mail processing as a burden to be dispensed with. One came in Saturday morning to process 142 pieces of mail in just over three hours, to "get rid of all the stuff." This same manager looked at the first piece of "hard" mail he had received all week, a standard cost report, and put it aside with the comment, "I never look at this."

These same five chief executives responded immediately to 2 of the 40 routine reports they received during the five weeks of my study and to 4 items in the 104 periodicals. They skimmed most of these periodicals in seconds, almost ritualistically. In all, these chief executives of good-sized organizations initiated on their own — that is, not in response to something else — a grand total of 25 pieces of mail during the 25 days I observed them.

An analysis of the mail the executives received reveals an interesting picture — only 13% was of specific and immediate use. So now we have another piece in the puzzle: not much of the mail provides live, current information — the action of a competitor, the mood of a government legislator, or the rating of last night's television show. Yet this is the information that drove the managers, interrupting their meetings and rescheduling their workdays.

Consider another interesting finding. Managers seem to cherish "soft" information, especially gossip, hearsay, and speculation. Why? The reason is its timeliness; today's gossip may be tomorrow's fact. The manager who is not accessible for the telephone call telling about the fact that the company's biggest customer was seen golfing with the main competitor may read about a dramatic drop in sales in the next quarterly report. But then it's too late.

To assess the value of historical, aggregated, "hard" MIS information, consider two of the manager's prime uses for such information — to identify problems and opportunities[8] and to build one's own mental models of the things close around (e.g., how the organization's budget system works, how the customers buy the company's product, how changes in the economy affect the organization, and so on). Every bit of evidence suggests that the manager identifies decision situations and builds models, not with the aggregated abstractions an MIS provides, but with specific tidbits of data.

Consider the words of Richard Neustadt, who studied the information-collecting habits of Presidents Roosevelt, Truman, and Eisenhower:

> It is not information of a general sort that helps a President see personal stakes; not summaries, not surveys, not the *bland amalgams*. Rather . . . it is the odds and ends of *tangible detail* that pieced together in his mind illuminate the underside of issues put before him. To help himself he must reach out as widely as he can for every scrap of fact,

opinion, gossip, bearing on his interests and relationships as President. He must become his own director of his own central intelligence.[9]

The manager's emphasis on the verbal media raises two important points:

First, verbal information is stored in the brains of people. Only when people write this information down can it be stored in the files of the organization—whether in metal cabinets or on magnetic tape—and managers apparently do not write down much of what they hear. Thus the strategic data bank of the organization is not in the memory of its computers but in the minds of its managers.

Second, the manager's extensive use of verbal media helps to explain why the reluctance to delegate tasks. When we note that most of the manager's important information comes in verbal form and is stored only in the mind, we can well appreciate this reluctance. It is not as if the manager can hand a dossier over to someone; the manager must take the time to "dump memory"—to tell that someone everything known about the subject. But this could take so long that the manager may find it easier to do the task alone. Thus the manager is damned by a personal information system to a "dilemma of delegation"—to do too much one's self or to delegate to subordinates without adequate briefing.

4. *Folklore: Management is, or at least is quickly becoming a science and a profession.* By almost any definition of *science* and *profession*, this statement is false. Brief observation of any manager will quickly lay to rest the notion that managers practice a science. A science involves the enaction of systematic, analytically determined procedures or programs. If we do not even know what procedures managers use, how can we prescribe them by scientific analysis? And how can we call management a profession if we cannot specify what managers are to learn? For after all, a profession involves "knowledge of some department of learning or science" (*Random House Dictionary*).[10]

Fact: The managers' programs—to schedule time, process information, make decisions, and so on—remain locked deep inside their brains. Thus, to describe these programs, we rely on words like *judgment* and *intuition*, seldom stopping to realize that they are merely labels for our ignorance.

I was struck during my study by the fact that the executives I was observing—all very competent by any standard—are fundamentally indistinguishable from their counterparts of a hundred years ago (or a thousand years ago, for that matter). The information they need differs, but they seek it in the same way—by word of mouth. Their decisions concern modern technology, but the procedures they use to make them are the same as the procedures of the nineteenth-century manager. Even the computer, so important for the specialized work of the organization, has apparently had no influence on the work procedures of general managers. In fact, the manager is in a kind of loop, with increasingly heavy work pressures but no aid forthcoming from management science.

Considering the facts about managerial work, we can see that the manager's job is enormously complicated and difficult. The manager is overburdened with obligations; yet cannot easily delegate tasks. As a result, the manager is driven to overwork and is forced to do many tasks superficially. Brevity, fragmentation, and verbal communication characterize the work. Yet these are the very characteristics of managerial work that have impeded scientific attempts to improve it. As a result, the management scientist has concentrated efforts on the specialized functions of the organization, where the procedures could be easily analyzed and the relevant information quantified.[11]

But the pressures of the manager's job are becoming worse. Where before the manager needed only to respond to owners and directors, now the manager finds that subordinates with democratic norms continually reduce this freedom to issue unexplained orders, and a growing number of outside influences (consumer groups, government agencies, and so on) expect full attention. And the manager has had nowhere to turn for help. The first step in providing the manager with some help is to find out what the manager's job really is.

BACK TO A BASIC DESCRIPTION OF MANAGERIAL WORK

Now let us try to put some of the pieces of this puzzle together. Earlier, I defined the manager as that person in charge of an organization or one of its subunits. Besides chief executive officers, this definition would include vice presidents, bishops, foremen, hockey coaches, and prime ministers. Can all of these people have anything in common? Indeed they can. For an important starting point, all are vested with formal authority over an organizational unit. From formal authority comes status, which leads to various interpersonal relations, and from these comes access to information. Information, in turn, enables the manager to make decisions and strategies.

The manager's job can be described in terms of various "roles," or organized sets of behaviors identified with a position. My description, shown in Figure 1, comprises ten roles. As we shall see, formal authority gives rise to the three interpersonal roles, which in turn give rise to the three informational roles; these two sets of roles enable the manager to play the four decisional roles.

Interpersonal Roles

Three of the manager's roles arise directly from formal authority and involve basic interpersonal relationships.

1. First is the *figurehead* role. By virtue of the manager's position as head of an organizational unit, every manager must perform some duties of a ceremonial nature. The president greets the touring dignitaries, the supervisor attends the wedding of a lathe operator, and the sales manager takes an important customer to lunch.

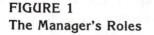

FIGURE 1
The Manager's Roles

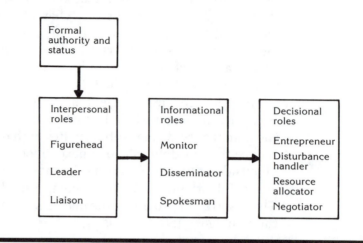

The chief executives of my study spent 12% of their contact time on ceremonial duties; 17% of their incoming mail dealt with acknowledgments and requests related to their status. For example, a letter to a company president requested free merchandise for a crippled schoolchild; diplomas were put on the desk of the school superintendent to be signed.

Duties that involve interpersonal roles may sometimes be routine, involving little serious communication and no important decision making. Nevertheless, they are important to the smooth functioning of an organization and cannot be ignored by the manager.

2. Being in charge of an organizational unit, the manager is responsible for the work of the people of that unit. Any actions in this regard constitute the *leader* role. Some of these actions involve leadership directly—for example, in most organizations the manager is normally responsible for hiring and training staff members.

In addition, there is the indirect exercise of the leader role. Every manager must motivate and encourage company employees, somehow reconciling their individual needs with the goals of the organization. In virtually every contact the manager has with employees, subordinates seeking leadership clues probe the actions: "Does the manager approve?" "How would the manager like the report to turn out?" "Is the manager interested in market share more than high profits?"

The influence of the manager is most clearly seen in the leader role. Formal authority vests the manager with great potential power; leadership determines in large part how much of it will be realized.

3. The literature of management has always recognized the leader role, particularly those aspects of it related to motivation. In comparison, until recently it has hardly mentioned the *liaison* role, in which the manager makes contacts outside the vertical chain of command. This is

remarkable in light of the finding of virtually every study of managerial work that managers spend as much time with peers and other people outside their units as they do with their own subordinates — and, surprisingly, very little time with their own superiors.

In Rosemary Stewart's diary study, the 160 British middle and top managers spent 47% of their time with peers, 41% of their time with people outside their unit, and only 12% of their time with their superiors. For Robert H. Guest's study of U.S. foremen, the figures were 44%, 46%, and 10%. The chief executives of my study averaged 44% of their contact time with people outside their organizations, 48% with subordinates, and 7% with directors and trustees.

The contacts the five CEOs made were with an incredibly wide range of people: subordinates; clients, business associates, and suppliers; and peers — managers of similar organizations, government and trade organization officials, directors on outside boards, and independents with no relevant organizational affiliations. The chief executives' time with and mail from these groups is shown in Figure 2. Guest's study of supervisors shows, likewise, that their contacts were numerous and wide ranging, seldom involving fewer than 25 individuals, and often more than 50.

As we shall see shortly, the manager cultivates such contacts largely to find information. In effect, the liaison role is devoted to building up the manager's own external information system — informal, private, verbal, but, nevertheless, effective.

Informational Roles

By virtue of the manager's interpersonal contacts, both with subordinates and with the network of contacts, the manager emerges as the nerve center of the organizational unit. The manager may not know everything, but most often the manager knows more than any staff member.

Studies have shown this relationship to hold for all managers, from street gang leaders to U.S. presidents. In *The Human Group*, George C. Homans explains how, because they were at the center of the information flow in their own gangs and were also in close touch with other gang leaders, street gang leaders were better informed than any of their followers.[12] And Richard Neustadt describes the following account from his study of Franklin D. Roosevelt:

> The essence of Roosevelt's technique for information-gathering was competition. "He would call you in," one of his aides once told me, "and he'd ask you to get the story on some complicated business, and you'd come back after a couple of days of hard labor and present the juicy morsel you'd uncovered under a stone somewhere, and *then* you'd find out he knew all about it, along with something else you *didn't* know. Where he got this information from he wouldn't mention, usually, but after he had done this to you once or twice you got damn careful about *your* information."[13]

You can see where Roosevelt "got this information" when you consider the relationship between the interpersonal and informational roles.

FIGURE 2

The Chief Executives' Contacts

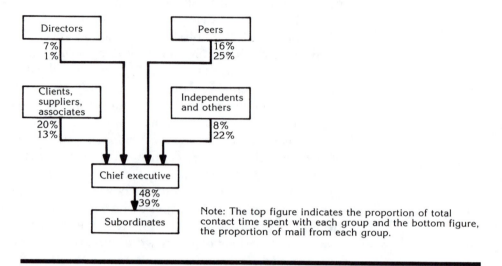

Note: The top figure indicates the proportion of total contact time spent with each group and the bottom figure, the proportion of mail from each group.

As leader, the manager has formal and easy access to every member of the staff. Hence, as noted earlier, the manager tends to know more about the unit than anyone else does. In addition, the liaison contacts expose the manager to external information to which the subordinates often lack access. Many of these contacts are with other managers of equal status, who are themselves nerve centers in their own organization. In this way, the manager develops a powerful data base of information.

The processing of information is a key part of the manager's job. In my study, the chief executives spent 40% of their contact time on activities devoted exclusively to the transmission of information; 70% of their incoming mail was purely informational (as opposed to requests for action). The manager does not leave meetings or hang up the telephone in order to get back to work. In large part, communication *is* the work. Three roles describe these informational aspects of managerial work.

1. As *monitor*, the manager perpetually scans the environment for information, interrogates liaison contacts and the subordinates, and receives unsolicited information, much of it as a result of the network of personally developed contacts. Remember that a good part of the information the manager collects in the monitor role arrives in verbal form, often as gossip, hearsay, and speculation. By virtue of his contacts, the manager has a natural advantage in collecting this soft information for the organization.

2. As a *disseminator*, the manager passes some privileged information directly to subordinates, who would otherwise have no access to it. The manager must share and distribute much of this information. Information gleaned from outside personal contacts may be needed within the organization. When subordinates lack easy contact with one another, the manager will sometimes pass information from one to another.

3. In the roll of *spokesperson*, the manager sends some information to people outside the unit — a president makes a speech to lobby for an organization cause, or a foreman suggests a product modification to a supplier. In addition, as part of the spokesperson roll, every manager must inform and satisfy the influential people who control the organizational unit. For the supervisor this may simply involve keeping the plant manager informed about the flow of work through the shop.

The president of a large corporation, however, may spend a great amount of time dealing with a host of influences. Directors and shareholders must be advised about financial performance; consumer groups must be assured that the organization is fulfilling its social responsibilities; and government officials must be satisfied that the organization is abiding by the law.

Decisional Roles

Information is not, of course, an end in itself; it is the basic input to decision making. One thing is clear in the study of managerial work: the manager plays the major role in the unit's decision-making system. As its formal authority, only the manager can commit the unit to important new courses of action; and as its nerve center, only the manager has full and current information to make the set of decisions that determines the unit's strategy. Four roles describe the manager as decision-maker.

1. As *entrepreneur* the manager seeks to improve the personal unit, to adapt it to changing conditions in the environment. In the monitor role, the president is constantly on the lookout for new ideas. When a good one appears, the manager initiates a development project for the supervisor or delegates to an employee (perhaps with the stipulation that the manager must approve the final proposal).

There are two interesting features about these development projects at the chief executive level. First, these projects do not involve single decisions or even unified clusters of decisions. Rather, they emerge as a series of small decisions and actions sequenced over time. Apparently, the chief executive prolongs each project so that it can fit into a busy, disjointed schedule, and so that the manager can gradually come to comprehend the issue, if it is a complex one.

Second, the chief executives I studied supervised as many as 50 of these projects at the same time. Some projects entailed new products or processes; others involved public relations campaigns, improvement of the cash position, reorganization of a weak department, resolution of a morale problem in a foreign division, integration of computer operations, various acquisitions at different stages of development, and so on.

The chief executive appears to maintain a kind of inventory of the development projects that are supervised — projects that are at various stages of development, some active and some in limbo. Like a juggler, the executive keeps a number of projects in the air; periodically, one comes down, is given a new burst of energy, and is sent back into orbit. At various intervals, new projects are put on-stream and old ones discarded.

2. The *disturbance-handler* role depicts the manager involuntarily responding to pressures. Here change is beyond the manager's control. Action must be taken because the pressures of the situation are too severe to be ignored: strike looms, a major customer has gone bankrupt, or a supplier reneges on a contract.

It has been fashionable, I noted earlier, to compare the manager to an orchestra conductor, just as Peter F. Drucker wrote in *The Practice of Management:*

> The manager has the task of creating a true whole that is larger than the sum of its parts, a productive entity that turns out more than the sum of the resources put into it. One analogy is the conductor of a symphony orchestra, through whose effort, vision, and leadership individual instrumental parts that are so much noise by themselves become the living whole of music. But the conductor has the composer's score and is only interpreter. The manager is both composer and conductor.[14]

Now consider the words of Leonard R. Sayles, who has carried out systematic research on the manager's job:

> The manager is like a symphony orchestra conductor, endeavoring to maintain a melodious performance in which the contributions of the various instruments are coordinated and sequenced, patterned and paced, while the orchestra members are having various personal difficulties, stage hands are moving music stands, alternating excessive heat and cold are creating audience and instrument problems, and the sponsor of the concert is insisting on irrational changes in the program.[15]

In effect, every manager must spend a good block of time responding to high-pressure disturbances. No organization can be so well run, so standardized, that it has considered every contingency in the uncertain environment in advance. Disturbances arise not only because poor managers ignore situations until they reach crisis proportions, but also because good managers cannot possibly anticipate all the consequences of the actions they take.

3. The *resource allocator* is the third decisional role. To the manager falls the responsibility of deciding who will get what in the personal organizational unit. Perhaps the most important resource the manager allocates is personal time. Access to the manager constitutes exposure to the unit's nerve center and decision maker. The manager is also charged with designing the unit's structure, that pattern of formal relationships that determines how work is to be divided and coordinated.

Also, in the role as resource allocator, the manager authorizes the important decisions of the unit before they are implemented. By retaining this power, the manager can ensure that decisions are interrelated; all must pass through a single brain. To fragment this power is to encourage discontinuous decision making and a disjointed strategy.

There are a number of interesting features about the manager's authorizing others' decisions. First, despite the widespread use of capital budgeting procedures—a means of authorizing various capital expenditures at one time—executives in my study made a great many authorization decisions on an ad hoc basis. Apparently, many projects cannot wait or simply do not have the quantifiable costs and benefits that capital budgeting requires.

Second, I found that the chief executives faced incredibly complex choices. They had to consider the impact of each decision on other decisions and on the organization's strategy. They had to ensure that the decision would be acceptable to those who influence the organization, as well as ensure that resources would not be overextended. They had to understand the various costs and benefits as well as the feasibility of the proposal. They also had to consider questions of timing. All of this was necessary for the simple approval of someone else's proposal. At the same time, however, delay could lose time, while quick approval could be ill considered and quick rejection might discourage the subordinate who had spent months developing a pet project.

One common solution to approving projects is to pick the man instead of the proposal. That is, the manager authorizes those projects presented by people whose judgment is trusted. However, this simple dodge can not always be used.

4. The *negotiator* is the final decisional role. Studies of managerial work at all levels indicate that managers spend considerable time in negotiations: the president of the football team is called in to work out a contract with the holdout superstar; the corporation president leads the company's contingent to negotiate a new strike issue; the supervisor argues a grievance problem to its conclusion with the shop steward. As Leonard Sayles puts it, negotiations are a "way of life" for the sophisticated manager.

These negotiations are duties of the manager's job; perhaps routine, they are not to be shirked. They are an integral part of the job, for only the manager has the authority to commit organizational resources in "real time," and only the manager has the nerve center information that important negotiations require.

The Integrated Job

It should be clear by now that the ten roles I have been describing are not easily separable. In the terminology of the psychologist, they form a gestalt, an integrated whole. No role can be pulled out of the framework and the job be left intact. For example, a manager without liaison contacts lacks external information. As a result, a manager can neither disseminate the information employees need nor make decisions that adequately reflect external conditions. (In fact, this is a problem for the new person in a managerial position, since effective decisions cannot be made until a network of contacts has been built up.)

Here lies a clue to the problems of team management.[16] Two or three people cannot share a single managerial position unless they can act as one entity. This means that they cannot divide up the ten roles unless they can very carefully reintegrate them. The real difficulty lies with the informational roles. Unless there can be full sharing of managerial information — and, as I pointed out earlier, it is primarily verbal — team management breaks down. A single managerial job cannot be arbitrarily split, for example, into internal and external roles, for information from both sources must be brought to bear on the same decisions.

To say that the ten roles form a gestalt is not to say that all managers give equal attention to each role. In fact, I found in my review of the various research studies that:

- Sales managers seem to spend relatively more of their time in the interpersonal roles, presumably a reflection of the extrovert nature of the marketing activity;

- Production managers give relatively more attention to the decisional roles, presumably a reflection of their concern with efficient work flow;

- Staff managers spend the most time in the informational roles, since they are experts who manage departments that advise other parts of the organization.

Nevertheless, in all cases the interpersonal, informational, and decisional roles remain inseparable.

TOWARD MORE EFFECTIVE MANAGEMENT

What are the messages for management in this description? I believe, first and foremost, that this description of managerial work should prove more important to managers than any prescription they might derive from it. That is to say, *the manager's effectiveness is significantly influenced by personal insight into the work*. The manager's performance depends on how well the pressures and dilemmas of the job are understood. Thus managers who can be introspective about their work are likely to be effective at their jobs.

1. *The manager is challenged to find systematic ways to share privileged information*. A regular debriefing session with key subordinates, a weekly memory dump on the dictating machine, the maintaining of a diary of important information for limited circulation, or other similar methods may ease the logjam of work considerably. Time spent disseminating this information will be more than regained when decisions must be made. Of course, some will raise the question of confidentiality. But managers would do well to weigh the risks of exposing privileged information against having subordinates who can make effective decisions.

If there is a single theme that runs through this article, it is that the pressures of the job drive the manager to be superficial in actions — to overload with work, encourage interruption, respond quickly to every stimulus, seek the tangible and avoid the abstract, make decisions in small increments, and do everything abruptly.

2. *Here again, the manager is challenged to deal consciously with the pressures of superficiality by giving serious attention to the issues that require it, by stepping back from tangible bits of information in order to see a broad picture, and by making use of analytical inputs.* Although effective managers have to be adept at responding quickly to numerous and varying problems, the danger in managerial work is that they will respond to every issue equally (and that means abruptly) and that they will never work the tangible bits and pieces of informational input into a comprehensive picture of their world.

As I noted earlier, the manager uses these bits of information to build models of her or his world. But the manager can also use the models of the specialists. Economists describe the functioning of markets, operations researchers simulate financial flow processes, and behavioral scientists explain the needs and goals of people. The best of these models can be searched out and learned.

In dealing with complex issues, the senior manager has much to gain from a close relationship with the management scientists of a personal organization. Only they have time to probe complex issues. An effective working relationship hinges on the resolution of what a colleague and I have called "the planning dilemma."[17] Managers have the information and the authority; analysts have the time and the technology. A successful working relationship between the two will be effected when the manager learns to share information and the analyst learns to adapt to the manager's needs. For the analyst, adaptation means worrying less about the elegance of the method and more about its speed and flexibility.

It seems to me that analysts can help the top manager especially to schedule time, feed in analytical information, monitor assigned projects, develop models to aid in making choices, design contingency plans for disturbances that can be anticipated, and conduct "quick-and-dirty" analysis for those that cannot. But there can be no cooperation if the analysts are out of the mainstream of the manager's information flow.

3. *The manager is challenged to gain control of personal time by turning obligations into advantages and by turning personal wishes into obligations.* The chief executives of my study initiated only 32% of their own contacts (and another 5% by mutual agreement). And yet to a considerable extent they seem to control their time. There were two key factors that enabled them to do so.

First, the unsuccessful manager blames failure on the obligations; the effective manager turns obligations to advantages. A speech is a chance to lobby for a cause; a meeting is a chance to reorganize a weak department; a visit to an important customer is a chance to extract trade information.

Second, the manager frees some time to do those things that perhaps no one else thinks are important by turning them into obligations. Free time is made, not found, in the manager's job; it is forced into the schedule. Hoping to leave some time open for contemplation or general planning is tantamount to hoping that the pressures of the job will go away. The manager who wants to innovate, initiates a project and obligates others to report back; the manager who needs certain environmental information establishes channels that will automatically keep him or her informed; the manager who has to tour facilities commits herself or himself publicly.

THE EDUCATOR'S JOB

Finally, a word about the training of managers. Our management schools have done an admirable job of training the organization's specialists—management scientists, marketing researchers, accountants, and organizational development specialists. But for the most part they have not trained managers.[18]

Management schools will begin the serious training of managers when skill training takes a serious place next to cognitive learning. Cognitive learning is detached and informational, like reading a book or listening to a lecture. No doubt much important cognitive material must be assimilated by the manager-to-be. But cognitive learning no more makes managers than it does swimmers. The latter will drown the first time they jump into the water if their coaches never take them out of the lecture hall, get them wet, and give them feedback on their performance.

In other words, we are taught a skill through practice plus feedback, whether in a real or a simulated situation. Our management schools need to identify the skills managers use, select students who show potential in these skills, put the students into situations where these skills can be practiced, and then give them systematic feedback on their performance.

My description of managerial work suggests a number of important managerial skills—developing peer relationships, carrying out negotiations, motivating subordinates, resolving conflicts, establishing information networks and subsequently disseminating information, making decisions in conditions of extreme ambiguity, and allocating resources. Above all, managers need to be introspective about their work so that they may continue to learn on their jobs.

Many of the manager's skills can, in fact, be practiced, using techniques that range from role playing to videotaping real meetings. And our management schools can enhance the entrepreneurial skills by designing programs that encourage sensible risk taking and innovation.

No job is more vital to our society than that of the manager. It is the manager who determines whether our social institutions serve us well or whether they squander our talents and resources. It is time to strip away the folklore about managerial work, and time to study it realistically so that we can begin the difficult task of making significant improvements in its performance.

REFERENCE NOTES

1   All the data from my study can be found in Henry Mintzberg, *The Nature of Managerial Work* (New York: Harper & Row, 1973).

2   Robert H. Guest, "Of Time and the Foreman," *Personnel*, May 1956, p. 478.

3   Rosemary Stewart, *Managers and Their Jobs* (London: Macmillan, 1967); see also Sune Carlson, *Executive Behavior* (Stockholm: Strömbergs, 1951), the first of the diary studies.

4   Francis J. Aguilar, *Scanning the Business Environment* (New York: Macmillan, 1967), p. 102.

5   Unpublished study by Irving Choran, reported in Mintzberg, *The Nature of Managerial Work*.

6   Robert T. Davis, *Performance and Development of Field Sales Managers* (Boston: Division of Research, Harvard Business School, 1957); George H. Copeman, *The Role of the Managing Director* (London: Business Publications, 1963).

7   Stewart, *Managers and Their Jobs;* Tom Burns, "The Directions of Activity and Communication in a Departmental Executive Group," *Human Relations* 7, no. 1 (1954): 73.

8   H. Edward Wrapp, "Good Managers Don't Make Policy Decisions," HBR September-October 1967, p. 91; Wrapp refers to this as spotting opportunities and relationships in the stream of operating problems and decisions; in his article Wrapp raises a number of excellent points related to this analysis.

9   Richard E. Neustadt, *Presidential Power* (New York: John Wiley, 1960), pp. 153–154; italics added.

10   For a more thorough, though rather different, discussion of this issue, see Kenneth R. Andrews, "Toward Professionalism in Business Management," HBR March-April 1969, p. 49.

11   C. Jackson Grayson, Jr., in "Management Science and Business Practice," HBR July-August 1973, p. 41, explains in similar terms why, as chairman of the Price Commission, he did not use those very techniques that he himself promoted in his earlier career as a management scientist.

12   George C. Homans, *The Human Group* (New York: Harcourt, Brace & World, 1950), based on the study by William F. Whyte entitled *Street Corner Society*, rev. ed. (Chicago: University of Chicago Press, 1955).

13   Neustadt, *Presidential Power*, p. 157.

14   Peter F. Drucker, *The Practice of Management* (New York: Harper & Row, 1954), pp. 341–342.

15   Leonard R. Sayles, *Managerial Behavior* (New York: McGraw-Hill, 1964), p. 162.

16   See Richard C. Hodgson, Daniel J. Levinson, and Abraham Zaleznik, *The Executive Role Constellation* (Boston: Division of Research,

Harvard Business School, 1965), for a discussion of the sharing of roles.

17 James S. Hekimian and Henry Mintzberg, "The Planning Dilemma," *The Management Review*, May 1968, p. 4.

18 See J. Sterling Livingston, "Myth of the Well-Educated Manager," HBR January-February 1971, p. 79.

QUESTIONS

1. How would you define a manager's job?

   _____

   _____

   _____

2. What knowledge, likes, and attitudes should a person have to perform the job of manager?

   _____

   _____

   _____

3. Would you ever want to be a manager? Explain.

   _____

   _____

   _____

4. Do you think certain people are cut out for leadership and others are not? Explain.

   _____

   _____

   _____

Pygmalion in Management

In George Bernard Shaw's *Pygmalion*, Eliza Doolittle explains:
"You see, really and truly, apart from the things anyone can pick up (the dressing and the proper way of speaking, and so on), the difference between a lady and a flower girl is not how she behaves, but how she's treated. I shall always be a flower girl to Professor Higgins, because he always treats me as a flower girl, and always will; but I know I can be a lady to you, because you always treat me as a lady, and always will."

Some managers always treat their subordinates in a way that leads to superior performance. But most managers, like Professor Higgins, unintentionally treat their subordinates in a way that leads to lower performance than they are capable of achieving. The way managers treat their subordinates is subtly influenced by what they expect of them. If a manager's expectations are high, productivity is likely to be excellent. If his expectations are low, productivity is likely to be poor. It is as though there were a law that caused a subordinate's performance to rise or fall to meet his manager's expectations.

The powerful influence of one person's expectations on another's behavior has long been recognized by physicians and behavioral scientists and, more recently, by teachers. But heretofore the importance of managerial expectations for individual and group performance has not been widely understood. I have documented this phenomenon in a number of case studies prepared during the past decade for major industrial concerns. These cases and other evidence available from scientific research now reveal:

- What a manager expects of his subordinates and the way he treats them largely determine their performance and career progress.

- A unique characteristic of superior managers is their ability to create high performance expectations that subordinates fulfill.

- Less effective managers fail to develop similar expectations, and, as a consequence, the productivity of their subordinates suffers.

Source: Reprinted by permission of the Harvard Business Review. *"Pygmalion in Management" by J. Sterling Livingston (July/August 1969). Copyright © 1969 by the President and Fellows of Harvard College; all rights reserved.*

- Subordinates, more often than not, appear to do what they believe they are expected to do.

IMPACT ON PRODUCTIVITY

One of the most comprehensive illustrations of the effect of managerial expectations on productivity is recorded in studies of the organizational experiment undertaken in 1961 by Alfred Oberlander, manager of the Rockaway District Office of the Metropolitan Life Insurance Company.[1] He had observed that outstanding insurance agencies grew faster than average or poor agencies and that new insurance agents performed better in outstanding agencies than in average or poor agencies, regardless of their sales aptitude. He decided, therefore, to group his superior men in one unit to stimulate their performance and to provide a challenging environment in which to introduce new salesmen.

Accordingly, Oberlander assigned his six best agents to work with his best assistant manager, an equal number of average producers to work with an average assistant manager, and the remaining low producers to work with the least able manager. He then asked the superior group to produce two thirds of the premium volume achieved by the entire agency the previous year. He described the results as follows:

> Shortly after this selection had been made, the men in the agency began referring to this select group as a "super-staff" since, due to the fact that we were operating this group as a unit, their esprit de corps was very high. Their production efforts over the first 12 weeks far surpassed our most optimistic expectations . . . proving that groups of men of sound ability can be motivated beyond their apparently normal productive capacities when the problems created by the poor producer are eliminated from the operation.
>
> Thanks to this fine result, over-all agency performance improved 40 percent and stayed at this figure.
>
> In the beginning of 1962 when, through expansion, we appointed another assistant manager and assigned him a staff, we again utilized this same concept, arranging the men once more according to their productive capacity.
>
> The assistant managers were assigned . . . according to their ability, with the most capable assistant manager receiving the best group, thus playing strength to strength. Our agency over-all production again improved by about 25–30 percent, and so this staff arrangement was continued until the end of the year.
>
> Now in this year of 1963, we found upon analysis that there were so many men . . . with a potential of half a million dollars or more that only one staff remained of those men in the agency who were not considered to have any chance of reaching the half-million-dollar mark.[2]

Although the productivity of the "super-staff" improved dramatically, it should be pointed out that the productivity of men in the lowest unit, "who were not considered to have any chance of reaching the half-million-dollar mark," actually declined and that attrition among these men increased. The performance of the superior men rose to meet their managers' expectations, while that of the weaker men declined as predicted.

Self-fulfilling Prophesies

However, the "average" unit proved to be an anomaly. Although the district manager expected only average performance from this group, its productivity increased significantly. This was because the assistant manager in charge of the group refused to believe that he was less capable than the manager of the "super-staff" or that the agents in the top group had any greater ability than the agents in his group. He insisted in discussions with his agents that every man in the middle group had greater potential than the men in the "super-staff," lacking only their years of experience in selling insurance. He stimulated his agents to accept the challenge of outperforming the "super-staff." As a result, in each year the middle group increased its productivity by a higher percentage than the "super-staff" did (although it never attained the dollar volume of the top group).

It is of special interest that the self-image of the manager of the "average" unit did not permit him to accept others' treatment of him as an "average" manager, just as Eliza Doolittle's image of herself as a lady did not permit her to accept others' treatment of her as a flower girl. The assistant manager transmitted his own strong feelings of efficacy to his agents, created mutual expectancy of high performance, and greatly stimulated productivity.

Comparable results occurred when a similar experiment was made at another office of the company. Further confirmation comes from a study of the early managerial success of 49 college graduates who were management-level employees of an operating company of the American Telephone and Telegraph Company. David E. Berlew and Douglas T. Hall of the Massachusetts Institute of Technology examined the career progress of these managers over a period of five years and discovered that their relative success, as measured by salary increases and the company's estimate of each man's performance and potential, depended largely on the company's expectations of them.[3]

The influence of one person's expectations on another's behavior is by no means a business discovery. More than half a century ago, Albert Moll concluded from his clinical experience that subjects behaved as they believed they were expected to.[4] The phenomenon he observed, in which "the prophecy causes its own fulfillment," has recently become a subject of considerable scientific interest. For example:

> In a series of scientific experiments, Robert Rosenthal of Harvard University has demonstrated that a "teacher's expectation for her pupils' intellectual competence can come to serve as an educational self-fulfilling prophecy."[5]

An experiment in a summer Headstart program for 60 preschoolers compared the performance of pupils under (a) teachers who had been led to expect relatively slow learning by their children, and (b) teachers who had been led to believe their children had excellent intellectual ability and learning capacity. Pupils of the second group of teachers learned much faster.[6]

Moreover, the healing professions have long recognized that a physician's or psychiatrist's expectations can have a formidable influence on a patient's physical or mental health. What takes place in the minds of the patients and the healers, particularly when they have congruent expectations, may determine the outcome. For instance, the havoc of a doctor's pessimistic prognosis has often been observed. Again, it is well known that the efficacy of a new drug or a new treatment can be greatly influenced by the physician's expectations—a result referred to by the medical profession as a "placebo effect."

Pattern of Failure

When salesmen are treated by their managers as supersalesmen, as the "super-staff" was at Metropolitan Rockaway District Office, they try to live up to that image and do what they know supersalesmen are expected to do. But when salesmen with poor productivity records are treated by their managers as *not* having "any chance" of success, as the low producers at Rockaway were, this negative expectation also becomes a managerial self-fulfilling prophecy.

Unsuccessful salesmen have great difficulty maintaining their self-image and self-esteem. In response to low managerial expectations, they typically attempt to prevent additional damage to their egos by avoiding situations that might lead to greater failure. They either reduce the number of sales calls they make or avoid trying to "close" sales when that might result in further painful rejection, or both. Low expectations and damaged egos lead them to behave in a manner that increases the probability of failure, thereby fulfilling their managers' expectations. Let me illustrate:

Not long ago I studied the effectiveness of branch bank managers at a West Coast bank with over 500 branches. The managers who had had their lending authority reduced because of high rates of loss became progressively less effective. To prevent further loss of authority, they turned to making only "safe" loans. This action resulted in losses of business to competing banks and a relative decline in both deposits and profits at their branches. Then, to reverse that decline in deposits and earnings, they often "reached" for loans and became almost irrational in their acceptance of questionable credit risks. Their actions were not so much a matter of poor judgment as an expression of their willingness to take desperate risks in the hope of being able to avoid further damage to their egos and to their careers.

Thus, in response to the low expectations of their supervisors, who had reduced their lending authority, they behaved in a manner that led to larger credit losses. They appeared to do what they believed they were expected to do, and their supervisors' expectations became self-fulfilling prophecies.

POWER OF EXPECTATIONS

Managers cannot avoid the depressing cycle of events that flow from low expectations merely by hiding their feelings from subordinates. If a manager believes a subordinate will perform poorly, it is virtually impossible for him to mask his expectations, because the message usually is communicated unintentionally, without conscious action on his part.

Indeed, a manager often communicates most when he believes he is communicating least. For instance, when he says nothing, when he becomes "cold" and "uncommunicative," it usually is a sign that he is displeased by a subordinate or believes he is "hopeless." The silent treatment communicates negative feelings even more effectively, at times, than a tongue-lashing does. What seems to be critical in the communication of expectations is not what the boss says, so much as the *way he behaves*. Indifferent and noncommittal treatment, more often than not, is the kind of treatment that communicates low expectations and leads to poor performance.

Common Illusions

Managers are more effective in communicating low expectations to their subordinates than in communicating high expectations to them, even though most managers believe exactly the opposite. It usually is astonishingly difficult for them to recognize the clarity with which they transmit negative feelings to subordinates. To illustrate again:

The Rockaway district manager vigorously denied that he had communicated low expectations to the men in the poorest group who, he believed, did not have "any chance" of becoming high producers. Yet the message was clearly received by those men. A typical case was that of an agent who resigned from the low unit. When the district manager told the agent that he was sorry he was leaving, the agent replied, "No, you're not; you're glad." Although the district manager previously had said nothing to the man, he had unintentionally communicated his low expectations to his agents through his indifferent manner. Subsequently, the men who were assigned to the lowest unit interpreted the assignment as equivalent to a request for their resignation.

One of the company's agency managers established superior, average, and low units, even though he was convinced that he had no superior or outstanding subordinates. "All my assistant managers and agents are either average or incompetent," he explained to the Rockaway district manager. Although he tried to duplicate the Rockaway results, his low opinions of his men were communicated — not so subtly — to them. As a result, the experiment failed.

Positive feelings, on the other hand, often do not come through clearly enough. For example:

Another insurance agency manager copied the organizational changes made at the Rockaway District Office, grouping the salesmen he rated highly with the best manager, the average salesmen with an average manager, and so on. However, improvement did not result from the move. The Rockaway district manager therefore investigated the situation. He discovered that the assistant manager in charge of the high-performance unit was unaware that his manager considered him to be the best. In fact, he and the other agents doubted that the agency manager really believed there was any difference in their abilities. This agency manager was a stolid, phlegmatic, unemotional man who treated his men in a rather pedestrian way. Since high expectations had not been communicated to the men, they did not understand the reason for the new organization and could not see any point in it. Clearly, the way a manager *treats* his subordinates, not the way he organizes them, is the key to high expectations and high productivity.

Impossible Dreams

Managerial expectations must pass the test of reality before they can be translated into performance. To become self-fulfilling prophecies, expectations must be made of sterner stuff than the power of positive thinking or generalized confidence in one's fellow men — helpful as these concepts may be for some other purposes. Subordinates will not be motivated to reach high levels of productivity unless they consider the boss's high expectations realistic and achievable. If they are encouraged to strive for unattainable goals, they eventually give up trying and settle for results that are lower than they are capable of achieving. The experience of a large electrical manufacturing company demonstrates this; the company discovered that production actually declined if production quotas were set too high, because the workers simply stopped trying to meet them. In other words, the practice of "dangling the carrot just beyond the donkey's reach," endorsed by many managers, is not a good motivational device.

Scientific research by David C. McClelland of Harvard University and John W. Atkinson of the University of Michigan[7] has demonstrated that the relationship of motivation to expectancy varies in the form of a bell-shaped curve (as shown on page 179).

The degree of motivation and effort rises until the expectancy of success reaches 50%, then begins to fall even though the expectancy of success continues to increase. No motivation or response is aroused when the goal is perceived as being either virtually certain or virtually impossible to attain.

Moreover, as Berlew and Hall have pointed out, if a subordinate fails to meet performance expectations that are close to his own level of aspirations, he will "lower his personal performance goals and standards, his . . . performance will tend to drop off, and he will develop negative attitudes toward the task activity or job."[8] It is therefore not surprising that failure of subordinates to meet the unrealistically high expectations of their managers leads to high rates of attrition; such attrition may be voluntary or involuntary.

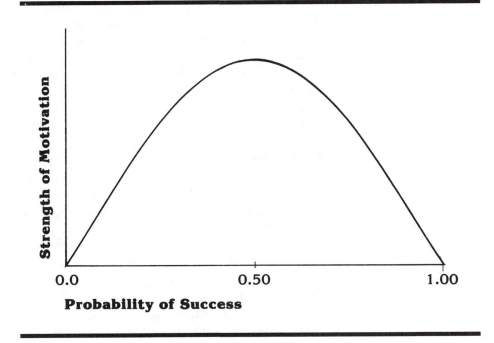

Strength of Motivation (y-axis)

Probability of Success (x-axis): 0.0   0.50   1.00

Secret of Superiority

Something takes place in the minds of superior managers that does not occur in the minds of those who are less effective. While superior managers are consistently able to create high performance expectations that their subordinates fulfill, weaker managers are not successful in obtaining a similar response. What accounts for the difference?

The answer, in part, seems to be that superior managers have greater confidence than other managers in their own ability to develop the talents of their subordinates. Contrary to what might be assumed, the high expectations of superior managers are based primarily on what they think about themselves—about their own ability to select, train, and motivate their subordinates. What the manager believes about himself subtly influences what he believes about his subordinates, what he expects of them, and how he treats them. If he has confidence in his ability to develop and stimulate them to high levels of performance, he will expect much of them and will treat them with confidence that his expectations will be met. But if he has doubts about his ability to stimulate them, he will expect less of them and will treat them with less confidence.

Stated in another way, the superior manager's record of success and his confidence in his ability give his high expectations credibility. As a consequence, his subordinates accept his expectations as realistic and try hard to achieve them.

The importance of what a manager believes about his training and motivational ability is illustrated by "Sweeney's Miracle,"[9] a managerial and educational self-fulfilling prophecy:

James Sweeney taught industrial management and psychiatry at Tulane University, and he also was responsible for the operation of the Biomedical Computer Center there. Sweeney believed that he could teach even a poorly educated man to be a capable computer operator. George Johnson, a black man who was a former hospital porter, became janitor at the computer center; he was chosen by Sweeney to prove his conviction. In the morning, George Johnson performed his janitorial duties, and in the afternoon Sweeney taught him about computers.

Johnson was learning a great deal about computers when someone at the university concluded that, to be a computer operator, one had to have a certain I.Q. score. Johnson was tested, and his I.Q. indicated that he would not be able to learn to type, much less operate a computer.

But Sweeney was not convinced. He threatened to quit unless Johnson was permitted to learn to program and operate the computer. Sweeney prevailed, and he is still running the computer center. Johnson is now in charge of the main computer room and is responsible for training new employees to program and operate the computer.

Sweeney's expectations were based on what he believed about his own teaching ability, not on Johnson's learning credentials. What a manager believes about his ability to train and motivate subordinates clearly is the foundation on which realistically high managerial expectations are built.

THE CRITICAL EARLY YEARS

Managerial expectations have their most magical influence on young men. As subordinates mature and gain experience, their self-image gradually hardens, and they begin to see themselves as their career records imply. Their own aspirations, and the expectations of their superiors, become increasingly controlled by the "reality" of their past performance. It becomes more and more difficult for them, and for their managers, to generate mutually high expectations unless they have outstanding records.

Incidentally, the same pattern occurs in school. Rosenthal's experiments with educational self-fulfilling prophecies consistently demonstrate that teachers' expectations are more effective in influencing intellectual growth in younger children than in older children. In the lower grade levels, particularly in the first and second grades, the effects of teachers' expectations are dramatic.[10] In the upper grade levels, teachers' prophecies seem to have little effect on a child's intellectual growth, although they do affect his motivation and attitude toward school. While the declining influence of teachers' expectations cannot be completely explained, it is reasonable to conclude that younger children are more malleable, have fewer fixed notions about their abilities, and have less well-established reputations in the schools. As they grow, particularly if they are assigned to "tracks" on the basis of their records, as is now often done in public schools, their beliefs about their intellectual ability and their teachers' expectations of them begin to harden and become more resistant to influence by others.

Key to Future Performance

The early years in a business organization, when a young man can be strongly influenced by managerial expectations, are critical in determining his future performance and career progress. This is shown by a study at American Telephone and Telegraph Company:

Berlew and Hall found that what the company initially expected of 49 college graduates who were management-level employees was the most critical factor in their subsequent performance and success. The researchers concluded: "The 0.72 correlation between how much a company expects of a man in his first year and how much he contributes during the next five years is too compelling to be ignored."[11]

Subsequently, the two men studied the career records of 18 college graduates who were hired as management trainees in another of the American Telephone and Telegraph Company's operating companies. Again they found that both expectations and performance in the first year correlated consistently with later performance and success.[12]

Berlew and Hall summarized their research by stating:

> Something important is happening in the first year. . . .. Meeting high company expectations in the critical first year leads to the internalization of positive job attitudes and high standards; these attitudes and standards, in turn, would first lead to and be reinforced by strong performance and success in later years. It should also follow that a new manager who meets the challenge of one highly demanding job will be given subsequently a more demanding job, and his level of contribution will rise as he responds to the company's growing expectations of him. The key . . . is the concept of the first year as a *critical period for learning*, a time when the trainee is uniquely ready to develop or change in the direction of the company's expectations.[13]

Most Influential Boss

A young man's first manager is likely to be the most influential person in his career. If this manager is unable or unwilling to develop the skills the young man needs to perform effectively, the latter will set lower standards for himself than he is capable of achieving, his self-image will be impaired, and he will develop negative attitudes toward his job, his employer, and — in all probability — his career in business. Since his chances of building a successful career with his employer will decline rapidly, he will leave, if he has high aspirations, in hope of finding a better opportunity. If, on the other hand, his manager helps him achieve his maximum potential, he will build the foundation for a successful career. To illustrate:

With few exceptions, the most effective branch managers at a large West Coast bank were mature men in their forties and fifties. The bank's executives explained that it took considerable time for a man to gain the knowledge, experience, and judgment required to handle properly credit risks, customer relations, and employee relations.

However, one branch manager, ranked in the top 10% of the managers in terms of effectiveness (which included branch profit growth, deposit growth, scores on administrative audits, and subjective rankings by superiors), was only 27 years old. This young man had been made a branch manager at 25, and in two years he not only improved the performance of his branch substantially but also developed his younger assistant manager so that he, in turn, was made a branch manager at 25.

The man had had only average grades in college, but, in his first four years at the bank, he had been assigned to work with two branch managers who were remarkably effective teachers. His first boss, who was recognized throughout the bank for his unusual skill in developing young men, did not believe that it took years to gain the knowledge and skill needed to become an effective banker. After two years, the young man was made assistant manager at a branch headed by another executive, who also was an effective developer of his subordinates. Thus it was that when the young man was promoted to head a branch, he confidently followed the model of his two previous superiors in operating his branch, quickly established a record of outstanding performance, and trained his assistant (as he had been trained) to assume responsibility early.

Contrasting records: For confirming evidence of the crucial role played by a person's first bosses, let us turn to selling, since performance in this area is more easily measured than in most managerial areas. Consider the following investigations:

In a study of the careers of 100 insurance salesmen who began work with either highly competent or less-than-competent agency managers, the Life Insurance Agency Management Association found that men with average sales aptitude test scores were nearly five times as likely to succeed under managers with good performance records as under managers with poor records; and men with superior sales aptitude scores were found to be twice as likely to succeed under high-performing managers as under low-performing managers.[14]

The Metropolitan Life Insurance Company determined in 1960 that differences in the productivity of new insurance agents who had equal sales aptitudes could be accounted for only by differences in the ability of managers in the offices to which they were assigned. Men whose productivity was high in relation to their aptitude test scores invariably were employed in offices that had production records among the top third in the company. Conversely, men whose productivity was low in relation to their test scores typically were in the least successful offices. After analyzing all the factors that might have accounted for these variations, the company concluded that differences in the performance of new men were due primarily to differences in the "proficiency in sales training and direction" of the local managers.[15]

A study I conducted of the performance of automobile salesmen in Ford dealerships in New England revealed that superior salesmen were concentrated in a few outstanding dealerships. For instance, 10 of the top 15 salesmen in New England were in 3 (out of approximately 200) of the dealerships in this region; and 5 of the top 15 men were in one highly successful dealership; yet 4 of these men previously had worked for other dealers without achieving outstanding sales records. There seemed to be little doubt that the training and motivational skills of managers in the outstanding dealerships were the critical factor.

Astute Selection

While success in business sometimes appears to depend on the "luck of the draw," more than luck is involved when a young man is selected by a superior manager. Successful managers do not pick their subordinates at random or by the toss of a coin. They are careful to select only those who they "know" will succeed. As Metropolitan's Rockaway district manager, Alfred Oberlander, insisted: "Every man who starts with us is going to be a top-notch life insurance man, or he would not have received an invitation to join the team."[16]

When pressed to explain how they "know" whether a man will be successful, superior managers usually end up by saying something like, "The qualities are intangible, but I know them when I see them." They have difficulty being explicit because their selection process is intuitive and is based on interpersonal intelligence that is difficult to describe. The key seems to be that they are able to identify subordinates with whom they can probably work effectively — men with whom they are compatible and whose body chemistry agrees with their own. They make mistakes, of course. But they "give up" on a subordinate slowly because that means "giving up" on themselves — on their judgment and ability in selecting, training, and motivating men. Less effective managers select subordinates more quickly and give up on them more easily, believing that the inadequacy is that of the subordinate, not of themselves.

DEVELOPING YOUNG MEN

Observing that his company's research indicates that "initial corporate expectations for performance (with real responsibility) mold subsequent expectations and behavior," R. W. Walters, Jr., director of college employment at the American Telephone and Telegraph Company, contends that: "Initial bosses of new college hires must be the best in the organization."[17] Unfortunately, however, most companies practice exactly the opposite.

Rarely do new graduates work closely with experienced middle managers or upper-level executives. Normally, they are bossed by first-line managers who tend to be the least experienced and least effective in the organizaton. While there are exceptions, first-line managers generally are either "old pros" who have been judged as lacking competence for higher levels of responsibility, or they are younger men who are making the transition from "doing" to "managing." Often, these managers lack the knowledge and skill required to develop the productive capabilities of their subordinates. As a consequence, many college graduates begin their careers in business under the worst possible circumstances. Since they know their abilities are not being developed or used, they quite naturally soon become negative toward their jobs, employers, and business careers.

Although most top executives have not yet diagnosed the problems, industry's greatest challenge by far is the underdevelopment, underutilization, and ineffective management and use of its most valuable resource—its young managerial and professional talent.

Disillusion and Turnover

The problem posed to corporate management is underscored by the sharply rising rates of attrition among young managerial and professional personnel. Turnover among managers one to five years out of college is almost twice as high now as it was a decade ago, and five times as high as two decades ago. Three out of five companies surveyed by *Fortune* magazine in the fall of 1968 reported that turnover rates among young managers and professionals were higher than five years ago.[18] While the high level of economic activity and the shortage of skilled personnel have made job-hopping easier, the underlying causes of high attrition, I am convinced, are underdevelopment and underutilization of a work force that has high career aspirations.

The problem can be seen in its extreme form in the excessive attrition rates of college and university graduates who begin their careers in sales positions. Whereas the average company loses about 50% of its new college and university graduates within three to five years, attrition rates as high as 40% in the *first* year are common among college graduates who accept sales positions in the average company. This attrition stems primarily, in my opinion, from the failure of first-line managers to teach new college recruits what they need to know to be effective sales representatives.

As we have seen, young men who begin their careers working for less-than-competent sales managers are likely to have records of low productivity. When rebuffed by their customers and considered by their managers to have little potential for success, the young men naturally have great difficulty in maintaining their self-esteem. Soon they find little personal satisfaction in their jobs, and, to avoid further loss of self-respect, leave their employers for jobs that look more promising. Moreover, as reports about the high turnover and disillusionment of those who embarked on sales careers filter back to college campuses, new graduates become increasingly reluctant to take jobs in sales.

Thus, ineffective first-line sales management sets off a sequence of events that ends with college and university graduates avoiding careers in selling. To a lesser extent, the same pattern is duplicated in other functions of business, as evidenced by the growing trend of college graduates to pursue careers in "more meaningful" occupations, such as teaching and government service.

A serious "generation gap" between bosses and subordinates is another significant cause of breakdown. Many managers resent the abstract, academic language and narrow rationalization typically used by recent graduates. As one manager expressed it to me: "For God's sake, you need a lexicon even to talk with these kids." Noncollege managers often are particularly resentful, perhaps because they feel threatened by the bright young men with book-learned knowledge that they do not understand.

For whatever reason, the "generation gap" in many companies is eroding managerial expectations of new college graduates. For instance, I know of a survey of management attitudes in one of the nation's largest companies which revealed that 54% of its first-line and second-line managers believed that new college recruits were "not as good as they were five years ago." Since what a manager expects of a subordinate influences the way he treats him, it is understandable that new graduates often develop negative attitudes toward their jobs and their employers. Clearly, low managerial expectations and hostile attitudes are not the basis for effective management of new men entering business.

CONCLUSION

Industry has not developed effective first-line managers fast enough to meet its needs. As a consequence, many companies are underdeveloping their most valuable resource — talented young men and women. They are incurring heavy attrition costs and contributing to the negative attitudes young people often have about careers in business.

For top executives in industry who are concerned with the productivity of their organizations and the careers of young employees, the challenge is clear: it is to speed the development of managers who will treat their subordinates in ways that lead to high performance and career satisfaction. The manager not only shapes the expectations and productivity of his subordinates, but also influences their attitudes toward their jobs and themselves. If he is unskilled, he leaves scars on the careers of the young men, cuts deeply into their self-esteem, and distorts their image of themselves as human beings. But if he is skillful and has high expectations of his subordinates, their self-confidence will grow, their capabilities will develop, and their productivity will be high. More often than he realizes, the manager is Pygmalion.

"O the despair of Pygmalion, who might have created a statue and only made a woman!"

— Alfred Jarry, 1873–1907
L'Amour Absolu

REFERENCE NOTES

1   See "Jamesville Branch Office (A)," MET003A, and "Jamesville Branch Office (B), MET003B (Boston, Sterling Institute, 1969).

2   "Jamesville Branch Office (B)," p. 2.

3   "Some Determinants of Early Managerial Success," Alfred P. Sloan School of Management Organization Research Program #81-64. (Cambridge, Massachusetts Institute of Technology, 1964), pp. 13–14.

4   Robert Rosenthal and Lenore Jacobson, *Pygmalion in the Classroom* (New York, Holt, Rinehart, and Winston, Inc., 1968), p.11.
5   Ibid., Preface, p. vii.
6   Ibid., p. 38.
7   See John W. Atkinson, "Motivational Determinants of Risk-Taking Behavior," *Psychological Review*, Vol. 64, No. 6, 1957, p. 365.
8   David E. Berlew and Douglas T. Hall, "The Socialization of Managers: Effects of Expectations on Performance," *Administrative Science Quarterly*, September 1966, p. 208.
9   See Robert Rosenthal and Lenore Jacobson, op. cit., pp. 3–4.
10 Ibid., pp. 74–81.
11 "Some Determinants of Early Managerial Success, pp. 13–14.
12 "The Socialization of Managers: Effects of Expectations on Performance," p. 219.
13 Ibid., pp. 221–222.
14 Robert T. Davis, "Sales Management in the Field," HBR January–February 1958, p. 91.
15 Alfred A. Oberlander, "The Collective Conscience in Recruiting," address to Life Insurance Agency Management Association Annual Meeting, Chicago, Ill., 1963, p. 5.
16 Ibid., p. 9.
17 "How to Keep the Go-getters," *Nation's Business*, June 1966, p. 74.
18 Robert C. Albrook, "Why It's Harder to Keep Good Executives," *Fortune*, November 1968, p. 137.

QUESTIONS

1. Can you personalize the Pygmalion phenomenon? Is there someone in your life who saw something in you and expected the best . . . so you gave it? Is there someone who expected the worst . . . so you gave it?

   _____

   _____

   _____

2. Do you enjoy the idea of developing others — as teacher, coach, supervisor, leader? Have you had experience in this area? Describe.

   _____

   _____

   _____

Managers Can
Drive Their
Subordinates Mad

Managers, no less than other people, have personality quirks. Little things they do on occasion drive their subordinates "up the wall." In the main, however, subordinates tolerate their manager's quirks because for the most part the manager's style is acceptable and for many subordinates it is much more than that. But what happens to subordinates when a manager seems to be all quirks, when there is no in-between?

As an administrator, J. Edgar Hoover struck many as an erratic autocrat, banishing agents to Siberian posts for the most whimsical reasons and terrorizing them with so many rules and regulations that adherence to all of them would have been an impossibility.[1] Hoover viewed his directorship as infallible; subordinates soon learned that dissent equaled disloyalty. No whim of Hoover's was considered too insignificant to be ignored. For example, nonobedience to participation in an antiobesity program was likely to incur his wrath, and rumor had it that chauffeurs had to avoid making left turns while driving him (apparently his car had once got struck by another car when he was making a left turn).

If it originated from Hoover, a trivial and unimportant order changed in meaning. Even if the directive was unclear, subordinates would have to take some form of calculated action and, it was said, should expect trouble if they did not take the directive seriously. Nurtured by the organizational participants, these directives often assumed a life of their own. Only appearances of and actual slavish obedience to the rules, and statistical accomplishments such as monetary value of fines, number of convictions, or apprehended fugitives counted. And problems arose if the figures did not increase each year.

Naturally, those agents who embraced the concept of the director's omnipotence were more likely to succeed. To ensure compliance, inspectors would be sent out to field offices in search of violations (the breaking of some obscure rule or instruction). If a "contract was out" on the special agent in charge of the office, a "violation" would inevitably be found.

Apparently, the inspector's own future at the FBI was at stake if no violations were discovered because then, in turn, a contract might be issued on *him*. If one wanted to survive in the organization, participation in many of these absurdities was often unavoidable. Many of these bizarre activities seem to have been treated as quite normal aspects of organizational life and were carried out with great conviction.

While Hoover at the FBI, Hitler in the days before the collapse of the Third Reich, and, even more recently, Jim Jones at the mass suicide in Guyana are newsworthy examples of what leaders can do to their subordinates when they lose touch with reality, the effects of dependence also occur in less heralded tales.

The president of a faltering company in the apparel industry seemed increasingly unwilling to face the declining profit position of his company. Even two months before the banks eventually took control, the president held meetings during which nonexistent orders, the development of new revolutionary machinery, and the introduction of new innovative products were discussed. These new developments were supposed to turn the company around and dramatically change its position in the industry. The president ignored the dismal profit and loss picture, inefficiencies in production, and poor sales performance, attributing them to unfair industry practices by competitors, or even sabotage, and assured his managers that change was imminent and the company would be out of the red shortly.

Sadly enough, these glorious ideas were far removed from reality. While the president seemed to originate most of these fantasies, his close associates not only participated in them but also encouraged his irrational thoughts and actions. The rare subordinate who expressed his disbelief was looked on with contempt, found himself ostracized and threatened with dismissal. Among the small but increasingly isolated group of managers the belief persisted that everything was not lost. Miraculous developments were just around the corner. Only when the banks took control was the spell finally broken.

What is striking about both these anecdotes is the shift of what appear as delusions and unusual behavior patterns from the originator of these activities to one or more others who are closely associated with him or her. These associates not only take an active part but also frequently enhance and elaborate on these delusions. The delusions seem to escalate in intensity when the people involved try to solve problems concerned with an already deteriorating situation. They inevitably aggravate the situation, make it worse, and become correspondingly more and more reluctant to face external reality. Feeling most comfortable in their own chosen, closed environment, they do not welcome the opinion of outsiders, seeing them as threatening the status quo and disturbing their tunnel vision.

Also noticeable in these two examples is just how contagious the behavior of a senior executive can be, and how devastating its effect on his subordinates and his organization. In Hoover's case, the reaction of his subordinates further encouraged him to continue in his dysfunctional behavior. Perhaps the particular mission of Hoover's organization may have contributed to the fact that very few subordinates were willing to refuse to participate in some of these bizarre activities. Regardless, many conformed to his wishes and some may actually have believed in the appropriateness and importance of his actions. In the second example, again the process of mental contagion is central.

In psychiatric literature, mental contagion is a recurring theme. This particular process of influence, which usually goes together with some form of break with reality occurring among groups of individuals, is generally known as *folie à deux* — that is, shared madness. Although folie à deux as a way of interaction has been limited to seriously disturbed relationships between two people, a broader definition of this particular psychological process may be helpful in understanding the interactions between leaders and followers in organizations.

One may gain insight into what is frequently described as an "eccentric" leadership style if one studies emotionally charged superior-subordinate relationships characterized by some kind of impaired ability to see things realistically within the context of folie à deux. One may discover that this phenomenon, with various degrees of intensity, is a regular occurrence in organizations and can be considered one of the risks of leadership.

A senior executive should not underestimate the degree of influence he wields in his organization. Recognizing dependency — need for direction — as one of man's most universal characteristics, a manager should be aware that many of his subordinates will sacrifice reality for its sake, participating in even irrational decisions without mustering a critical stand and challenging what is happening. . . .

To preserve the dependency, both subordinates and superiors create closed communities, losing touch with the immediate reality of the organization's environment to the detriment of organizational functioning. When the reality is not abandoned completely, however, this phenomenon is often difficult to recognize. But in view of its damaging consequences, even in a limited form, it deserves serious attention. I will explore this aspect of leadership, hoping to help managers diagnose and prevent the incidence of its potentially disastrous effects.

DYNAMICS OF FOLIE À DEUX

We have seen that folie à deux is marked by contagious irrational behavior patterns, but how does it occur in organizations?

Suppose a senior executive under the strain of leadership, trying to cope with often disconcerting imagery around power and control in addition to the general pressures of the business environment, gradually loses touch with the organization's reality. Also this individual's charismatic personality may once have attracted executives with highly ungratified dependency needs to the organization. Or it may have been the organizational climate itself which was conducive to a reawakening of these executives' dependency needs.

Whatever the reason, during their association with the organization these managers may have become dependent on the senior executive. Although strong, these needs do not at first completely overpower all other behavior patterns. What changes dependency needs into folie à deux? When both senior executive and subordinates become dependent on each other in a situation which offers few outside sources of gratification, their complete commitment to each other can be taken as symptomatic.

At some point, triggered by an event usually associated with a depriving experience of the past, the senior executive may become preoccupied with some delusionary ideas (and this is not necessarily a conscious process), one of which being that his subordinates are taking unfair advantage of him. As a result, he develops a certain amount of hostility. But, at the same time, since the subordinates' expressions of attachment finally fulfill his own dependency needs which have been ungratified for so long, he experiences guilt about this feeling of hostility.

In spite of lingering resentment, therefore, the senior executive is extremely reluctant to give up his relationships with his subordinates. They may be among the few close relationships he has been able to establish. Consequently, to defend himself against his own emerging hostility toward his subordinates, he externalizes it and attributes the hostility to others.

The senior executive absolves the closely associated executives of responsibility for these feelings; it is "the others" who are to blame. This blame can take many forms, eventually encapsulating everything that may be going wrong with the company. The senior executive, who has been the originator of this process, now needs his subordinates to support his delusionary ideas and actions. He needs that support not only because the ideas are his defense against hostility but also because he may lose his feelings of closeness with his subordinates if he does not get it. There seems to be only one option—namely, to induce his subordinates to participate.

If a subordinate resists, the senior executive will become overtly hostile, including him in his vision of "the other camp"—the enemy. Naturally, the subordinate's level of anxiety will rise. A double-bind situation develops for the subordinate; he will have to choose between the loss of gratification of his dependency needs and exposure to the wrath of the senior executive, on the one hand, and the loss of reality, on the other.

In many instances, the subordinate will solve this intrapsychic conflict by giving in to the psychological ultimatum, "identify with the aggressor." He thus satisfies his own dependency needs and deflects the hostility of the senior executive. Separation from the person who started this process is viewed as much more of a direct, tangible loss than the loss of reality.

Identifying with the aggressor usually implies participating in his or her persecutory fantasies. The shared delusions are usually kept well within the realms of possibility and are based on actual past events or certain common expectations. Because the accusations contain a bit of reality, this process is difficult to discern. Through participation in these fantasies, the subordinates maintain their source of gratification, lower their anxiety and guilt level, and express their anger in a deflected form by directing it toward others. The process is mirrorlike; the actions of the initiator of the process become reflected in those of the subordinates and vice versa and can be viewed as the outcome of an effort to save the alliance from breaking up.

Now let us look at some of these dynamics in greater detail.

Getting Trapped

In organizations, folie à deux can be one of the pitfalls of leadership. Often, however, this dimension of leadership is not seen for what it is, and contagious behavior patterns are more often than not accepted and rationalized as being merely side products of an eccentric or autocratic leadership style.

Take, for example, the behavior and actions of the first Henry Ford, who had been acclaimed not only a mechanical genius but also, after the announcement of the five-dollar day, as a philanthropist. Because of the darker sides of his actions, however, this image eventually changed. While the public merely ridiculed his escapades, for the employees of the Ford Motor Company the situation was not a laughing matter. His despotic one-man rule and his continuous search for enemies increasingly had repercussions in every function of the company. He began to view Wall Street bankers, labor unions, and Jews as his enemies, seeing each group as supposedly endangering his complete control over the company and obstructing him in his grandiose plans (e.g., the Peace ship mission, his idea to stop the First World War, or his senatorial campaign).

At one point there may have been an element of reality to some of Ford's notions (i.e., the labor union movement), but over time what there was got lost. One can regard the relationship between the senior Henry Ford and his lieutenants Liebold, Sorenson, and, particularly, Bennett in the context of folie à deux. Using a system of intimidation, helped by a large number of Detroit underworld characters, Bennett spread terror in the organization, a process originally instigated by Henry Ford but performed by Bennett and his henchmen.

Executives who did not participate in the idiosyncrasies of Henry Ford and his close associates were fired. The Model T, which carried the company to its original success, eventually became a burden. Regardless, reinforced in his behavior by his close subordinates, Henry Ford stuck to his original strategy of a cheap car for the masses, making even suggestions of modification taboo. Only in 1927, after the Model T had been in production for 19 years, and only after an incredible loss of market share to General Motors, was Henry Ford willing to make a model change.

This example illustrates how contagious a senior executive's behavior can be and how originally functional behavior can become increasingly damaging to the organization and even bring the company close to bankruptcy. Henry Ford's subordinates only encouraged his views, although it remains open to question which subordinates were only conforming and which were truly believing in their actions.

A more contemporary example involves the behavior of a manager of an isolated plant in a mining community who had developed the belief that the head office wanted to close down the production facility. The recent introduction by the head office of a new factory control system started him in his belief, and regular visits by head office staff to implement the new control system only reinforced these ideas, which he communicated to his subordinates and which were widely accepted. Although the production figures were more than adequate, a collusion began to develop among plant personnel. Eventually the plant manager and his subordinates began to falsify information to show the plant in an even more favorable light. Only a spot check by the internal auditor of the head office brought these malpractices to light.

In many of these instances, however, a major question remains. How much of the behavior of the subordinates can be accurately described in the context of folie à deux, and how much is mere compliance to the eccentric leadership style of a senior executive? The latter situation is illustrated by this example:

The division head of a company in the machinery equipment industry would habitually mention the advanced product technology used in his plants to each visitor of the company and at talks at trade association meetings. On promotion trips abroad, he was always trying to obtain license arrangements for his technology. And occasionally he would be successful. But, in spite of the fact that the company was turning out a high-quality product, there was nothing unique about the technology. As a matter of fact, most competitors were using comparable or even more advanced technological processes. Although most of his subordinates were aware of the actual state of affairs, they were unwilling to confront the division head with the facts. Compliance seemed easier than confrontation.

It is worth noting that mere compliance, if continued long enough, can evolve into stronger alliances, possibly resulting in active participation in these irrational actions. These examples also emphasize some of the characteristics of folie à deux; for example, the relative isolation of the actors, their closeness, the existence of a dominant partner, and the emergence of delusionary ideas.

The Search for Scapegoats

Interaction that contains elements of folie à deux can contribute to collusion among subgroups that fosters and maintains organizational myths and fantasies often only remotely related to the reality of the situation. In these instances, for some cliques, the organization's overall objectives and strategies become of lesser interest than tactical considerations. As concern for the maintenance of various irrational notions consumes more energy, there is less congruence between specific actions and available information.

It appears as if the members of these groups live in a polarized world that no longer includes compromise or the acceptance of differences. Everyone is pressured to choose sides. It is also a world where one continuously has to be on one's guard against being singled out as a target for unfriendly actions. In such an organization, scapegoating becomes a predominant activity directed not only toward individuals within the organization but also toward such groups as the government, labor unions, competitors, suppliers, customers, or consumer organizations. What may have been a well-thought-out program may become distorted. For instance, alertness to the environment, which at one time may have been an organizational strength, can turn into a watch for imminent attack — a caricature of its original purpose.

Because of structural arrangements, subgroups frequently overlap with departments or other units. When this happens, people jealously guard areas of responsibility; territorialism prevails. The determination of boundaries between departments can lead to disputes. Seeking or accepting help from other groups may be considered a weakness or even a betrayal.

For example, in a large electronics company a vice president of production development began to imagine that two of his colleagues, a vice president of R&D and a vice president of manufacturing, wanted to get rid of him. He perceived that his two colleagues were trying to reorganize his department out of existence and incorporate it into their own functional areas. At every available opportunity, he communicated this concern to his subordinates and expected them to confirm his own suspicions. Disagreement was not tolerated; resistance resulted in either dismissal or transfer to another department. Gradually, many of his executives began to believe in his statements and to develop a siege mentality which led to a strong sense of group cohesion.

Relationships between this group and members of other departments became strained. What were once minor interdepartmental skirmishes deteriorated into open warfare. Committee meetings with members of other departments became public accusation sessions about the withholding of information, inaccurate data, and intrusion into each others' territory. In addition, because of his recurring complaints about poor quality of delivered material and late deliveries, the vice president's contacts with some of his suppliers deteriorated. (A subsequent examination by a new vice president found that most of these accusations were unwarranted.)

Eventually, managers of other departments began to avoid contact with product development people, thereby confirming their suspicions. Over time, the rest of the company built up a number of separate, fairly informal information systems to avoid any dealings with the product development group. Finally, after the product development group made a number of budgetary mistakes because of distorted information, the president transferred the vice president and reorganized the department.

In this example one can see how excessive rivalry and suspicion can lead people to adopt a narrow perspective of organizational priorities and become defensive and controlling. Without integrating mechanisms to counterbalance their effect, these attitudes can fractionate an organization. Understandably, organizational participants will take refuge in policies and procedures, collusive activities, and other forms of organizational gamesmanship. Cooperation will disappear and priorities will become distorted.

Where elements of folie à deux seep into organizations, conflict becomes stifling, creativity is discouraged, and distrust becomes the prevailing attitude. Instead of taking realistic action, managers react to emergencies by withdrawing or scapegoating. Fear will be the undercurrent of the overall organizational climate. As ends and means become indistinguishable, the organization will drift along, losing touch with originally defined corporate goals and strategies.

ENTREPRENEURIAL DANGERS

Because of the great intensity and closeness that develop in small isolated groups, entrepreneurial ventures tend to be particularly susceptible to folie à deux behavior patterns. In many instances the venture begins because the entrepreneur tries to overcome his or her feelings of dependency, helplessness, and rejection by adopting an opposite posture, a financial and psychological risk-taking style. In addition, the entrepreneur may have a strong need for achievement, control, and power, as well as an intense concern for autonomy.[2]

The relationship between entrepreneur and enterprise is usually an involved and conflict-ridden one in which the company has great emotional significance for the individual. Frequently, this type of attachment may lead to growth and succession crises, episodes aggravated by developments of a folie à deux nature, as the following example shows:

The president and founder of a medium-size electronics company often expressed concern about the need for more professional management in his company. He liked to state that the entrepreneurial phase had been passed and that the time had come to make organizational changes, prepare to go public, and plan for succession. To that end, he became personally involved in the recruitment of MBAs at various business schools. His charismatic appeal and his strong advocacy of professional management attracted a great number of MBAs. The MBA influx was balanced, however, by a steady exodus of many of the same MBAs who soon realized the difficulties in conforming to the president's demands.

Under the guise of being "a happy family," the founder felt he could intrude into the private affairs of his subordinates. What he presented as the great deal of responsibility that he would delegate to the newcomers turned out to be poorly defined assignments without much authority, which frequently led to failure. A person's career advancement depended on his or her closeness to the president, compliance with his wishes, and willingness to participate in often irrational behavior patterns. Exile to various obscure sales offices became the price of resistance. Eventually, the company had to pay a toll for this leadership, but the president blamed the steady drop in sales and profits on government intervention, union activities, and sabotage by a number of singled out employees.

Hoarding of information, playing of favorites, inconsistent handling of company policies, and, generally, creating ambiguous situations constitute a common phenomenon in entrepreneurial companies. Because the company's survival does depend on the entrepreneur, many subordinates are easily drawn into supporting him even when what he does may be irrational. Those unwilling to participate leave, while conformers and ones susceptible to folie à deux relationships remain.

This phenomenon may explain why in so many entrepreneurial companies a strong layer of capable middle managers is missing. In situations of folie à deux-like behavior, those who remain will spend a great part of their energies on political infighting and supporting the irrational behavior and beliefs of the entrepreneur. These activities can become even more intense if members of the entrepreneur's family are employed in the company so that family and organizational dynamics become closely intertwined.

MANAGEMENT OF FOLIE À DEUX

Assuming a folie à deux pattern occurs in an organization, what can be done to cope with it? How can managers prevent getting stuck in this peculiar circular process? How can they recognize the symptoms?

Before outlining the steps managers can take, I want to stress that some aspects of what might look like folie à deux are not always organizationally undesirable. As I indicated earlier, in the initial phases interpersonal processes that could lead to folie à deux may be a source of strength contributing to team building, commitment to goals and strategies, or even the establishment of effective environmental scanning mechanisms. Unfortunately, in the long run, interpersonal relationships that in extreme form typify folie à deux may become a danger to the organization's operations and even its survival.

The first steps in the containment of folie à deux are recognizing those individual and organizational symptoms:

1. *Check out your managers.* Managers likely to initiate this type of behavior usually show specific personality characteristics. For example, they may appear to possess a lot of personal charm and seductiveness, qualities that may have been originally responsible for their personal attractiveness. A closer look, however, will reveal that this behavior is often a cover-up for attitudes of conceit, arrogance, demonstrative self-sufficiency and self-righteousness. Individuals prone to folie à deux find it extremely difficult to alter their concepts and ideas; their actions often contain a rigid quality.

Because of his need to dominate and control other people, this type of executive usually stands out. He will deeply resent any form or use of authority by others. He seems to be continually on his guard, prepared to fight suspected, often imagined, dangers. Hyperalertness, hypersensitivity, and suspiciousness of others tend to become ways of life. Frequently, he is preoccupied with people's hidden motives and searches for confirmation of his suspicions. He evinces a great concern about details, amplifying and elaborating on them. Not surprisingly, the creation and maintenance of a state of interpersonal tension in the organization will be one of the effects of such behavior.

Such an executive will easily feel slighted, wronged, or ignored. Lack of trust and confidence in others can make him extremely self-conscious, seclusive, reserved, and moody. Frequently, there is querulousness, insensitivity, and a lack of consideration of others. Dramatic mood swings can be observed. If an attitude of friendliness and companionship temporarily prevails, such behavior will be quickly shattered by the slightest provocation, after which the full force of hate, mistrust, and rage may break loose. A sense of playfulness and humor seems to be lacking.

When behavior of a folie à deux nature starts to spread, the influenced persons may show similar behavior patterns, but in most instances not of such an intensive nature. For all the participants in this form of mental contagion, a key problem remains the existence of highly ungratified dependency needs. It is exactly those needs that the instigators of this process fulfill. By being directive, self-assured, and willing to take complete control, these executives attract those followers who need to be treated this way.

2. *Look at their organizations.* The danger signals of folie à deux can also be detected by looking at possible peculiarities of the organization's culture and ways of operation. One symptom is unusual selection and promotion procedures that largely reflect a senior executive's idiosyncracies rather than a concern for a candidate's overall managerial capabilities. Strange, selective, and unsystematic decision-making patterns, erratic information systems, and excessive control and extreme secrecy can also often be taken as danger signs.

Other indications may be a department's preoccupation with details at the cost of overall company effectiveness, and excessive manifestation of various stress symptoms in the organization, such as a large turnover of executives and a high degree of absenteeism. One can also view frequent changes in organizational goals, and existence of grandiose, unrealistic plans, and insistence on supposed conspiracies, or the actual creation of the latter, as other signs.

Whatever the exact nature of the disturbing behavior pattern or process one notices, one should keep folie à deux processes in mind as a possible cause. Once symptoms are recognized, managers need to take corrective action, as well as to design systems and procedures that will counteract folie à deux:

1. *Establish a trusting relationship.* When folie à deux is in full swing the manager involved is beyond helping himself. For the person who started this process, the route back to reality is particularly difficult. A disposition toward delusional thinking can be difficult to overcome. Appeal to the manager's logic and reality does not help; on the contrary, it might

evoke uncompromising, hostile, and aggressive reactions. Rather, in these instances, one has to establish some degree of trust and closeness with the affected manager to make him willing to entertain the possibility that his assumptions of the organizational environment are invalid.

This change in attitudes is not going to be arrived at easily, but without a change it will not be possible for an affected manager to make a realistic self-appraisal of inner strengths and weaknesses. Substituting reality for fantasies is likely to be a slow and difficult process involving reintegration and adjustment of many deeply ingrained behavior patterns. Because of the intensity of the delusions, in many instances these persons may need professional guidance.

The outlook for the affected followers is more positive and usually less dramatic. Frequently, merely the removal of the closeness with the affected senior executive will be sufficient to break the magic spell. Some form of disorientation may occur at the beginning, but proper guidance by other nonaffected executives will soon help to bring the managers back into more normal, reality-oriented behavior patterns.

2. *Monitor your own susceptibilities.* One way to make the occurrence of this behavior less likely is to be aware of your own susceptibility to it. Most people are to some extent vulnerable. We like to be taken care of at times and do not seriously object when others make decisions for us. It is sometimes easy to relax and not be responsible, to have someone to follow, to guide our behavior. Moreover, an activity such as scapegoating has its attractive sides; blaming others for things you may be afraid of but tempted to do yourself creates not only a sense of moral righteousness but also a sense of satisfaction about your own behavior. Furthermore, as long as the interpersonal interactions retain a firm base in reality, these behavior patterns are not disturbing or dangerous. Unfortunately, the slide into irrational action is easy.

To prevent yourself from entering into a folie à deux pattern you should periodically take a critical appraisal of your own values, actions, and interpersonal relationships. Because it is hard to recognize your own possible "blind spots" and irrational behavior patterns, you might consider getting help in this appraisal process from outside the organization. Also a certain amount of courage is needed to face these confrontations with yourself.

Nonetheless, the executives with the willingness to test and reevaluate reality will be the ones who in the end possess real freedom of choice, acting out of a sense of inner security. Ability for self-examination enhances a person's identity, fosters adaptation to change, and limits susceptibility to controlling influence. Because these qualities form the basis for mature working relationships, mutual reality-oriented problem solving, and a healthy organizational climate, they deter episodes of folie à deux.

3. *Solicit the help of interested parties.* Awareness of the occurrence of folie à deux is of limited help when the instigator is a powerful senior executive who happens to be a major shareholder. Occasionally, however, in such instances, the support of a countervailing power such as the govern-

ment or a union may be necessary to guide the organization away from possible self-destructive adventures. Naturally, other possible interested parties who could blow the whistle are customers, suppliers, and bankers.

The situation becomes somewhat less problematic when the chief executive officer is not a major shareholder since the board of directors and the shareholders can play a more active monitoring role. One of their responsibilities will be to watch for possible danger signs. Naturally, the possibility always exists that board members will be drawn into the delusionary activities of a senior executive. Such an event is, of course, less likely to happen with a board of outside directors.

Regardless, because boards traditionally follow the directives of the CEO, the possibility of folie à deux indicates how important the selection of board members is. Important criteria in this selection process will be independence, a sense of identity, diversity of background, and reality orientation which can neutralize a folie à deux process.

4. *Reorient the work climate and structure.* Organizational solutions to folie à deux become more feasible when the instigator is not a senior executive officer. Then confrontation, transfer, or, in serious cases, dismissal will be sufficient to stop the process. Also important, however, are the systems and procedures in an organization. For instance, reward systems that promote irrational behavior also give it implicit approval. Thus it is crucial to foster a healthy climate where irrational processes cannot take root.

Supporting individual responsibility and independence of mind in the organization, as well as selecting and promoting managers who behave accordingly, can be a buffer against folie à deux. An organizational culture of mutual collaboration, delegation, open conflict resolution, and respect for individuality will expose a process of mental contagion before it can spread. Such organizational patterns will lessen dependency needs and force conflict into the open, thus counteracting the incidence of vicious circles in interpersonal behavior.

Objective information systems can also assist managers to focus on reality, as can using many different sources for information gathering and processing. Interdepartmental committees and formal control systems can fulfill a similar function.

Contemporary pressures toward participative management, or work democratization, are other ways of preventing, or at least limiting, the emergence or proliferation of folie à deux. These structural changes can reduce the power of senior executives and restrict the advantage they may take of their subordinates' dependency needs.

REFERENCE NOTES

1 "The Truth about Hoover," *Time*, December 22, 1975.
2 See my article, "The Entrepreneurial Personality: A Person at the Crossroads," *Journal of Management Studies*, 1977, 14(I), 34.

QUESTIONS

1. Have you ever seen a boss have a negative influence on the judgment or behavior of a subordinate? Describe.

   _____

   _____

   _____

2. Have you ever seen the opposite condition — where a subordinate exerts negative influence on the personality of the boss? Discuss.

   _____

   _____

   _____

3. What strategies and principles would you recommend so that bosses and subordinates do not become victims of unhealthy dependency?

   _____

   _____

   _____

CASES

What Happened When I Gave Up the Good
Life and Became President   202

A Different Style of Leadership   210

Mr. Black, Ms. Blue, and Mr. White   214

The Full Court Press   216

The Forklift Fiasco   221

What Happened When
I Gave Up the Good Life
and Became President

A rather extraordinary thing happened to me this year. Last spring I was without a job—I'd been without one for two years, in fact—and on the whole was enjoying life immensely. In June, however, I had to go back to work. Since working is a common enough experience among adults, and since I'm thirty-five, I don't expect any special sympathy over my reappearance in the U.S. labor force. But the job I got was something special. I became president and chief executive of a $20-million enterprise in deep trouble. . . .

The company I've now gone to work for is Eberhard Faber Inc., the family business. It was founded by my great-grandfather in 1849, and is one of the oldest, and I think the best, manufacturers of pencils and other stationery supplies in the U.S. Its domestic operations are based in a plant at Mountaintop, outside Wilkes-Barre, Pennsylvania, but it also has subsidiaries in Germany and Canada, partnerships in Venezuela and Colombia, and licensees in Brazil, Argentina, Peru, El Salvador, Turkey, and the Philippines. The company seemed to be thriving when I was growing up, and it occurred to me at a fairly early age that, if I wanted to, I could run it one day.

THE VIEW FROM GREENPOINT

Actually, I have been somewhat ambivalent about this prospect over the years. I remember that in the summer of 1953, just before I went off to college at Princeton, I worked as a stock boy in the shipping department. The company was then located in a sprawling thirteen-building complex in the Greenpoint section of Brooklyn. I used to take my lunch up to the roof, sit under the huge letters of the Eberhard Faber sign there, and gaze across the East River at the United Nations Building, trying to decide what to make of my life. At that point I was inclined to be a man of letters. In college I edited the *Daily Princetonian*. Later I won a

Fulbright Teaching Fellowship, under which I taught American literature at the University of Caen in Normandy. And later still I spent two years in Paris writing fiction.

However, I also kept my hand in at the company. In 1960–61, I worked as an executive trainee (unpaid) at the new Mountaintop offices. In the spring of 1965, I came back for another, somewhat longer tour of duty: I worked as assistant treasurer, then assistant secretary, and finally secretary of the corporation. I'd been attending board meetings of the company since I was twenty-one, and in 1966, when I was twenty-nine, I became a director.

Then, in 1969, I decided to leave the company. I was bored with my duties, the enterprise seemed to run perfectly well without me, and I wanted to write. Besides, I felt that I wanted to extract more fun out of life than I'd been doing. . . .

Anyway, in March, 1969, I quit the company and took up the good life in Belle Mead. Unfortunately, the company began running into trouble at about the same time. There was, I'm afraid, no connection between my departure and the company's new problems.

HARD TIMES IN THE PENCIL GAME

Some of the problems were built into the industry. The pencil business itself, which represents almost 40 percent of our revenues, had been substantially depressed during much of the postwar period. It is plagued by overcapacity, the result of seventeen companies sharing a market of only about $40 million, and chronically afflicted by ruinous price wars. The ball-point pen and increased computerization of many office operations have held down the market growth that might have been expected with a rising population. Efforts to diversify have not been entirely successful. In addition to pencils, Eberhard Faber Inc. now makes erasers, rubber bands, felt- and porous-tipped markers, a "whiteboard" visual-aid panel for schools, several kinds of adhesives, type cleaners, and more: and profit margins on quite a few of the lines are low.

But some of the company's problems in 1969 went beyond those of the industry. Labor relations deteriorated that year and there was an eleven-week strike. When the dust settled, the company had lost a lot of business, some of it permanently. The size of the final settlement further reduced profit margins on the bulk of the product line. Worst of all, there were indications that, even after the settlement, the union's relations with management were hostile and communication was bad. The directors were not surprised when the losses continued, and in fact deepened, during 1970.

Later, when it began to look as though 1971 would be even worse, the company called in Goggi & Race, a New York consulting firm, to get an outside appraisal of the problems. Specifically, the firm was asked what Eberhard Faber Inc. should do to straighten out its labor problems. After a long, hard look at the company, Paul Goggi reported to the board that the real problem wasn't labor—it was management. He went on to make some specific suggestions for improving the company's materials management and sales forecasting, reshaping the organizational structure, using our machinery and space more efficiently. Later, when the suggestions were not implemented rapidly enough, Goggi indicated forcibly that the company needed some executive changes.

For almost a century after it was founded, Eberhard Faber Inc. was run by, as well as owned by, members of the family. But a series of tragedies some three decades ago interrupted the family's managerial role. In 1945 my father and one of his brothers were drowned while trying to rescue me in the rough surf off the New Jersey shore; I was eventually rescued by another uncle, my mother's brother Duncan. Not long afterward, my grandfather died. My father had been the company's executive vice president; my grandfather had been president. In an effort to fill this large management vacuum, my great-uncle John took over as president—although he was in his nineties. Not surprisingly, Uncle John never did get a very firm grip on the company, and when he died in 1949 it was pretty much out of control.

KEEPING IT IN THE FAMILY

At this point, all logic pointed to selling the company, but my mother insisted that it stay in the family. She continued to insist on family control even after she had received some attractive offers for the company, and she stuck to this position after she was stricken by cancer and had to undergo major surgery. One potential buyer actually got a representative into her room at the hospital, when her condition was still critical, and attempted to do business right there. It is another cherished family tradition that my Uncle Duncan finally got rid of the man by brandishing a revolver at him. Luckily, my mother has the constitution of a Texas steer and the fighting spirit of an Irish terrier. She recovered, held on to the company, and became a vice president (for many years she handled public relations). She did not attempt to run the company, however, and no other Faber was available in the years after Uncle John's death.

I mention all these details because they help to explain why, when Paul Goggi said the company needed new management, I decided to offer my services as president. I had, of course, some large material reasons for being concerned about the company's future. Almost all my family's resources are tied up in the business. If it fails, the family is in trouble. But I wasn't just making an investment decision; a lot of family history and traditions were fed into the decision too. On top of everything else, I felt an obligation to try to do something for the company's employees, hundreds of whom I knew personally. I thought I could actually help the company.

A BEGINNING IN THE CAFETERIA

The board accepted my offer, and I took over as president on June 8. The first few hours were fairly rugged. I'd been up almost until dawn the night before I showed up at the office, working on a speech I had to deliver to the employees of Eberhard Faber Inc. I knew that the employees would be tense when they assembled for the meeting. They didn't know what they were going to be told, or even by whom. When they saw me appear at the podium of our cafeteria — it's the largest room available at Mountaintop, and it has to be used for meetings — they would realize the occasion was an important one, possibly an announcement that the company would be sold or moved elsewhere. The first thing I had to tell them, therefore, was that I was speaking to them as president of an ongoing enterprise. That would reassure them to some extent; however, there was no getting around the company's massive problems, and so I also had to let them know about the company's deteriorating financial position. Finally, I wanted to inspire them — to give them a feeling that they could turn the company around.

At Eberhard Faber Inc., the factory gets to work at seven, the office at eight. It was seven-thirty on an outrageously beautiful June morning when I pulled into the parking lot. I had an hour before the speech was to be delivered, and I didn't want to be seen, and start all sorts of rumors, during that hour. I scurried quickly up the stairs to the executive offices, feeling somewhat conspiratorial, and spent the ensuing hour with several other executives, trying to smile through the terror. Paul Mailloux, our new executive vice president, kept assuring me that arrangements for the meeting would go smoothly; I noticed, however, that he seemed unable to light his pipe.

Actually, there was a large complication about speaking to all the employees of our company. There were 523 of them at Mountaintop and the production workers were on two different shifts. The cafeteria, furthermore, holds only about seventy-five. In the end, my speech to the employees had to be delivered *eight times*.

I thought that the first session, which was for the management group, went fairly well. I could feel the sweat coursing down my arms and chest as I prepared for the second session, which was for the union committee. But that one seemed to go fairly well too, and when it was over the union president, Paul Butchko, came over and said, "As long as you play fair with us, we'll play fair with you." He had the same husky tone in his voice that I'd heard in mine during parts of the speech, and I suddenly realized that Butchko, who was about my own age, had a lot of new responsibilities to deal with too.

The speeches went on all through the day, which just got hotter every hour. By the time I'd finished Speech No. 8, for the night shift, I was completely exhausted. It was a Wednesday, and I briefly considered dropping by at the Westmoreland Club in downtown Wilkes-Barre to relax in the club's weekly poker game. But the evening papers were carrying our story, and I just didn't feel strong enough to face a crowd of well-wishers and answer questions about my new situation. I went home and slept like a log. . . .

CAGING THE PAPER TIGER

Obviously, I had a lot to learn about running the company, but I did have some advantages when I started out. I had, of course, a lot of help from our management team and from Goggi & Race. Because of my previous tours of duty in the company, I knew where the men's room was, so to speak. I was reasonably familiar with the plant operation, the sales distribution patterns, the organizational structure, and the daily routines. And, of course, I knew the people.

The first thing I had to learn about running the company concerned the mounds of paper that were now dumped on my desk — larger mounds than I'd ever seen in my life. Enormous, incomprehensible data-processing runs arrived daily. Tickler files, based on miscellaneous memoranda of past years, appeared promptly every Thursday, often leaving me mystified about whom to tickle, how to tickle them, and whether it really mattered. Job applications and resumes, acquisition and merger inquiries, advertising and sales bulletins, association newsletters, results from our test labs, interoffice memos, travel schedules of other executives, letters of congratulation on my appointment, brochures on the advantages of alternate plant sites, news about our community services, were all in the mound. Also, it seemed as though everyone in the company thought it prudent to send the new president a copy of every letter he wrote, if only as evidence of hard work.

I let this avalanche pour over me for a while; but finally, guided by a powerful instinct for survival, I took a deep breath, prayerfully apologized to the puritan God of Hard Work, and instructed my secretary to hide most of it in the closet. She now screens my mail ruthlessly. Sometimes letters don't get answered for a week, or at all, and sometimes an important document gets buried in the great mound, but I can't really believe it's affecting the bottom line.

The company's major problem at the time I took over was, of course, to stem the accelerating flow of losses and get onto a breakeven basis, at least. This meant, inevitably, that the operating budget had to be trimmed severely. There was also an urgent need to get a grip on our inventories, which were far too large in several product lines. Thus far we've reduced the budget by 18 percent and reduced the total inventory by about 25 percent. The inventory cutback enabled us to pay off our short-term loan and, in general, lower the pressures represented by our friendly bankers.

SELLING THE WHITEBOARD

The single most important business decision we faced concerned our "whiteboard" operations in Lansing, Michigan. We had acquired the Lansing operation in 1967, and it was losing money at a frightening rate. The product itself, which we call the Eberhard Faber-Board visual-aid panel, is a white panel that has some substantial advantages over ordinary composition or slate blackboards. It uses water and xylene-based markers as writing instruments, and the writing is a lot easier to read than anything chalked on blackboards; in addition, there's less glare and no smudging when you erase. Finally, the panel can be used as a projection screen.

Unfortunately, we badly misjudged the market for it. We had felt that its principal use would be in schools and colleges, and that it could easily ride on the coattails of our regular line, much of which is sold through school-supply houses and other educational distributors. We failed to see one large difficulty about selling it, however. The panel would be a capital item for the school, which meant that administrators who wanted to buy it would have to go through a quite different and more complicated approval process than they go through when they buy our pencils and erasers. Given the financial crisis that schools generally have been in recently, there just wasn't much heart to take on new lines. A few schools and colleges — one is the Massachusetts Institute of Technology — have been good customers, but in general we haven't had nearly as many educational sales as we'd counted on. The market has thus far turned out to be in industry and architects. We've sold the board to just about every major corporation in the U.S., and many have been repeat buyers. The whiteboard was even bought by Grumman for use in planning the production and testing of the lunar modules. (Grumman had the panels on tracks, and used groups of them to keep its people informed about the status of the modules as they went through the production process.)

The fact remained, however, that our total sales volume was not high enough to justify the kind of costs we were running up in the Lansing facility. And so I asked our management committee to meet and ponder three alternatives: sell the whiteboard operation to another company; liquidate it; or move it into the Mountaintop plant (which would reduce total corporate overhead charges). I indicated that the one option we did *not* have was doing nothing — that is, leaving the operation as it was.

At the first meeting the management committee was somewhat disposed to move the operation to Mountaintop. For one thing, moving it would be far less costly than liquidating it. For another, we still felt that the product had an exciting sales potential. At this point, however, we found ourselves confronting a question to which we had no answer: what kind of profit margin could we expect on the product if we did move it to Mountaintop? We asked George Flower, our treasurer, for an answer, and I adjourned the meeting.

At a second meeting on the whiteboard, we had Mr. Flower's projections in front of us. They showed a fair enough margin between our production costs and the selling price; the gross margin was close to the necessary minimum for product at Mountaintop. But it occurred to me to ask about the cost of selling the panels, and Mr. Mailloux's off-the-cuff reply indicated that it was far higher than our average. Suddenly everyone was scribbling numbers on his pad. I have a lot to learn about management, but I know, at least, that you're supposed to do your homework before meetings, not during them. Somewhat exasperated, principally at myself, I adjourned this meeting too and asked George Flower to project his figures all the way to the bottom line. When the new figures came in, they were clearly unsatisfactory.

The reason our selling expenses were so high was that many of our dealers hadn't been willing to devote much time to selling the panel. Therefore we'd had to direct our own sales and promotion effort directly to the ultimate consumer; on many orders we ended up doing all the selling ourselves. That wouldn't have been so bad except that, after we'd done the work, we were letting the dealers write up the orders — and take their standard commissions. With George Flower's new figures in front of him, our sales manager, Walt Krieger, proposed a selling program that was a lot more equitable. The program produced a projected net profit that seemed to make some sense. The decision to move the Lansing operation to Mountaintop was approved.

The moral I drew from this sequence of events was not to worship the false God of Gross Profit Margin. We now base all our product decisions on models that project to the bottom line. . . .

WAITING FOR A VERDICT

One morning a few weeks back, I was driving to my office and thinking about the day's business. Its main feature was a management-committee meeting with a lot of important business on the agenda — one entry was the future of the whiteboard. Brooding about the potential for big trouble in each of the situations, I suddenly felt that it might be a good idea to pull over to the side of the road. I opened the car door and parted with my breakfast. I was weak and found, to my dismay, that I couldn't stop trembling.

At any previous point in my life, I would have felt that the symptoms justified going home and getting into bed. This time, however, it seemed that the management-committee meeting absolutely had to take place, and that I had to be there for it. I drove to the drugstore, bought a bottle of mouthwash, and went to work.

As the story might indicate, I'm still not entirely at ease in my new way of life. Nevertheless, I'm actually having a lot of fun in the job. The prospect of turning our company around, of succeeding at that challenging task, has exhilarated me, just as it has the people working with me. Thus far we have met our short-term objectives; I believe that we'll meet our long-range ones as well, though it certainly will not be easy. I just hope I don't completely lose the ability to loaf.

QUESTIONS

1. Have you ever been unexpectedly challenged to accept responsibility or provide leadership? How did you feel? What did you do?

   _____

   _____

   _____

2. What experiences and training would you recommend for potential leaders? Describe.

   _____

   _____

   _____

3. Do you aspire to leadership responsibility? Do you have the interest? Do you have the aptitude? What are you doing to prepare?

   _____

   _____

   _____

A Different Style of Leadership

In my new position as Systems Engineer with BBG Industries, my initial assignment was in the Glass Research and Development Automations Section. My immediate supervisor. Al Sirroco, was given the mission of providing computer services for laboratory personnel and production, thus bridging the gap between data processing and process control. With a background in chemical engineering and computer sciences, Al was instrumental in pioneering the powerful and beneficial use of the computer as an aid to scientists and engineers. Utilizing a rented time-shared terminal, results were obtained that maximized calculation thruput and accuracy, thus providing concise historical records so vital in the research environment. Upper management was very impressed by Al's initial success in the realm of automation. The formation of the automation section was concrete evidence that management encouraged further growth in this field for BBG Industries.

Al faced the basic problem of obtaining group cohesiveness and coordination in order to build it into an effective organization. People in our group had diverse backgrounds, including a Ph.D. in mathematics, computer operators with high school diplomas, electrical engineers, and operations research personnel.

To overcome possible communications barriers among members of such a diverse unit, informal group meetings were held once a month. During such meetings each member could openly expound upon any problems requiring clarification, without any fear of retaliation. These staff meetings created an air of openness and relaxation of the status differences caused by differences in rank in our group. Each member had ample opportunity to make an informal presentation of what he or she was contributing to the group effort. Talk about work often spilled over to talk about personal life; the net effect was to produce a feeling of togetherness. After awhile one got the impression that any group member would help any other member with any kind of problem. One weekend, five of us helped bail out Tim, a computer operator, whose basement flooded in a rainstorm.

Our group obtained its first real surprise about Al's approach to managing people following a once-in-a-lifetime incident. An unfortunate

Source: Reprinted with permission from Andrew J. DuBrin (Robert E. Gmitter researched and wrote this case, with the exception of several editorial changes); Casebook of Organizational Behavior, Copyright 1977, Pergamon Press.

situation occurred at the computer center which required the immediate dismissal of a key senior analyst. Although quiet and seemingly introverted, the analyst was held in high esteem because of his diligence and his record of accomplishment. Everyone in the group wondered what violation necessitated such drastic action on Al's part.

Rumors spread that perhaps the systems analyst had been engaged in sabotage, physical attack upon a fellow worker, criminal activity, drug abuse, or maybe a combination of several of these. The day after the incident. Al summoned the group into his office for an important announcement. He informed us that the extreme dedication to job performance shown by this systems analyst had caused him to suffer a nervous breakdown. Al maintained that it was necessary for his safety and the safety of the group for this man to be immediately separated from the company.

Evidence to corroborate Al's explanation was discovered when the individual's desk was cleaned out. A note was found buried beneath some papers in one of the drawers. His writings reflected several approaches to suicide. Al instigated efforts, and received approval, for the analyst to undergo psychiatric help immediately at the company's expense. In addition, severance pay of six month's salary was granted to him, and the company agreed to help him find future employment once his condition improved.

Al's explanation and the suicide note seemed to satisfy everyone's curiosity. However, several weeks later the real cause for the dismissal of the systems analyst surfaced via the company grapevine. One night when the analyst was working late, the only other employee in the building was a female computer operator. While she was walking down the aisle between the office and the computer equipment, he unzipped his pants, exposing himself. Upset by the incident, the computer operator reported the analyst's exhibitionism to her father, a manager in the laboratory. The father demanded retaliation and subsequent criminal prosecution.

Al's handling of the situation was unique and the termination of the systems analyst placated the father. By firing the analyst, the operator was spared the embarrassment of confronting him again at work. Yet, a couple of people in the group felt that Al's handling of the situation was bizarre. Irv, a mathematician, expressed it this way:

"Al sure is cool under pressure, but he's also quite a moralist. Sure, the poor guy exposed himself once that we know of. We cannot estimate the probability that he would expose himself again given the same circumstances. Maybe the father who complained so bitterly was really just jealous of the systems analyst. Worst of all, I question the value of Al making up a phony story just to bury the incident. If we fired everybody in this company who displayed a little deviant behavior once in their lives, we would probably have a pretty thin work force."

Al's approach to leadership can also be understood in his handling of overtime work. Many times crucial projects required extended periods of late hours in order to meet critical deadlines. For exempt professionals, the lab rule stipulated that no compensation would be given, regardless of the time expended in discharging one's responsibilities.

Al informally modified the rule for his group. The term "E-Time," for earned time, could be accumulated by each member for extra hours worked. This was an honor system with responsibility left entirely to the individual. Earned time could be cashed in by trading it for time off with pay when the project load lessened. Al's policy minimized the long, arduous hours of extended toil and promoted excellent group morale.

Al strived constantly to support individual accomplishments and to foster creativity in the glass industry. The Director of Research required a monthly meeting to discuss his group's progress, concepts, improvements, and future goals. Although key projects were mandatory in the agenda, voluntary participation and the initiation of topics were allowed at these important meetings. Each member of the group was encouraged by Al to make his contribution.

Al's impact upon people can be illustrated in his dealings with Kiwabi, a senior mathematician in the group. Kiwabi was advised to present a radical technique for the regression analysis of process data which reduced the time and amount of data, yet maintained qualitative accuracy. His brief presentation in the limelight impressed upper management and paved the way toward Kiwabi obtaining a fully-paid leave of absence to obtain his Ph.D.

A study I had made of various computer systems for process control, as to their power and cost, was scheduled by Al for one of these meetings. My presentation led to future study of this same topic, which verified my findings. Not only was my career as a systems engineer brightened because of it, but the company benefited by obtaining more efficient computer systems with the latest technology at the maximum return upon investment. I honestly believe that without Al's prodding and guidance this study would not have come to fruition.

Supplementing our exposure at meetings, Al would circulate, via inter-lab memos, accomplishments and proposals of his personnel. By this mechanism, all pertinent managers and head scientists were made aware of the existence of group members. It also provided a first-rate opportunity for interface with groups requiring our supportive capabilities in the field of automation.

Al also scheduled trips to the plants to introduce us, explain our function, and relate our specialties. Plant associates could depend upon our expertise to assist them with problems. One such problem solved by our group was the correct depositing of raw materials, such as sand and dolomite, into holding bins. Predetermined amounts of raw material are required for each raw batch composition of glass before heating. The existing manual method had caused production upset due to the wrong ingredients in the bins. An automated, batch unloading protection system was designed, developed, and implemented by our group.

You can understand Al's comprehensive approach to managing people only by sampling the kind of things he did for people. Al would arrange trips for us to other companies, such as Mead Paper, to exchange technological applications and broaden our knowledge of automation. Al also encouraged a few of us to write articles for trade journals, and even provided help in this area. On the basis of these efforts a couple of us have achieved some national recognition.

Al had a keen sense of the ever persistent technological changes taking place in the world of automation. To maintain the group's expertise, Al would submit a list of appropriate courses relevant to each individual's background. Participation and attendance at symposia and conferences were integrated into the work schedule. One of Al's pet projects was to get us involved in the Process Control Workshop at Purdue University. The Workshop consisted of international representation dedicated to standardization of the principles of process control automation.

For my money, Al is a top manager. But not everybody agrees with me. One of the skeptics in our groups said, "If Al walked into my office at 4:30 and reminded me to brush my teeth because it was good for me, I wouldn't be surprised. It would fit his leadership style."

QUESTIONS

1. Evaluate Al Sirroco's handling of the systems analyst problem. What would you have done if you were the supervisor?

_____

_____

_____

2. What style of leadership do you prefer? Would you want a leader like Al? Discuss the pros and cons.

_____

_____

_____

Mr. Black, Ms. Blue, and Mr. White

Recently you were promoted from the job of first-level supervisor to that of middle management, and you now have under your supervision several of your former equals. You get along well with them, and there is no resentment about your advancement because they recognize that you are the best person available for the job.

You know from past associations that you will have to straighten out three of these subordinates; the rest are all right. The three are Black, Blue, and White. Black has always been against the organization, Blue has always been snowed under by work, and White has always been a permissive supervisor.

Black, the anticompany employee, always sides with his subordinates against the organization and sympathizes with them when things go wrong. He wants conditions to be perfect and is always pointing out the defects in the company and finding fault with the way the organization is run. (Conditions, while not perfect, are above average.) Black does his job grudgingly and does not get along well with the other people in the organization.

Blue, on the other hand, is snowed under by her work; she carries the whole load of the department on her shoulders. Her subordinates take no initiative, and she is continually correcting their mistakes. Blue sees that whatever little work comes out of her section is letter-perfect even if she has to have her employees do their jobs over and over again and she has to put on the finishing touches herself. Often her subordinates are standing around waiting for her to get around to checking their work. They know their jobs but wait for Blue to make all the decisions.

Finally, there is White, the permissive supervisor. Instead of running his employees, he is letting them run him. His subordinates do their jobs in any manner they wish. They do not respect White's authority, and they raise so many objections that he lets them do whatever they want. Often they boast of how they tell him off.

All the other supervisors under your jurisdiction are doing a good job. You would like to take the easy way out and fire Black, Blue, and White,

Source: William J. McLarney and William M. Berliner, Management Training: Cases and Principles, *5th ed. (Homewood, Ill.: Richard D. Irwin, Inc., 1970), 34–35. Reprinted with permission.*

but they have been with the company for quite a while. Besides, you feel that, if you can lick these problems, you will receive quite a bit of recognition from upper management.

QUESTIONS

1. How would you go about straightening out Black?

   _____

   _____

   _____

2. How would you go about straightening out Blue?

   _____

   _____

   _____

3. How would you go about straightening out White?

   _____

   _____

   _____

The Full Court Press

Newport Mutual Insurance Company has a regular program of superior-subordinate counseling that has been in operation for close to five years. The core ingredient of the program entails a three-way meeting of the person being counseled about job improvement, his or her boss, and a human resource specialist on assignment from the home office. Prior to the meeting, according to the format of the program, the superior confers briefly with the human resource specialist to discuss the plan for the subordinate's development.

Bonnie Fraser, Branch Manager of the Richmond, Virginia Office and a 16-year veteran in the casualty insurance business, was scheduled to meet with Rudy Bonbright, the Human Resource Specialist from the Home Office. As Branch Manager for the last three years, Bonnie's performance was rated as satisfactory by her superiors. Any criticism about her performance seemed to center around her devoting an unusual amount of attention to the personal development of her subordinates, sometimes at the expense of performing some of the other functions required of her position.

With this criticism about her performance in the back of his mind, Rudy Bonbright began his discussion of the development of personnel at the Richmond Branch.

RUDY: "How are things going for you here, Bonnie? I mean how are your people coming along?"

BONNIE: "Quite satisfactorily, I would say. Our sales are up slightly and we are getting a better mix of business. We have added substantially to our commerical lines and are getting our share of the desirable lines of coverage. Nobody in the office is in danger of being dismissed for poor performance and most of the 20 people here are showing signs of making positive strides in their development. I am personally working with six of the people on their development. The other people are being helped along by their supervisor, but sometimes I'm concerned that part of their development gets lost in the press of everyday business matters. I do what I can to insure that such a situation does not happen with the people reporting directly to me."

Source: *Reprinted with permission from Andrew J. DuBrin*, Casebook of Organizational Behavior, *Copyright 1977, Pergamon Press.*

RUDY: "Maybe we could begin by talking about a specific person among the six you are working with directly. With whom shall we begin?"

BONNIE: "A good starting point would be Russ Atkins, my Field Sales Manager. As you know, he is responsible for most of the recruitment, selection, and training of our new sales personnel. I assist him on many of the selection decisions, but maintaining a field force is mostly his job. He's a good man, with potential for advancement, provided that he overcomes a few developmental needs."

RUDY: "In your opinion, what are his developmental needs?"

BONNIE: "Number one, I don't think Russ is a very effective planner. There are times when he honestly comes into the office with no plan of attack for what he should be doing. He just waits for an assignment or for the phone to ring. One phone call can send him into a three-hour diversion. He also doesn't seem to have a master plan for recruiting a steady supply of new sales personnel. He figures enough people are eager to sell insurance to make it unnecessary for him to draw up elaborate schemes for recruiting new personnel.

"I'm developing a gnawing concern that part of Russ's problems — one thing that is holding him back — is that he is less self-confident than a Field Sales Manager should be. Maybe this could be the factor underlying his other developmental needs."

RUDY: "And what might that be?"

BONNIE: "I think that Russ lacks a killer instinct. He's not mean enough, and this rubs off on the sales people he is trying to develop. Of course, I don't believe in the old-fashioned stereotype of an insurance salesman who badgers prospects into buying more insurance than they need. In my branch, I try to disseminate the idea that a representative for Newport Mutual is a professional insurance consultant — somebody who has the good of the client in mind at all times. Yet, there are times when a prospect needs a little convincing.

"As part of our sales training program, the Field Sales Manager accompanies the inexperienced salesperson on as many sales calls as may be needed. It is crucial for the Field Sales Manager to demonstrate how important it is to close a sale. Not much skill is required in talking to insurance prospects about their insurance problems. A salesperson is paid to close a few big ones. And here is where a little bit of the killer instinct is required. After the prospect is in clear view, you have to get that harpoon in and wheel him on to your boat."

RUDY: "How does Russ Atkins feel about your diagnosis of his needs for development?"

BONNIE: "Russ has a mixed reaction to some of my observations. I think he partially agrees. He seems to be at least fairly responsive to some of our agreed upon action plans for overcoming his developmental needs."

RUDY: "What are these action plans that you have developed?"

BONNIE: "They involve some reading, some attendance at the right kind of training program. But rather than go into detail about them now, why don't we wait until our three-way conference. We can carefully review them in Russ's presence. Then we won't be going over the same ground twice."

RUDY: "Good idea. Why don't we meet with Russ now. Can we use the conference room? It's somewhat neutral territory. If we meet in your office, Russ may unconsciously interpret it as a use of double authority to exert force to get him to improve."

(Bonnie, Rudy, and Russ meet in the conference room.)

BONNIE: "Russ, you have met Rudy before. He's the human resource man from the Home Office who's here to help us with the superior-subordinate development program."

RUSS: "Oh, sure, I remember you came by about six months ago. I understand that today is my turn. I've been looking forward to this meeting. It's always good to get an objective third party's opinion about something as important as your career development."

RUDY: "To begin, Russ, could you review for me what your career goals are?"

RUSS: "Sure thing. I'm in field sales now and I see it as a logical stepping stone to reaching my ultimate goal of a top management position in the marketing wing of an insurance company. At age 28, a Field Sales Manager is a fine perch for further advancement. I would assume that if things go well, I will be eligible for a Branch Manager position in a couple of years or less."

RUDY: "I see. That sounds logical to me. Statistically speaking, a very small proportion of people ever get to be Vice Presidents of Marketing, but it's well worth aiming high."

BONNIE: "As things stand now, what will you need to do as an individual to reach those heights? In other words, is there anything that could be blocking you from reaching your goal?"

RUSS: "It's mostly a question of more of the same. More experience that will improve me across the board. We all need improvement. Just like anybody else in business, I could benefit from being more intelligent, creative, and luckier."

BONNIE: "But what about some of the specific needs for growth that apply to you, Russ Atkins, as an individual?"

RUSS: "Yes, I almost forgot about them, didn't I? Number one, you told me that I should plan my activities more effectively. That might be true to some extent, but my job as Field Sales Manager doesn't lend itself very well to careful planning. You never know which sales representative is going to ask for your help or which of the big customers might want to talk to you. Aside from the duties of a Field Sales Manager, I also handle my share of key accounts."

RUDY: "What action plan have you worked out to improve your skills as a planner?"

RUSS: "I believe that just by being aware of the importance of planning, you can improve your skills in that area. Also, at the request of Bonnie, I've been reading a couple of books that give a manager a lot of good tips on planning his work day. One I recall is an old book of Drucker's, *The Effective Executive* (1967). I've made some progress in reading it and it looks useful. Bonnie, of course, has her own sure-fire techniques of forcing me into becoming a better planner."

RUDY: "What are those?"

RUSS: "She bought me a huge Executive Daily Planner which requires that you keep a meticulous diary of what you do and everything you plan to do. One section of each month's diary asks you to list your plans for the week, month, year, and, finally, a three-year projection. The idea is sound and I make casual use of it. At least every other day, Bonnie asks me how my Executive Planner is going. She follows my diary very closely while I interpret it as a rough guide for action."

BONNIE: "Yes, I do think that such a desk planner is a useful step in improving your planning skills on a day-by-day basis. It requires careful follow-up, otherwise it is easily forgotten."

RUSS: "Okay, now let's talk about Bonnie's insistence that I need to be more aggressive, more of a killer. She also tells me that I should be more self-confident. I agree to some extent, but I don't want to overdo it. A fine line exists between assertiveness and being obnoxious— particularly here in Richmond. I think you can get away with more assertiveness in the New York area. It's a cultural expectation."

RUDY: "What improvement programs have you worked out to match these developmental needs?"

RUSS: "Bonnie has influenced me a lot here, too. First, let's take the self-confidence angle. I don't feel lacking in self-confidence, but I do agree that I, like anybody else, could benefit from acting more self-confident in more situations. Bonnie was helpful in arranging for the company to pay my tuition to the Dale Carnegie Sales Program. I found it effective, even though it is somewhat on the emotional, rah, rah side. Excuse the expression, but I don't want to come across to others like the stereotype of an insurance salesman.

"Bonnie's follow-up to my experiences at Dale Carnegie is worth talking about. She would ask me every week if I felt I was getting anything out of the program, if I were becoming more self-confident. That kind of follow-up can get annoying."

BONNIE: "I didn't mean to annoy you. It's just that any kind of developmental experience requires frequent attention. If you ask yourself periodically what you are getting out of a training program, you are more likely to derive some benefits from it. It's another way of reminding yourself to put into practice the principles that you learn during the training sessions."

RUDY: "Are there any other concerns you have about the way Bonnie monitors your developmental program?"

RUSS: "Yes, I think she plain puts too much effort and time into the development of her subordinates, particularly me. She can get a little cloying at times, despite her good intentions. Another thing she's been pushing is for me to attend assertiveness training. Her point is that perhaps this is just the kind of growth I need to become more self-confident and more of a 'killer.' I'm not so sure I'm that unassertive, but I was willing to give it a try. As things worked out, I did attend a few sessions and I found them intriguing. For one, I learned that I'm much less of a basket case than Bonnie thinks. Most of the other people in the group are far less assertive than I am."

BONNIE: "Then you did get something out of the program. It gave you more confidence in yourself. You realize some more of your strengths."

RUSS: "I guess I should be thankful for that. I'm not objecting to the fact that you pointed me toward an assertiveness training program. What does irritate me is the way you keep a weekly check on my progress. At least once a week you ask me, 'Do you feel yourself becoming more assertive?'"

RUDY: "Then you object to Bonnie's coaching techniques."

RUSS: "At least some aspects of her coaching. What I dislike most is her full court press."

RUDY: (After the meeting): "Bonnie, I think you are pressing too hard with Russ. He may be showing some resistance to being overdeveloped by the company. We want our managers to participate with enthusiasm in human resource development, but we also have to watch out for an overemphasis in this area. Remember that all development is really self-development."

QUESTIONS

1. Have you ever known or had a supervisor who was concerned about the personal/professional development of an employee? Describe.

_____

_____

_____

2. Have you ever known or had a supervisor who showed no interest in employee development? Discuss.

_____

_____

_____

3. If you were a supervisor, what principles and practices would you use regarding employee development?

_____

_____

_____

The Forklift Fiasco

There are three fork-lift truck operators in the warehouse. Two of them are young employees who have both been warned twice (the second warning in writing) about careless operation of the trucks. Last week one of them (Jack) made a fast turn and spilled a shipment. The dropped cartons had to be opened and inspected and a number of damaged items sent back for repair.

The supervisor said it was inexcusable carelessness and gave him a three-day layoff. He warned all truck operators that any damage with trucks would be punished by layoff from here on.

Today Ray Harrison, the third truck operator, ran into a door frame overhead and spilled the entire load he was carrying. He had simply failed to lower the truck. He is a valued employee and has never had an accident before or any disciplinary record in all his years on the job. He is a friend and neighbor of the supervisor and they ride to work together. Everyone is watching to see what the supervisor is going to do about it.

QUESTIONS

1. If a supervisor makes a threat, is it necessary to carry it out?

_____

_____

_____

2. Have you ever been punished for a mistake on the job? Was the action fair? Explain.

_____

_____

_____

Source: William J. McLarney and William M. Berliner, Management Training: Cases and Principles, 5th ed. (Homewood, Ill.: Richard D. Irwin, Inc., 1970), 599. Reprinted with permission.

APPLICATION

Train the Trainer   224

Train The Trainer

Directions

The following pages are divided into four "frames." Read each frame and fill in the blanks as you progress. Begin by reading frame number one on page 225. Complete it by writing your answer in the blank space provided. Then, turn the page and check your answer. After you have checked your answer, go on to frame number two *on the next page*. Note that the first three frames set the pattern; after that, you are not told where to find the answer or the next frame.

DO NOT READ DOWN THE PAGE.

Keep turning forward each time.

You will find clues to help you with the blanks and questions as you go along. If you read carefully and remember what you read, you will usually get the right answer at each step before turning the page. If you do get an answer wrong—that is, the correct answer is totally different from what you were thinking and is not just another way of saying the same thing—think about why the printed response is right before going on.

By reading carefully and thinking about your answers, you will find that, when finished, you can remember almost everything you have studied.

Source: Naomi Miller, based on How to Train Others, *The Procter & Gamble Company, 1965.*

WHY GOOD TRAINING
IS IMPORTANT

1. Every year a number of people are trained for new jobs in all types of organizations. Training is important because a poor job of training usually means _____ performance for the trainee when he assumes responsibility for the new job.

   Answer is on page 2. Frame number 2 is on page 3.

---

21. *If you have come here from frame number 1, you goofed. Go back to frame number 1 and read the instructions again.*

    To begin with, suppose I asked you, "How do I get to the Campbell County Court House from here?" If you knew the answer, you would probably _____ me how to get there.

---

41. If your trainee has taken good _____ that he can use later, he may not need to rely so much on his _____ when he begins trying to apply what you have taught him.

---

61. And the reason for this mistake can easily be traced back to the _____ 's failure to explain to the _____ exactly _____ he was to do the job in the particular way he was trained.

Correct Answers

1. poor

21. tell

41. notes
    memory

61. trainer
    trainee
    why

2. If training seems important to the organization, it probably seems even more important to the trainee. If a person is poorly trained, his performance will probably also be _____.

Answer is on page 4. Frame number 3 is on page 5.

---

22. By telling me this, you might realistically assume you had taught me something — how to get to the Campbell County Court House. This is natural, because it often seems that all that is needed to teach someone something is just _____ him how to do it.

---

42. Of course, note taking will not be appropriate for all the details of the job. Some important parts can only be learned by practice. Think about it, though, and name a few things that it would be a good idea to take notes on in learning your job:

_____

_____

_____

_____

---

62. This happens very often in training. The trainee knows what he's supposed to do and how to do it, but because he doesn't know _____, he guesses at the reason, makes a wrong guess, and finishes by making a big _____.

Correct Answers

2. poor

---

22. telling

---

42. Your answer should include some things you do not have to remember in detail, but that you need to refer to from time to time.

---

62. why
mistake

3. How do you recognize a poorly trained person? What is his job performance usually like compared with one who has been well trained and knows what he is doing? In your own experience, you have probably seen poorly trained employees make mistakes and perform careless work. Consequently, the q _____ of work is not as good.

Answer is on page 6. Frame number 4 is on page 7.

---

23. However, telling or explaining as a method of _____, all by itself, has some obvious shortcomings. For one thing, you really don't know how clearly your trainee understands what you are saying, and even if he does understand at the time, later he will probably _____ exactly what you said.

---

43. Another thing about notes. You may have some notes of your own that you could give to your trainee. You may think that since he will not have to take them himself, you will be doing him a _____ and saving him _____.

---

63. Think of some examples of parts of your job where it would be especially important that your trainee understand why he must do things a particular way.

Correct Answers

3. quality

---

23. teaching, training
    forget

---

43. favor
    time, work

---

63. Your answer: You should be a better judge of these things than anyone
    else. Did you consider quality, quantity, safety, cost, interpersonal
    relations, communications, etc.?

4. So, he often does work of low _____. In addition, he has not learned the easiest and most efficient way to do things. As a result, he often does not get as _____ work done in the same amount of time as a well-trained person.

   Answer is on next page.

---

24. *Note: Read this frame ONCE only — don't look back at it.*

    Suppose I want to teach you to draw a particular figure on a piece of paper and I say: "It's easy. Just make a rectangle that is twice as high as it is wide; draw a line across the middle; draw diagonal lines connecting every right angle; and last, draw lines connecting the four angles closest to the center of the figure."

    Go to the next frame right now.

---

44. Sometimes this can be a good idea, and sometimes not. If the notes are on something the trainee does not have to know (he just needs a place to look it up), by all means, give him your _____ so that he doesn't have to take his own.

---

64. In training another person then, you will want to make sure that, for all parts of the job, he knows: _____ to do, _____ to do it, and, so easy to overlook, _____ he should do it just that way.

Correct Answers

4. quality
   much

   Frame 5 is on page 9.

---

24. *Go on to the next frame.*

---

44. notes

---

64. what
    how
    why

5. It is probable that the employee who doesn't know how to do his job is going to be pushing a lot _____ just to keep up. And when you are pushing (especially if you have never really learned what the hazards are on the job), you are much more likely to have an _____ or make a serious _____.

   Answer is on next page.

---

25. Now, without looking back at the directions, draw the figure I described to you. I can probably afford to give you $1000 for every one you can draw correctly. But, go ahead and try.

    Use a piece of scratch paper; then go on to the next frame.

---

45. However, if he does have to learn it—that is, he must have it in his head because there is not enough time to look up answers—it is best to have him take his own notes. If he has to think it through well enough to put it into his own words, he will be more likely to _____ it later.

THE IMPORTANCE
OF CORRECTING

65. Next, how can you tell whether your trainee is really learning so that you may make corrections promptly? The surest way, of course, is to let him actually _____ the job, and then watch to see if any _____ are made.

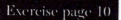

Correct Answers

5. faster, harder
   accident
   mistake

   Frame 6 is on page 11.

---

25. It looks like this:

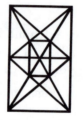

If you got it right, you cheated. But don't worry, I didn't get to the Campbell County Court House either without some groping.

---

45. remember

---

65. do, practice, perform
    mistakes, errors

6. Put yourself in the employee's place. What does the poorly trained employee feel like?

- The _____ of his work is not high.

- He may be working _____ while getting less done.

- And on top of everything else (especially if he is on a job that has any real hazards), he may take a careless shortcut that may land him in the _____.

26. You forgot! Or maybe you remembered, but never really had it straight in the first place. That is frequently what happens when you rely only upon _____ someone how to do something.

46. Deciding if you should give your trainee your notes, or have him take his own, depends upon whether _____, or he _____.

66. Sometimes, when the trainee is trying out what you have taught him, he may make mistakes without being fully aware of them. To prevent mistakes from becoming a habit, you should _____ him promptly.

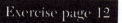

Correct Answers

6. quality
   harder
   hospital

26. telling

46. he has to *learn* it
    just needs a record for reference

66. correct

7. List four ways a poorly trained employee's work habits are likely to be different from those of a well-trained employee.

   1. _____

   2. _____

   3. _____

   4. _____

---

27. So, what should you do? It is unreasonable not to use telling. But it is reasonable to look for something else you can do in _____ to telling — at least when what you are trying to teach is at all complicated.

---

47. If he should learn the material:

         1. Have him take his own notes.

   Choose: *or*

         2. Give him yours

---

67. At the time you _____ him, it is always best to have the trainee _____ over the part of the job he did incorrectly. In this way, he learns to do it right immediately after you have _____ him.

Correct Answers

7. lower quality
   not as fast or efficient
   has to work a lot harder to keep up
   more likely to work carelessly

---

27. addition

---

47. no.1; take his own notes

---

67. correct
    do, try
    corrected

8. And the employee really doesn't know what to do about it because the training program is over and he did not _____. How do you think he feels? _____.

---

28. One good addition would be to give the trainee something to look at or watch — that is, in addition to telling him what to do, you can _____ him what to do.

---

48. If he does not need to learn it, but just needs it for reference:

        1. Have him take his own notes

Choose: or

        2. Give him yours

---

68. Even though you can see what he is doing by watching him, it is not easy to tell whether he knows _____ he is doing it.

Correct Answers

8. learn
   he probably feels terrible

---

28. show, demonstrate to

---

48. no. 2; give him yours

---

68. why

9. This happens, of course. And when it does, who do you think suffers most? _____

_____

_____

29. When you are teaching a job that has several steps, the trainee is much more likely to remember the steps if you _____ as you go along.

49. Taking notes can be a bother (even on things important to remember). If you leave it up to your trainee and don't say anything about it yourself, he probably _____ take as good notes as he should. Be sure you, as the trainer, _____ him to take notes on things you think will be useful later.

69. To find out if he knows the reasons behind what he is doing, you will have to get him to tell you. This means you have to _____.

Correct Answers

9. The poorly trained person suffers, or maybe the organization. It depends on how you look at it. But nobody wins.

---

29. demonstrate

---

49. will not
    encourage, tell, etc.

---

69. ask questions

WHO IS MOST RESPONSIBLE
FOR THE SUCCESS OF
A TRAINING PROGRAM?

10. No matter how the training is presented, if a person does not learn something, it is assumed that he just did not _____ hard enough; he is lazy; or just plain _____.

---

30. Now, try to draw the figure again. You have already had a look at it, so don't look back. Do it from memory and then CHECK IT.

---

50. Remember, if the trainee fails to do the right things to learn the job because he doesn't know any better, and you do know better, it is _____ responsibility. The _____ is more responsible than anyone else for the success of the training program.

HOW TO ASK QUESTIONS

70. What kinds of questions? Well, what do you think of one like this? "Charlie, I've just spent five hours teaching you how to bone an elephant. Do you understand it all, Charlie, or do you have any questions?" Is this a good question?

Correct Answers

10. try, work, study
     dumb, stupid

---

30. *You might have gotten it this time but if you didn't, you're not alone.*

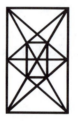

---

50. your
     trainer

---

70. No, it is not. Chances are that Charlie will say yes, that he understands it, and will hope for the best. Then, the next time he gets an elephant on his bench, he will ruin it good and proper.

11. You do not have to look only in the work setting to see this happening. Anywhere—in the public schools, for example—if the student doesn't learn, it is usually assumed to be the _____'s own fault.

31. If you didn't get it right this time (and even if you did, chances are that I could have prevented it by making the drawing a little more complicated), there are still a couple of things we could do to improve learning. This time you had a clearer picture to start with, but didn't have anything to look at while you were drawing, so you had to rely on your _____ .

51. To review a few of the things discussed to this point: the simplest and yet, by itself, least effective way to teach someone to do something would be _____ .

71. Anyone can answer a "Do you understand?" question about anything, and you don't know a single thing about whether he really understands it. All you know is that he _____ he understands it.

Correct Answers

11. student's

---

31. memory

---

51. telling, explaining — just tell them how to do it

---

71. thinks or says

12. However, as more research is done on the conditions under which people "learn" or "do not learn," there appear to be more and more things the trainer can do to help the trainee _____ the job and learn it well. This, more often than not, means if the trainee has not learned, the _____ has not taught.

HOW TO HELP YOUR TRAINEE
NOT TO FORGET

32. Instead of having to wait between seeing the picture and drawing it, you probably could have done better if you had drawn the figure _____ after seeing it the first time. Once you had drawn it correctly the first time, you would probably be able to continue drawing it _____ and _____ without mistakes.

---

52. The next thing you might consider doing to give a clearer picture is

_____

_____ .

---

72. So, if you are the trainer, and the trainer is really _____ for the success of the training program, you had better find a _____ way of asking questions.

Correct Answers

12. learn
    trainer, leader

---

32. immediately, right
    again and again, over and over

---

52. showing, demonstrating—don't just tell, but show how to do it

---

72. responsible
    better, different, good

13. In this exercise you are going to learn some things that will help you do a good job of _____ a person to do anything. However, from what has been suggested so far, who would you say is more responsible than anyone else for the success of a training program? _____ .

33. So, here is an important point: When you are teaching someone to do something, it is a good idea to let him not only watch you do it, but actually _____ it himself, and to do it as _____ as possible after you tell and show him how to do it.

53. There are two additional ways to help a person not to forget what you have told and shown him. These were:

1. _____

2. _____

73. If you ask a trainee questions that make him think about what he's been taught, and put this into his own words, you will probably be able to tell whether he really _____ what you have been teaching.

Correct Answers

13. training, teaching
    the trainer

---

33. do, try, practice
    soon

---

53. 1. Let him try it out or practice; the earlier, the better.
    2. Encourage him to take notes.

---

73. understands, knows

HOW TO BEGIN

14. Think of some of the courses that you have taken. One of the first things your instructor probably did before getting into the details of the subject was to give a broad overview of what the whole _____ would cover.

34. Of course, there are times when it will not be possible to let the trainee practice _____ away. There may be safety hazards, or there may be too much money at stake, or there may be other reasons for putting practice off until the trainee knows a little more. But, whenever possible, let the trainee _____ what you have taught, and let him do it _____ after you teach it, even if it is only a small part of the whole job.

54. There is still a very important thing you can do to help your trainee learn that has not been mentioned. Very few trainers do as much of this as they should. Look at the case in the following frame and see if you can spot it.

74. To test a person's understanding, you should ask questions that make him _____ and then put his thoughts into _____.

Correct Answers

14. course, subject

---

34. right
    do, try, practice
    soon

---

54. Go right on to the next frame.

---

74. think
    words

15. The reason for giving this _____ before getting into specific _____ is this: if a trainee knows where the course is going to take him in general, he will be more interested in the course and will do a better job _____ the details that come later.

---

35. Most trainees will not be able to understand some operations fully until they actually _____ them.

---

55. The trainer in the Accounting Department gives instructions to a new payroll employee on how to prepare the information needed in order to have checks ready for distribution on the scheduled payday. He first gives an overview of the total operation; then he explains and demonstrates the steps involved before taking the payroll to the Data Processing Department on Thursday, where it is always run on Friday morning; he gives the employee plenty of time to practice; and he reminds the trainee that the whole payroll should reach Data Processing before noon on Thursday. What would you say the trainer has neglected in this case?

---

75. Your trainee will not be able to answer such questions correctly unless he really _____ what you have been teaching him.

Correct Answers

15. big picture, overview, preview
    details
    learning

---

35. do, practice, try, perform

---

55. He failed to explain *why* the checks should reach Data Processing before noon Thursday.

---

75. understands, knows, comprehends

16. When you teach someone a job, it is best to start this same way. Don't start right in teaching little details of the job before you have told the trainee something about the _____ job.

---

36. There are many jobs a person must actually "learn in his muscles" as well as in his head. Typing is one example. This is another reason why _____ is so important, in addition to showing and telling.

THE IMPORTANCE
OF EXPLAINING WHY

56. This may at first seem to be a fairly unimportant point. After all, the trainer told him and even showed him what to do and how to do it. And if a person knows what and how, you might think it wouldn't matter if he knows _____ he's doing it.

---

76. In discussing the importance of asking questions, we are mainly talking about questions designed to find out if your trainee knows _____ he is doing the things he is doing.

Correct Answers

16. whole, total

36. practice, doing

56. why

76. why

17. Discuss the new employee's responsibilities in a general way. Tell him how his job fits in with other _____ in the department, and how the work of the _____ fits in with other departments in the organization.

---

37. In any case, you can seldom depend on a person's _____ a job well and correctly unless you have given plenty of opportunity to _____ during training.

---

57. But put yourself in the trainee's position here. The following week, the trainer has to be at a meeting in another department on Thursday morning. The trainee finds himself running behind schedule, but decides that since the payroll is not run until Friday, it will not matter. He completes the work and takes the payroll to Data Processing late on Thursday afternoon. He does not think that two or three hours could make much difference anyway.

---

77. However, you can use good questions all through the training program for other purposes as well. For example, you may feel safer about turning a trainee loose on some jobs if you ask him to explain to you _____ he is going to do before he does it.

Correct Answers

17. jobs, work, employees
    department

---

37. doing, learning, knowing
    do it personally, try it personally, practice it personally

---

57. *Go on to the next frame.*

---

77. what (and probably how as well)

18. To sum up, if you spend a few minutes giving the trainee the _____ picture before going into details, he probably will do a better job of picking up those _____ as you cover them later.

---

38. And remember: If there is a long delay between instruction and practice, the trainee is likely to _____ what you have taught him, or at least parts of it.

---

58. And is he right? Well, let's see. The trainee understood that the payroll run was made on Friday, so there should be no real rush. However, the real reason for having the payroll in Data Processing on Thursday afternoon is that the information has to be keypunched before the Friday morning run. So what happened? With the delay in receiving the payroll information, the keypunch operators had to work overtime, and it was not ready when the computer time was scheduled for the run. Since it was necessary to process the payroll, and something else could not be started and stopped, hundreds of dollars in computer time were lost. When the payroll was run, it caused the check distribution for the whole organization to be delayed a full day. Under the circumstances, what should the trainee have done when he was working on the payroll?

---

78. There may also be situations that don't happen very often on the job. If you have told the trainee what to do when these things happen, you can test his understanding at any time by _____

_____

_____.

Correct Answers

18. whole, big
    details

---

38. forget

---

58. He should have checked with the trainer or someone else in the depart-
    ment before making the change in the time schedule.

---

78. questioning him — that is, asking him to explain now what he will
    do when these situations come up later.

HOW TO TEACH ANYBODY
HOW TO DO ANYTHING

19. The principles discussed here should help you _____ anybody how to do anything. These principles are general and should be useful in any _____ you ever do (and it is likely that you will do a great deal of it).

---

39. Therefore, it is important to give the trainee a chance to practice

_____

_____

(when?).

---

59. Instead, he made the change without checking. What could the trainer have done during the training session that would have prevented this mistake from being made? _____

_____

_____

---

79. You might assume that if a trainee doesn't understand something, he will ask questions. How often do you think this turns out to be the case?

1. Never   2. Sometimes   3. Nearly always

Correct Answers

19. teach, train, instruct
training

---

39. as you go along — as soon as possible after each phase of instruction

---

59. He could have told him the reason for getting the payroll completed before noon on Thursday. He could have told him "why."

---

79. No. 2—*sometimes*; but often *never*, either because he is embarrassed, or because he isn't aware that he is confused.

20. For example, the principles would help you do a better job of teaching your child to tie his shoe, your husband to change a diaper, or your wife to grease the car. In short, these rules for effective training apply in teaching anybody to do _____.

40. Is there anything other than immediate practice that you can do to help your trainee remember? You can make sure he has a notebook, and you can encourage him to take _____ for himself on what he learns.

60. If the trainee had been well trained in this case, he probably _____ have made the mistake.

80. Since the trainee frequently will not ask questions when he should, it is especially important that the _____ does ask questions— the kinds of questions that make the trainee _____ and _____. Then you can be sure he _____ what you have taught him.

Correct Answers

20. anything

Stop. Go back to page 1, frame 21.

---

40. notes

Go back to page 1, frame 41.

---

60. would not

Go back to page 1, frame 61.

---

80. trainer
think
put his thoughts into words
understands

Go to top of next page for Final Review. Page 41.

FINAL REVIEW

For a final review of what has been covered here, suppose you look at the following examples and see what, if anything, looks wrong with each. In each case the person talking is the trainer. What should he have done differently?

Go on to Review Question Number 1 on page 43.

---

2. "I can't understand how she could make a mistake like that. I explained to her what she was supposed to do, and told her to ask questions if there was anything she didn't understand."

See page 42 for the answer.

---

4. "No need to take any notes on landing, Leonard. I'll just give you mine and you can memorize them after you're in the air."

See page 42 for the answer.

---

6. "One thing to remember about de-fusing Z-bombs, John, is that unless you disconnect this wire *first* and *then* that one and *then* that one, you'll blow up the whole southside. Now, let me ask you a question, John. Do you understand how to make these disconnections? You say you think so? Fine, suppose you go over there and try one."

See page 42 for the answer.

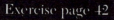

Answers

2. Telling or explaining usually isn't enough; the trainer should show, too. Also, trainees are often embarrassed to ask questions, so the trainer should ask questions that test understanding.

Go to Review Question 3 on page 43.

4. Have trainee take his own notes if he has to learn it, and start learning it at the same time.

Go to Review Question 5 on page 43.

6. Show as well as tell; let trainee practice; ask questions that test understanding — not just "Do you understand?"

Go to Review Question 7 on page 43.

1. "How do you do, Frank. My name is Helen and I am going to be your trainer. This is a very complex job, and the first thing I want to show you about it is what to do if this screw comes loose. First you. . ."

See page 44 for the answer.

3. "You will have a lot to learn on this job, Alice. I have counted exactly 1,479 different things I do in the average week. Now, suppose you watch me do them the first week, and then the second week you try to do it yourself while I watch."

See page 44 for the answer.

5. "I have an unabridged dictionary I could let you use, Evelyn, but I always feel you will find it more useful if you copy one of your own."

See page 44 for the answer.

7. "What's that, Ed? You say you thought the reason you were told to wear gloves when you handle that stuff was to keep your hands warm, and your hands got too warm so you took the gloves off and now. . .if you'll stand still and stop shouting a minute, Ed, I'll take a look at it."

See page 44 for the answer.

Answers

1. Start with a broad view of the whole job — get into the details next.
   Go back to page 41 for frame 2.

---

3. Practice soon after learning, otherwise your trainee forgets what you have said by the time you are ready to let him try it himself.
   Go back to page 41 for frame 4.

---

5. If the notes are only for reference and not to be memorized, use any accurate reference available instead of having the trainee make notes of his own.
   Go back to page 41 for frame 6.

---

7. Tell *why* as well as what and how, and you will save a lot of grief and misunderstanding.

   The End

APPENDIX A

Background Information, Teaching Suggestions, and Testing and Grading

The Human Side of Work is a series of desk books for managers, hand-books for practitioners, and workbooks for students. These are applied books that combine behavior theory with business practice. Each book teaches central concepts and skills in an important area of the world of work. The set of eight books includes stress management, communication skills, employee motivation, leadership principles, quality of work life, managing for excellence, employee participation, and the role of ethics.

Each book combines theory with practice, gives commonsense answers to real-life problems, and is easy to read and fun to use. The series may be used as a set or as stand-alone books. The subject areas are made more forceful and the impact greater by the self-evaluation questionnaires and practical exercises that are used for personal development.

AUDIENCE

The Human Side of Work is written for two audiences. One audience includes managers and professionals interested in personal and professional development on their own or within the context of a management development program. Another audience includes students in human relations, organization behavior, and other management-related courses.

The material is appropriate for use at the four-year college and university level as well as in community colleges, proprietary schools, extension programs, and management training seminars.

CONTENT AND STYLE

The difference between most organization behavior texts and *The Human Side of Work* can be compared to the difference between a lecture and a seminar. Although both are good educational vehicles, the lecture is better for conveying large amounts of information, while the seminar is better for developing skills. The good lecture is interesting and builds knowledge; the good seminar is stimulating and builds competency. *The Human Side of Work* emphasizes the interactive, seminar approach to learning.

The writing style is personal and conversational, with minimal professional jargon. True-life examples clarify points under consideration. Concepts are supported by stories and anecdotes, which are more meaningful and easy to remember than facts, figures, and lists. Each book includes learning activities to bridge the gap between classroom theory and on-the-job practice.

The Human Side of Work is more than a series of textbooks. These are "learning" books that actively involve the reader in the learning process. Our goal has been to include material that is interesting to read, relates to the reader's own concerns, and is practical to use. The following captures the spirit of our effort:

I Taught Them All

I have taught in high school for ten years. During that time, I have given assignments, among others, to a murderer, an evangelist, a pugilist, a thief, and an imbecile.

The murderer was a quiet little boy who sat on the front seat and regarded me with pale blue eyes; the evangelist, easily the most popular boy in school, had the lead in the junior class play; the pugilist lounged by the window and let loose at intervals with a raucous laugh that startled even the geraniums; the thief was a gay-hearted Lothario with a song on his lips; and the imbecile, a soft-eyed little animal seeking the shadows.

The murderer awaits death in the state penitentiary; the evangelist has lain a year in the village churchyard; the pugilist lost an eye in a brawl in Hong Kong; the thief, by standing on tiptoe, can see the windows of my room from the county jail; and the once gentle-eyed little moron beats his head against a padded wall in the state asylum.

All of these young men once sat in my room, sat and looked at me gravely across worn brown desks. I must have been a great help to those pupils — I taught them the rhyming scheme of the Elizabethan sonnet and how to diagram a complex sentence.

Naomi John White

The focus of *The Human Side of Work* is self-discovery and personal development as the reader "learns by doing." The material covered is authoritative and up to date, reflecting current theory and practices. The level of material is appropriate for all levels of expertise (new and experienced managers) and all levels of education (undergraduate and graduate).

TESTING AND REVIEW PROCESS

The Human Side of Work has been tested and refined in our classes at Northern Kentucky University. The information and activities have been used with hundreds of organizations and thousands of employees in business, industry, and government. Users include American Telephone and Telegraph Co., International Business Machines Corp., John Hancock, Marriott Corporation, Sun Oil, and Ford Motor Co. in the private sector and the Department of Transportation, the Environmental Protection Agency, the Internal Revenue Service, the National Institutes of

Health, and state governments in the public sector. The following are sample evaluations:

Good for student participation. My students like the exercises and learning instruments, and the fact each is a stand-alone book that is bite-size. Their reaction: "Everyone should read them!"

Joseph F. Ohren, Eastern Michigan University

A comprehensive series dealing with employee development and job performance. Information is presented in an interesting and easy-to-use style. Case studies and readings help teach the topics, and applications make the material more meaningful. It is an excellent guide for the practicing manager. Ideal as desk books.

David Duncan, IBM

I am a non-traditional student. As one who has worked for over twenty years, I thoroughly enjoyed the material. An understanding of the world of work is presented in a way that is usable at any level of an organization. The books present a common sense approach to management.

Naomi Miller, Northern Kentucky University

Best I've seen on the people side of work. Helps the person. Helps the company. Good for personal and management development. Popular with participants from all backgrounds.

Charles Apple, University of Michigan

This is an easy-to-read, comprehensive series in organization behavior. It puts theory into relevant, usable terminology. Methods for identifying and solving human relations problems are pinpointed. It sets the stage for understanding how people, environment and situations interact in an organization.

David Sprouse, AT&T

TEACHING FORMATS

The Human Side of Work is versatile and can be used in many formats:

- for seminars and training programs
- as classroom texts
- as supplemental information and activities

The following is a discussion of each option.

Seminars and Training Programs

Books used for seminars and training programs should be selected to meet the objectives and needs of the participants — communication, stress, leadership, etc. Material can be mixed and matched for training programs in personal development, professional development, management development, and team building. Material in each book is appropriate for a variety of time periods: one-half day (3 to 4 hours), one full day (6 to 8 hours), and two full days (12 to 16 hours).

The books provide excellent learning activities and questionnaires to encourage participation and personalize the subject. Books then serve as "take-home" material for further reading and personal development. In this format, study quizzes are rarely used for grading, and homework assignments are seldom given. See the following table for appropriate audiences, program focus, and recommended books when using *The Human Side of Work* for seminars and training programs.

Classroom Texts

The series is appropriate for use as texts in college courses in human relations, organization behavior, and organizational psychology. The following is a sample lesson plan using the set for a one-semester course:

Week	Focus on the Person	
1	Stress	Part One, Part Two
2	Stress	Part Three, Part Four
3	Communication	Part One, Part Two
4	Communication	Part Three, Part Four
5	Human Behavior	Part One, Part Two
6	Human Behavior	Part Three
7	Ethics	Part One, Part Two
8	Ethics	Part Three, Part Four

	Focus on the Organization	
9	Morale	Part One, Part Two
10	Morale	Part Three
11	Leadership	Part One, Part Two
12	Leadership	Part Three, Part Four

USING THE HUMAN SIDE OF WORK FOR SEMINARS AND TRAINING PROGRAMS

Appropriate Audiences	Program Focus	Recommended Books
Personal and professional development	Focus on the individual	* Stress Without Distress: Rx for Burnout * Communication: The Miracle of Dialogue * Human Behavior: Why People Do What They Do * Ethics at Work: Fire in a Dark World * Morale: Quality of Work Life (optional) * Performance: Managing for Excellence (optional)
New and experienced managers	Focus on management	* Morale: Quality of Work Life * Leadership: Nine Keys to Success * Performance: Managing for Excellence * Groupstrength: Quality Circles at Work * Stress Without Distress: Rx for Burnout (optional) * Communication: The Miracle of Dialogue (optional) * Human Behavior: Why People Do What They Do (optional) * Ethics at Work: Fire in a Dark World (optional)
Employee development and team building	Focus on the organization	* Communication: The Miracle of Dialogue * Morale: Quality of Work Life * Groupstrength: Quality Circles at Work * Stress Without Distress: Rx for Burnout (optional) * Human Behavior: Why People Do What They Do (optional) * Performance: Managing for Excellence (optional)

Popular seminar and program titles with corresponding books are as follows:

Managing Change: Personal and Professional Coping Skills	* Stress Without Distress: Rx for Burnout
Communication: One to One; One to Many	* Communication: The Miracle of Dialogue
Human Relations and the Nature of Man	* Human Behavior: Why People Do What They Do
Business Ethics and Corporate Culture	* Ethics at Work: Fire in a Dark World
Quality of Work Life	* Morale: Quality of Work Life
The Human Side of Management	* Leadership: Nine Keys to Success
Managing for Productivity: People Building Skills	* Performance: Managing for Excellence
Employee Involvement: If Japan Can Do It, Why Can't We?	* Groupstrength: Quality Circles at Work

13	Performance	Part One, Part Two
14	Performance	Part Three
15	Groupstrength	Part One, Part Two
16	Groupstrength	Part Three

Related Activities and Homework Assignments

Week	Suggested Readings, Cases and Applications
1	*Anatomy of an Illness as Perceived by the Patient* (reading) *The Price of Success* (case)
2	*Death of a Salesman* (reading) *Scientific Relaxation* (application)
3	*Barriers and Gateways to Communications* (reading) *The Power of Vocabulary* (application)
4	*The Dyadic Encounter* (application) *Attitudes toward Women Working* (application)
5	*The Human Side of Enterprise* (reading) *Significant People and Critical Events* (application)
6	*Values Auction* (application) *Personal and Interpersonal Growth* (application)
7	*If Hitler Asked You to Electrocute a Stranger, Would You?* (reading) *How Could the Jonestown Holocaust Have Occurred?* (reading)
8	*Values Flag* (application) *The Kidney Machine* (application)
9	*Work* (reading) *The Joe Bailey Problem* (application)
10	*The Coffee Break* (case) *In Search of Excellence* (application)
11	*What Happened When I Gave Up the Good Life and Became President* (case) *Black, Blue, and White* (case)
12	*The Forklift Fiasco* (case) *Train the Trainers* (application)
13	*Games Mother Never Taught You* (reading) *How Will You Spend Your Life?* (application)

14	*How to Manage Your Time: Everybody's No. 1 Problem* (reading)
	Chrysler's Turnaround Strategy (case)
15	*Groupthink* (reading)
	The Dean Practices Participative Management (case)
16	*Decisions, Decisions, Decisions* (reading)
	The Bottleneck (application)

This format for a one-semester course uses selected readings, cases, and applications from all eight books. For a two-semester course, additional readings, cases, and applications are provided.

Another popular format is to use fewer books in a one-semester course, and to use these more thoroughly. The books can be selected by the instructor or the class. For example, stress, communication, morale, and leadership may be best suited for a given group.

Testing and Grading

When using *The Human Side of Work* as classroom texts, study quizzes in each book can be used to evaluate content knowledge. Although quiz scores can be used to assign formal grades, students learn best when they are also asked to apply the concepts in some personal way. Examples include a term journal, a related research paper, a small-group project, a field assignment, and/or a self-improvement project.

Grades can be assigned on the basis of test scores and term project(s). Projects can be evaluated according to the three C's: clarity, comprehensiveness, and correctness. Half the course grade could be based on study quiz scores, and the other half on the term project(s).

Supplemental Information and Activities

The books in *The Human Side of Work* can provide supplemental information and activities for various college courses. State-of-the-art questionnaires and user-friendly exercises add variety and increase student involvement. Books matched with appropriate college courses are as follows:

Recommended Books	College Courses
Stress Without Distress: Rx for Burnout	Personal Development
	Personal Health
	Human Relations
	Organization Behavior
	Organizational Psychology
	Supervisory Development

Communication: The Miracle of Dialogue	Personal Development Communications Human Relations Organization Behavior Organizational Psychology Supervisory Development
Human Behavior: Why People Do What They Do	Personal Development Human Relations Organization Behavior Organizational Psychology Supervisory Development
Ethics at Work: Fire in a Dark World	Personal Development Business Ethics Human Relations Organization Behavior Organizational Psychology Supervisory Development
Morale: Quality of Work Life	Personnel/Human Resources Human Relations Organization Behavior Organizational Psychology Supervisory Development
Leadership: Nine Keys to Success	Management Principles Human Relations Organization Behavior Organizational Psychology Supervisory Development
Performance: Managing for Excellence	Management Principles Human Relations Organization Behavior Organizational Psychology Supervisory Development
Groupstrength: Quality Circles at Work	Personnel/Human Resources Human Relations Organization Behavior Organizational Psychology Supervisory Development

When used as supplemental material, books are rarely tested for grades. The emphasis is on using the questionnaires, exercises, cases, and applications to increase interest and participation and to personalize the subject.

APPENDIX B

Additional References

ADDITIONAL REFERENCES

The following books are recommended for further reading in the area of leadership. Each is included because of its significance in the field, support to this text, and value for further personal development.

Bennis, Warren G. *Leaders: The Strategies for Taking Charge.* New York: Harper & Row Publishers, Inc., 1985.

Blake, Robert Rogers. *The Managerial Grid: Key Orientations for Achieving Production Through People.* Houston, Texas: Gulf Publishing Co., 1964.

Blake, Robert Rogers. *The New Managerial Grid.* Houston, Texas: Gulf Publishing Co.,1978.

Blanchard, Kenneth H. *The One-Minute Manager.* New York: William Morrow & Co., Inc.,1982.

Drucker, Peter. *Management: Tasks, Practices, Responsibility.* New York: Harper & Row Publishers, Inc., 1974.

Drucker, Peter. *Managing for Results.* New York: Harper & Row Publishers, Inc., 1964.

Hart, Michael H. *The One Hundred.* New York: Beaufort Books, 1985.

Hegarty, Christopher. *How to Manage Your Boss.* Mill Valley, Calif.: Whatever Publishing, Inc., 1980.

Hersey, Paul. *Situational Leadership.* New York: Warner Books, 1985.

Iacocca, Lee A. *Iacocca, an Autobiography.* New York: Bantam Books, Inc., 1984.

Lewin, Kurt. *Field Theory as Human-Science.* New York: Gardner Press, 1976.

Mager, Robert Frank. *Analyzing Performance Problems.* Belmont, Calif.: Fearon Pitman Publishers, 1970.

Mager, Robert Frank. *Developing Attitudes Toward Learning.* Belmont, Calif.: Fearon Publishers, 1968.

Odiorne, George S. *How Managers Make Things Happen.* Englewood Cliffs, N.J.: Prentice-Hall, Inc., 1961.

Peters, Thomas J. *Passion for Excellence.* New York: Random House, 1985.

Stogdill, Ralph M. *Handbook of Leadership.* New York: Free Press, 1981.

Stogdill, Ralph M., and Alvin E. Coons. *Leader Behavior: Its Description and Measurement.* Columbus, Ohio: Ohio State University Press, 1980.

Townsend, Robert. *Up the Organization.* New York: Alfred A. Knopf, Inc., 1981.

Townsend, Robert. *Further Up the Organization.* New York: Alfred A. Knopf, Inc., 1984.

Uris, Auren. *The Executive Deskbook.* Florence, Ken.: Van Nostrand Reinhold Co., 1979.

Uris, Auren. *Techniques of Leadership.* New York: McGraw-Hill, Inc., 1953.

APPENDIX C

Suggested Films

The following films are excellent learning aids. These are supplementary media that can enrich a class or training program. They are ideal for small-group discussion, panel debates, and question-and-answer periods. Topics are listed in the order in which they appear in the text.

A PASSION FOR EXCELLENCE
(Public Broadcasting Service (PBS), 45 min.)

This film is an excellent public lecture by Thomas Peters, author of the book, *Passion for Excellence*. It is ideal for all business groups, especially people in leadership positions. It is current, humorous, and educational. Award winner; highest rating.

PBS Video
475 L'Enfant Plaza, S.W.
Washington, DC 20014

UP THE ORGANIZATION
(Time-Life, 30 min.)

Robert Townsend, who wrote the book that outraged the business world, gives his personal views on such topics as the chief executive, personnel department, and management consultants. An excellent film.

Time-Life Films
43 West 16th Street
New York, NY 10011

A NEW LOOK AT MOTIVATION
(CRM, 32 min.)

Affiliation, power, and achievement are examined as they are expressed in a work environment; each is related to personality characteristics.

CRM Educational Films
Del Mar, CA 92014

MANAGEMENT BY EXAMPLE
(BNA, 25 min.)

This film defines tough-mindedness in Joe Batten's terms. Strike a piece of granite a hard blow, he says, and it will break because it is hard, cold, brittle. Strike leather the same blow, and it will scarcely show a dent. It is warm, resilient, but tough. So a tough-minded manager is not solely a disciplinarian, but one whose primary drive is to build himself, his subordinates, his organization. Above all, he sets an example of integrity.

BNA Films
5615 Fishers Lane
Rockville, MD 20852

LEADERSHIP: STYLE OR CIRCUMSTANCE?
(CRM,27 min.)

This film separates leadership into two broad categories: relationship oriented and task oriented, the former being a democratic form, the latter more directive and forceful. Both styles have their uses, depending on specific situations. Ways of developing new leaders and ensuring the effectiveness and longevity of such leaders once they are on the job are discussed.

CRM Educational Films
Del Mar, CA 92014

THEORY X AND THEORY Y: THE WORK OF DOUGLAS MC GREGOR, PART I AND PART II (BNA, 30 min. each)

Warren Bennis, Richard Beckhard, and John Paul Jones interpret and explain the findings of the late Douglas McGregor regarding the assumptions management is prone to make about its employees. McGregor labeled these assumptions Theory X and Theory Y. Theory X is a way of looking at human capabilities that regards them as potentially static, unimprovable, and not very impressive. Theory Y assumes an ultimate faith in man's potential for growth and development through learning and a belief that human nature responds to the challenge of a responsible, satisfying job. In Part I, "Description of the Theory," examples and discussion are devoted to a comparison of the two sets of assumptions. In Part II, "Application of the Theory," the viewer is shown why a Theory Y manager will be more likely to elicit greater production from employees.

BNA Films
5615 Fishers Lane
Rockville, MD 20852

THE GRID APPROACH TO CONFLICT SOLVING
(BNA, 33 min.)

The conflict grid is described and demonstrated in this film. Blake and Mouton help managers plot themselves, others, and the group on the grid.

BNA Films
5615 Fishers Lane
Rockville, MD 20852

THE MANAGERIAL GRID IN ACTION
(BNA, 33 min.)

Blake and Mouton explain the grid; various grid styles are demonstrated in a company manager's meeting.

BNA Films
5615 Fishers Lane
Rockville, MD 20852

THE ONE-MINUTE MANAGER
(BTD, 40 min.)

An exceptional presentation by the author of the book *The One-Minute Manager*, this film is excellent for use in supervisory and management development programs. It is practical and highly recommended.

Blanchard Training and Development
2048 Alder Grove, Suite B
Escondido, CA 92025

DELEGATING
(CRM, 28 min.)

Delegation saves managers time and motivates people. The film covers delegation's four fundamental steps.

CRM Education Films
Del Mar, CA 92014

PRODUCTIVITY AND THE SELF-FULFILLING PROPHECY: THE PYGMALION EFFECT
(CRM, 31 min.)

This film reenacts Robert Rosenthal and Lenore Jacobson's experiment with elementary school children that shows how expectations and labels often color reactions to people's behavior. It's an excellent film for managers, teachers, and parents.

CRM Educational Films
Del Mar, CA 92014

COACHING
(CRM, 24 min.)

Improve employee skills on the job by teaching managers and supervisors how to coach. The film describes a five-step process to sharpen coaching skills and raise worker job performance.

CRM Educational Films
Del Mar, CA 92014

THE POWER OF REINFORCEMENT
(CRM, 25 min.)

A little praise can go a long way. Examine several positive reinforcement programs that have made companies millions and discover their secret. Winner of five film awards.

CRM Educational Films
Del Mar, CA 92014

WORKING WITH DIFFICULT PEOPLE
(CRM, 25 min.)

How do managers handle difficult customers or employees? Here are four helpful steps to minimize the negative effects of difficult personalities, whether they are aggressive or passive.

CRM Educational Films
Del Mar, CA 92014

RESOLVING CONFLICTS
(CRM, 22 min.)

Every manager and supervisor gets caught in the middle of conflicts, whether they like it or not. Learn how to do the most good with the least confusion from this clear-cut film.

CRM Educational Films
Del Mar, CA 92014

STUDY QUIZ ANSWERS

Part One	Part Two	Part Three	Part Four
1. a	1. a	1. d	1. b
2. c	2. a	2. b	2. b
3. a	3. b	3. a	3. d
4. e	4. d	4. e	4. c
5. a	5. a	5. b	5. f
6. a	6. d	6. d	6. e
7. c	7. a	7. b	7. c
8. c	8. b	8. b	8. j
9. a	9. e	9. a	9. c
10. d	10. b	10. b	10. e
11. d		11. f	11. a
12. b			12. a
13. a			13. e
14. b			14. b
15. a			15. d
16. b			16. b
17. a			17. c
18. c			
19. a			
20. c			
21. d			

APPENDIX E

The Relationship of the Quiz Questions and the Discussion and Activities to the Part Objectives

The following chart shows the relationship of the quiz questions and the discussion and activities to the part objectives.

PART ONE

Objective Number	Quiz (Q), Discussion and Activities (D&A)	Objective Number	Quiz (Q), Discussion and Activities (D&A)
1	Q: 5, 16, 17, 18 D&A: 1	4	Q: 1, 10, 14, 15, 19, 20 D&A: 2
2	Q: 2, 18 D&A: 1	5	Q: 8, 12 D&A: 5
3	Q: 9 D&A: 3	6	Q: 3, 4, 6, 7, 11, 13, 21 D&A: 4

PART TWO

Objective Number	Quiz (Q), Discussion and Activities (D&A)	Objective Number	Quiz (Q), Discussion and Activities (D&A)
1	Q: 1, 2, 3, 6, 8, 9, 10 D&A: 1, 2, 3, 5	2	Q: 4, 5, 7 D&A: 4

PART THREE

Objective Number	Quiz (Q), Discussion and Activities (D&A)	Objective Number	Quiz (Q), Discussion and Activities (D&A)
1	Q: 6, 7, 10, 11 D&A: 1, 2, 3	2	Q: 1, 2, 3, 4, 5, 8, 9 D&A: 4, 5

PART FOUR

Objective Number	Quiz (Q), Discussion and Activities (D&A)	Objective Number	Quiz (Q), Discussion and Activities (D&A)
1	Q: 8, 14 D&A: 1, 5	4	Q: 15, 16, 17 D&A: 3, 4
2	Q: 5, 9 D&A: 1, 2	5	Q: 10 D&A: 6
3	Q: 1, 2, 3, 4, 6, 7, 11, 12, 13 D&A: 2		